Coastal California

John Doerper
Photography by Catherine Karnow and Galen Rowell

COMPASS AMERICAN GUIDES
An imprint of Fodor's Travel Publications

Compass American Guides: Coastal California

Editor: Diane Mehta
Designer: Tina R. Malaney
Compass Editorial Director: Paul Eisenberg
Compass Creative Director: Fabrizio La Rocca
Compass Senior Editor: Kristin Moehlmann
Production Editor: Jacinta O'Halloran
Photo Editor and Archival Researcher: Melanie Marin
Map Design: Mark Stroud, Moon Street Cartography

Cover photo (Surfers, Shelter Cove on the Lost Coast) by Catherine Karnow

Third Edition
ISBN 1–4000–1538–3
ISSN 1555–5852

The details in this book are based on information supplied to us at press time, but changes occur all the
time, and the publisher cannot accept responsibility for facts that become outdated or for inadvertent errors
or omissions.

Compass American Guides are available at special discounts for bulk purchases for sales promo-
tions or premiums. Special editions, including personalized covers, excerpts of existing books,
and corporate imprints, can be created in large quantities for special needs. For more information, write to Special Markets/Premium Sales, 1745 Broadway, MD 6-2, New York, NY 10019
or e-mail specialmarkets@randomhouse.com.

Compass American Guides, 1745 Broadway, New York, NY 10019
PRINTED IN CHINA

10 9 8 7 6 5 4 3 2 1

To Victoria, my favorite beach buddy.

C O N T E N T S

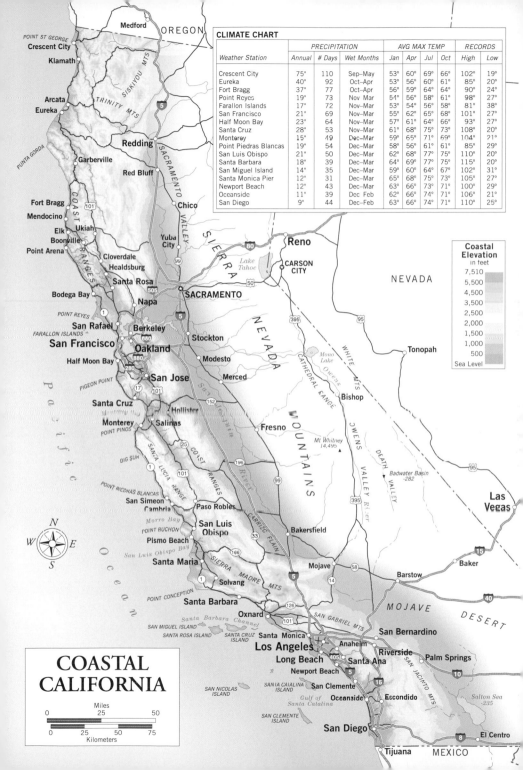

CLIMATE CHART

Weather Station	PRECIPITATION			AVG MAX TEMP				RECORDS	
	Annual	# Days	Wet Months	Jan	Apr	Jul	Oct	High	Low
Crescent City	75°	110	Sep–May	53°	60°	69°	66°	102°	19°
Eureka	40°	92	Oct–Apr	53°	56°	60°	61°	85°	20°
Fort Bragg	37°	77	Oct–Apr	56°	59°	64°	64°	90°	24°
Point Reyes	19°	73	Nov–Mar	54°	56°	58°	61°	98°	27°
Farallon Islands	17°	72	Nov–Mar	53°	54°	56°	58°	81°	38°
San Francisco	21°	69	Nov–Mar	55°	62°	65°	68°	101°	27°
Half Moon Bay	23°	64	Nov–Mar	57°	61°	64°	66°	93°	27°
Santa Cruz	28°	53	Nov–Mar	61°	68°	75°	73°	108°	20°
Monterey	15°	49	Dec–Mar	59°	65°	71°	69°	104°	21°
Point Piedras Blancas	19°	54	Dec–Mar	58°	56°	61°	61°	85°	29°
San Luis Obispo	21°	50	Dec–Mar	62°	68°	77°	75°	110°	20°
Santa Barbara	18°	39	Dec–Mar	64°	69°	77°	75°	115°	20°
San Miguel Island	14°	35	Dec–Mar	59°	60°	64°	67°	102°	31°
Santa Monica Pier	12°	31	Dec–Mar	65°	68°	75°	73°	105°	27°
Newport Beach	12°	43	Dec–Mar	63°	66°	73°	71°	100°	29°
Oceanside	11°	39	Dec–Feb	62°	66°	74°	71°	106°	21°
San Diego	9°	44	Dec–Feb	63°	66°	74°	71°	110°	25°

Coastal Elevation
in feet

7,510	
5,500	
4,500	
3,500	
2,500	
2,000	
1,500	
1,000	
500	
Sea Level	

COASTAL CALIFORNIA

Miles
0   25   50

Kilometers
0   25   50   75

Literary Extracts

Topical Essays

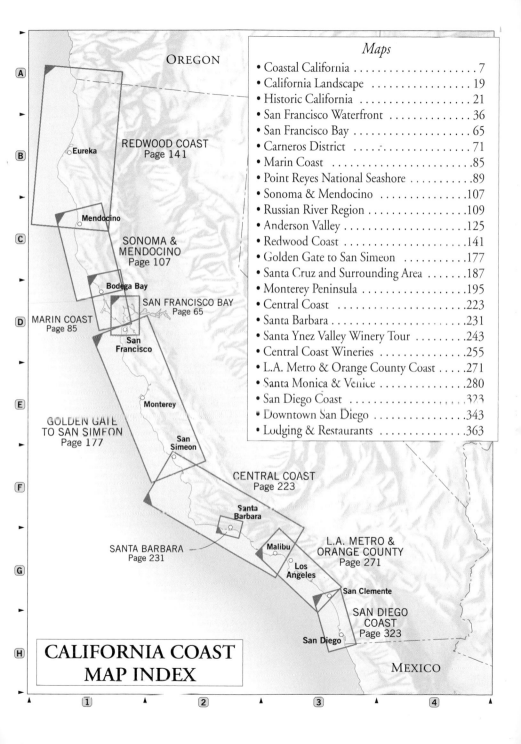

OREGON

REDWOOD COAST
Page 141

Eureka

Mendocino

SONOMA &
MENDOCINO
Page 107

Bodega Bay

SAN FRANCISCO BAY
Page 65

MARIN COAST
Page 85

San
Francisco

Monterey

GOLDEN GATE
TO SAN SIMEON
Page 177

San
Simeon

CENTRAL COAST
Page 223

Santa
Barbara

SANTA BARBARA
Page 231

Malibu

Los
Angeles

L.A. METRO &
ORANGE COUNTY
Page 271

San Clemente

SAN DIEGO
COAST
Page 323

San Diego

CALIFORNIA COAST
MAP INDEX

MEXICO

A B C D E F G H

1 2 3 4

O V E R V I E W

■ How to Use this Book

To long-distance drivers, the California coast is a 1,200-mile ribbon of highway running from Oregon to Mexico. But to most visitors, it's a beautiful stretch of shore within easy reach of either their home city or a major airport. Since most Californians live in one of the state's three great coastal metropolitan areas—San Francisco Bay Area, Los Angeles/Orange County, and San Diego—we have taken each of the metropolitan areas as a departure point, providing guides for an easy exploration of the coast by car from San Francisco, Los Angeles, or San Diego, as well as suggestions for trips farther afield.

■ San Francisco Bay *page 32*

San Francisco, more than any other California city, has fired the imagination of the world for more than 150 years. The city has been glorified in literature and vilified in the press, celebrated in song and story, and sometimes even praised and damned in one sentence. San Francisco has ever found a way to stay in the news (and the popular imagination), from the Gold Rush chaos and vigilantes of the 1850s to the Beat culture of the 1950s and the gay marriage revolution of the early 2000s. To many visitors, San Francisco is not as much a place as a state of mind. It is, of course, both.

■ Marin Coast *page 82*

From the cliffs of the Marin Headlands to the magnificent sweep of Point Reyes and the fishing boats of Bodega Bay, this is an awesomely beautiful area. Rolling hills rise above rocky headlands and offshore sea stacks. Coves, sea caves, and long, sandy beaches are perfect places for exploring on foot or by kayak. Along the way are comfortable inns and excellent restaurants.

■ Sonoma & Mendocino *page 104*

A wild and rural coast, where visitors can wander on long secluded beaches. Point Arena, Fort Bragg, and Mendocino all offer art galleries, inviting inns, and sophisticated restaurants. Vineyards thrive in sunny coastal valleys.

A quiet day looking out over the Pacific.

■ REDWOOD COAST *page 138*

Only a few towns brave the wildness of this lonely stretch, where steep coastal mountains merge with sandy shores. Along the rivers that flow into the ocean here grow the world's tallest trees—the most magnificent of California redwoods. These silent woods are perfect for contemplative walks. Small towns and villages like Shelter Cove, Ferndale, and Trinidad invite visitors to relax a while. Humboldt Bay, California's second-largest estuary, is a perfect place for watching birds from the shore or from a kayak.

■ GOLDEN GATE TO SAN SIMEON *page 174*

South of San Francisco, along the San Mateo County coast, lies a rural landscape and wide views of an indigo sea. The Santa Lucia Mountains push to the sea at Monterey, forming rocky coves that face green and turquoise waters. CA 1, which runs along seaward cliffs of the Big Sur coast, is one of the most gorgeous—as well as hair-raising—drives in the world. Elkhorn Slough and other estuaries make for great bird-watching. Santa Cruz, Monterey, Pacific Grove, and Carmel cater to travelers. Hearst Castle at San Simeon is a cultural showcase of a different kind—a monument to a nouveau riche fascination with European antiquities.

■ **CENTRAL COAST RIVIERA** *page 220*

Long, sandy beaches, the largest sand dunes in North America, rocky cliffs, monolithic Morro Rock, and warm ocean waters are highlights of this scenic stretch of coast. The old mission town of Santa Barbara, the loveliest on the Central Coast, adds a touch of Mediterranean elegance. Pismo Beach and Avila Beach are old-fashioned, folksy beach towns with splendid beaches and lots of sunshine. Morro Bay's compact waterfront has shops and restaurants; its beaches and those of Cayucos to the north are perfect for walking, bird-watching, and surfing.

■ **L.A. METRO AND ORANGE COUNTY** *page 268*

The western fringes of the West Coast's largest metropolitan area are known for beach culture, warm waters, and an effervescent, au courant lifestyle. A large crescent of sandy strand curves from the shores of Malibu past culturally sophisticated Santa Monica, down-to-earth Manhattan Beach, folksy Redondo, and the flower-bedecked bluffs of the Palos Verdes Peninsula. From Newport Beach south, rocky shores with pocket beaches dominate the coast before giving way to more sandy beaches that run south through San Clemente. This is a shore of sand, sun, palm trees, and extensive development.

■ **SAN DIEGO COAST** *page 320*

With its rocky shores, quiet coves, sandy beaches, and warm ocean waters, San Diego County is the Mediterranean shore of California. State-protected coastal lagoons add a touch of wildness, as do surfers who brave the breaking waves at some of the West's most famous surfing beaches. Gardens of subtropical flowers bloom all year long, and graceful palm fronds wave in the sea breeze. Along the Coast Highway are chic, sophisticated La Jolla, expensive Del Mar, and the historic sights of the city of San Diego. Mexico, just a few miles away, profoundly influences the area's music, cuisine, economy, and political life.

A pensive moment in the shade of the California redwoods.

INTRODUCTION

The California coast, with its wide, sandy beaches, flower-bedecked bluffs, surf-washed cliffs, and wild mountain ranges, is one of the most scenic places in the world. It is both rugged and urbane, with wilderness abutting the West Coast's most cultured cities.

Since most California residents live near the coast, you'll find it easy to switch back and forth between wilderness and civilization. Follow up a beach picnic of fresh oysters with dinner at an elegant restaurant; bird-, seal-, or whale-watching with a night at the opera; a day of hiking lonely trails with a stroll along an urban boulevard.

One unique aspect of this coast is the climate: in summer, when inland valleys and mountains swelter in the heat, the coast is cool; in winter, when inland areas are cold—even frosty—much of the coast is delightfully mild. Even if the weather is too cool for swimming or sunbathing, it's rarely wet enough to make beach combing or hiking unpleasant.

The color of sky and ocean vary with the seasons, and sometimes with the time of the day. The sea can be a deep royal blue or indigo, battleship gray, a translucent green, turquoise, or a reddish brown like redwood bark. The sky can be intensely cerulean, pale golden, glaringly white with the intense light of the summer sun, or pearly gray with fog. For most of the coast, the horizon is a long dark line broken only now and then by the outline of a fishing boat or freighter, but off the Southern California coast, islands, previously hidden by haze, appear out of nowhere, and the outlines of offshore oil rigs and passing ships may be etched sharply into the sky.

The California coast is as much a state of mind as it is a place. Its people, and the stories and myths they have woven around this magic coast, are as captivating as the spectacular scenery.

This book introduces you to many of these: it will tell you what the beaches are like and whether they are good for sunbathing, swimming, surfing, diving, or beachcombing; it will take you on trails and into backwaters; it will visit villages and towns and tell you where to find the best food and most comfortable lodging; and it will take you on winery tours. Anecdotes and historical stories will introduce you to the people of the coast and to their way of thinking, because this coast is as filled with things to do as it is with natural beauty.

Roosevelt elk graze on a misty slope along the Lost Coast.

LANDSCAPE & HISTORY

Imagine yourself aboard a Manila galleon, one of the Spanish treasure ships that, once every year in the mid-1700s, made the trip from Manila across the wild Pacific Ocean on the prevailing westerly winds, then scooted south to Acapulco on the California Current and favorable winds.

Storms have driven you a bit north of the standard route. As the galleon turns south you catch glimpses of a rocky, surf-washed shore over which tower huge conifers. The pilot turns the ship's bow out to sea, for he sees whitewater and spume ahead, indicating that a reef runs far out into the ocean from the shore, posing danger to the galleon. Soon the water turns muddy, and huge driftwood logs, with roots as big around as whales, bob in the waves. You suspect that large rivers flow into the ocean here. You want to land at an estuary to take on fresh water, but the pilot counsels against it, reminding you that several galleons have sunk off this coast since the Manila trade began.

Suddenly a huge headland emerges from the fog: Cape Mendocino. You're back on the regular galleon route. Steep mountains loom forbiddingly off the starboard bow. A few leagues south, cliffs give way to sand dunes—still overtowered by those huge trees, some of which you estimate must be more than 50 *brazos* tall.

After you pass a large sandy hook reaching far into the ocean (later named Point Arena), the galleon once again runs along a shore of rocky cliffs. Sea otters watch you from the safety of kelp beds and sea lions bark from offshore rocks. You pass a rocky headland sheltering a secure harbor (later to be known as Bodega Bay) and, shortly after, sail past Point Reyes, whose white cliffs were likened to the cliffs of Dover by that notorious pirate, Francis Drake. Just south you note a muddy discoloration of the water. Surely a large river must flow into the ocean through a gap in these steep headlands, but the pilot points to the unbroken wall of cliffs and a white line of the surf and says it's impossible. He refuses to risk the ship by sailing closer to shore. Yet it is here that in 1769 a land expedition led by Gaspar de Portola discovers San Francisco Bay, the greatest harbor on the coast, and in 1775 your acquaintance Manuel de Ayala will brave the entrance and moor in the vast protected waters off beautiful Angel Island.

Now, the forest-clad mountains retreat from the shore. Coastal terraces are covered with meadows of lush grass, studded with oaks, pines, and cypresses.

Mission San Gabriel *in San Gabriel, east of Los Angeles, was painted by Ferdinand Deppe in 1832.*

Occasionally, you spot herds of deer and elk. Lagoons, marked by swarms of water-fowl and shorebirds, interrupt a grim line of cliffs.

South of Point Año Nuevo, where huge elephants seals loll on the beaches, the shore recedes at Santa Cruz to form a vast bay with a long crescent of sandy beach. At its southern end a rocky headland, covered with pines and cypresses growing almost to the water's edge, shelters the bay. The sand here is so white you think at first it must be snow. Surely this must be the port of Monterey, described by Sebastian Vizcaino in his logs 150 years earlier.

South of this bay there is no safe anchorage for a hundred leagues or more. Tall mountains rise straight from the sea, their southern slopes covered with meadows and oaks. As the galleon scuds ahead of the wind, every sail set and drawing well, the mountains give way to rolling hills. You see miles of sand dunes, a few almost as high as mountains, before you reach Point Conception, the most notorious cape on the coast, a place of fogs and storms. But you're lucky—you have the wind and current on your side. Racing past the dreaded rocks, you suddenly find yourself in a changed world. Sun shines above a cobalt-blue sea, highlighting the white sands and tawny hills of the shore and setting off the chain of Channel Islands in dark relief against the sea. You can clearly see the large domed huts of the natives on the bluffs. As you sail past San Miguel Island (where Juan Cabrillo, the explorer, died and was buried 200 years ago), the natives approach the galleon in their canoes, hoping to trade fruit and meat for fish hooks and trinkets.

Sailing between the islands and the shore, you note that the landscape becomes drier, more barren; scrub and chaparral rather than forest cover the seaward slopes of mountains rising from the sea. The air is warm, the light fine and clear. A large plain opens up to the east. Grass and cactus dominate the vegetation of the coastal terraces, but here and there copses of oaks and pines interrupt the open prairies.

Every few leagues, the line of cliffs is broken by freshwater lagoons. From the heaving deck of the galleon, you can just make out the tops of the tule and willow thickets, and see the line of thick-trunked sycamore trees marching down to the sea along stream and river banks.

Soon you sail past Point Loma and stop for a few days at the sheltered harbor of San Diego with its long sand spit. Rumor has it that this will be the site of Alta California's first presidio and mission to be established by the Viceroy of Mexico. Just south of here, the pilot tells you, the land turns very dry. You've reached the desert shores of the California Peninsula, and the pilot turns the galleon's bow seaward. From here to Cabo San Lucas you will sail far out to sea, to avoid the hidden reefs of this arid shore. And then, 1,534 miles south of San Diego, you will reach Acapulco with your treasure ship.

■ FIRST IMMIGRANTS

The shape of the land has determined the human history of the coast. Access was easiest from the valleys and forests of the Pacific Northwest, and by 9,000 years ago settlers had edged down into California. From every other direction access was difficult. Deserts and the Sierra Nevada have defined the modern state's eastern and southern boundaries. Its western coast, in many places rocky and rough, faced 1,200 miles of ocean.

The individual tribes and tribelets who reached California began to settle into a stable way of life sometime between 7,000 and 5,000 years ago, enjoying a staple diet of wild grains, flower seeds, acorns, small and large game, fish, and shellfish.

LANDFORMS

- Mountainous and rocky coastline
- Terraces and steep cliffs
- Bays and sandy beaches
- Fault zones

CALIFORNIA LANDSCAPE

Miles
0   25   50

0   25   50   75
Kilometers

① Terraces and steep cliffs
(Half Moon Bay)

② Mountainous and rocky coastline
(Big Sur Coast)

③ Bays and sandy beaches
(Laguna Beach)

POINT ST GEORGE

Rattlesnake Mtn
3,668
Preston Peak
7,309
Baldy Peak
6,775

Mt Shasta
14,162

CAPE MENDOCINO
Coskie 2,151
Grogan Fault

Lassen Peak
10,456

TRINITY MTS
SISKIYOU MTS
CASCADE RANGE

PUNTA GORDA
Horse Mtn
4,087

Maacama Fault
Sardine Peak
8,134

COAST RANGES
SACRAMENTO VALLEY
SIERRA

Cold Springs Mtn
2,736
POINT ARENA

Lake
Tahoe

Big Mtn
2,675

NEVADA

Eagle Peak
11,845

POINT REYES
Mt Tamalpais
2,571
San Francisco Bay

Hayward Fault
Mt Diablo
3,849
YOSEMITE
VALLEY

Mono
Lake

WHITE MTS

PILLAR POINT
Half Moon Bay
Langley Hill
1,242

Mission Fault
Mt Hamilton
4,213

CATHEDRAL RANGE

Owens River

PIGEON POINT
San Gregorio Fault

Calaveras Fault

San Joaquin River

MOUNTAINS

OWENS VALLEY

DEATH VALLEY

Furnace Creek
Fault

Monterey Bay
POINT PINUS

SAN JOAQUIN VALLEY

POINT SUR
BIG SUR

SANTA LUCIA RANGE
SANTA CRUZ MTS
San Andreas Fault

Mt Whitney
14,495
Badwater Basin
-282

②
Cone Peak
5,155

COAST RANGES

Owens Valley
Fault

PAHRUMP VALLEY

Mount Mars
2,674

Rinconada Fault
Morro Bay
POINT BUCHON

CARRIZO PLAIN

River

Garlock Fault
Lockhart Fault

San Luis Obispo Bay

SIERRA MADRE MTS

Sawmill Mtn
8,818

TEHACHAPI MTS

MOJAVE   DESERT

POINT ARGUELLO
San Rafael Mtn
6,593
Tranquillon Mtn
2,159
POINT CONCEPTION

La Cumbre Peak
3,985

Santa Barbara Channel
CHANNEL ISLANDS

SAN GABRIEL MTS

San Andreas
Fault

CHOCOLATE MTS

Colorado River

Santa Monica Bay
POINT VICENTE

③
San Jacinto Mtn
10,804
Palomar Mtn
6,140

SAN JACINTO MTS

SANTA CATALINA
ISLAND
SAN NICOLAS
ISLAND

Gulf of
Santa Catalina

VALLECITO MTS

Salton Sea
-235

SAN CLEMENTE
ISLAND

La Jolla Peak
1,567
Cuyamaca Peak
6,512

POINT LOMA
San Diego
Bay

While most of the coastal tribes collected shellfish from tidal rocks, only a few native people developed seaworthy boats. The Tolowa and Yurok in the far northwest used their sturdy redwood dugouts to visit the offshore sea stacks; the Chumash of the Central Coast also built large canoes (a technology they shared with the neighboring Gabrielinos) in which they paddled across the Santa Barbara Channel to the Channel Islands, where a large part of the tribe lived.

It was a peaceful life, with little or no warfare. Battles might be fought, but the action consisted mostly of shouting and threatening gestures with hunting weapons.

According to anthropologist Alfred Kroeber, the Indians of the Northern California coast were not pressed for food. He noted that there were almost no references, either in myth or tradition, to famines.

■ SPANISH GALLEONS AND BRITISH BUCCANEERS

Navigator Juan Rodriguez Cabrillo was the first European explorer to touch the California shore. In September of 1542, he sailed into San Diego Bay (which he named "San Miguel") and took possession for Spain, hoping that on this voyage north he'd find gold. He found none, although he was the first to report on the seafaring Chumash of the Santa Barbara Channel. He did not return from this voyage, dying of an injury he received while disembarking on the rocky shore of one of the Channel Islands on January 3, 1543. Cabrillo's crew continued exploring the coast after their captain's demise, but with little success. Because they found no gold, their reports were filed away and forgotten.

But the Spanish would soon return to the region. The pride of their colonial fleet—the great Manila galleons—sailed between the port of Acapulco, in Mexico, and Manila, in the Philippines. Once a year, large well-armed galleons, loaded with silver, wafted west from Acapulco by favorable trade winds. In Manila, the silver was traded for silks, porcelain, pearls, rubies, sapphires, and assorted knickknacks, as well as nutmeg, cinnamon, and other spices at reasonable prices. The goods were then transshipped in Acapulco, sent across the Atlantic, and sold in Europe at fabulous profits.

Galleon captains soon discovered that the quickest way back from the Philippines to Mexico was along a northern route, which brought the ships to the coast of California at about the latitude of Cape Mendocino. Here the galleons picked up the California current and sailed south on the prevailing northerly

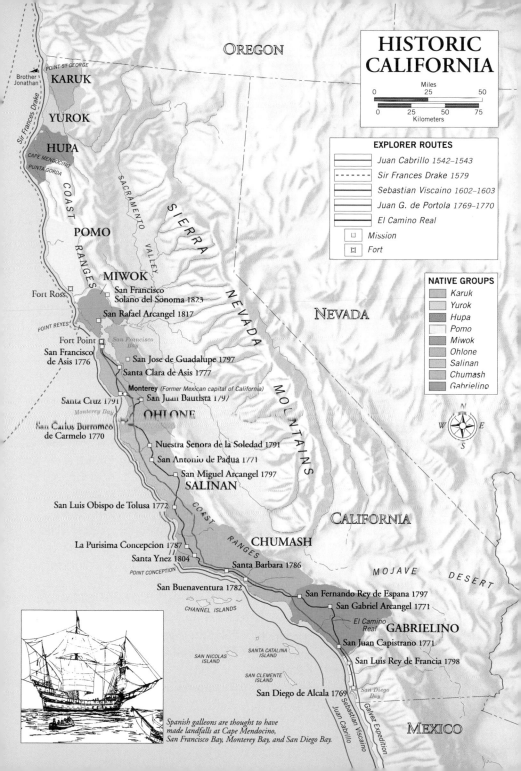

HISTORIC CALIFORNIA

Miles
0 — 25 — 50

Kilometers
0 — 25 — 50 — 75

EXPLORER ROUTES

Juan Cabrillo 1542–1543
Sir Frances Drake 1579
Sebastian Viscaino 1602–1603
Juan G. de Portola 1769–1770
El Camino Real
□ Mission
⊡ Fort

NATIVE GROUPS

Karuk
Yurok
Hupa
Pomo
Miwok
Ohlone
Salinan
Chumash
Gabrielino

OREGON

KARUK

YUROK

HUPA

POMO

MIWOK

OHLONE

SALINAN

CHUMASH

GABRIELINO

NEVADA

CALIFORNIA

MOJAVE DESERT

MEXICO

POINT ST GEORGE
Brother Jonathan
CAPE MENDOCINO
PUNTA GORDA

COAST RANGES

SACRAMENTO VALLEY

SIERRA NEVADA MOUNTAINS

Fort Ross

POINT REYES

Fort Point
San Francisco Bay
San Francisco de Asis 1776

San Francisco Solano del Sonoma 1823
San Rafael Arcangel 1817
San Jose de Guadalupe 1797
Santa Clara de Asis 1777
Monterey (Former Mexican capital of California)
San Juan Bautista 1797
Santa Cruz 1791
Monterey Bay
San Carlos Borromeo de Carmelo 1770
Nuestra Senora de la Soledad 1791
San Antonio de Padua 1771
San Miguel Arcangel 1797
San Luis Obispo de Tolusa 1772
La Purisima Concepcion 1787
Santa Ynez 1804
POINT CONCEPTION
San Buenaventura 1782
Santa Barbara 1786

COAST RANGES

CHANNEL ISLANDS

SAN NICOLAS ISLAND
SANTA CATALINA ISLAND
SAN CLEMENTE ISLAND

San Fernando Rey de Espana 1797
San Gabriel Arcangel 1771
El Camino Real
San Juan Capistrano 1771
San Luis Rey de Francia 1798
San Diego de Alcala 1769
San Diego Bay

Juan Cabrillo
Sebastian Viscaino
Galvez Expedition

N W E S

Sir Frances Drake

Spanish galleons are thought to have
made landfalls at Cape Mendocino,
San Francisco Bay, Monterey Bay, and San Diego Bay.

SAFE HARBOR ALONG THE COAST

In 1603, Sebastian Vizcaino, under commission of the Viceroy of Mexico, set out to map and explore the California coast, with three ships and 200 men. Although navigator Juan Cabrillo had first described Monterey some 60-odd years before, Vizcaino was the first to map the area and describe it carefully.

Among the ports of greater consideration which I discovered was one in thirty-seven degrees of latitude which I called Monterey. . . . It is all that can be desired for commodiousness and as a station for ships making the voyage to the Philippines. . . . This port is sheltered from all winds, while on the immediate coast there are pines from which masts of any desired size can be obtained, as well as live oaks and white oaks, rosemary, the vine, the rose of Alexandria, a great variety of game, such as rabbits, hares, partridges, and other sorts of species found in Spain . . . .

This land has a genial climate, its waters are good, and it is very fertile—judging from the varied and luxuriant growth of trees and plants.

—Sebastian Vizcaino, Publication of the Historical Society
of Southern California, from ship's logs of 1603

winds. The Spanish tried to keep their lucrative trade route secret, but the news was quickly learned by British buccaneers, who intercepted the galleons off the California and Mexican coasts. None other than Sir Francis Drake, English man-about-town and buccaneer, was the first to challenge the Spanish supremacy in what was then known as the South Seas.

In 1577, Drake sacked and pillaged unprotected Spanish settlements all along the west coast of the Americas. Off Lima, Peru, he captured the treasure ship *Cacafuego,* his richest prize. He sailed as far north as 48 degrees, but after failing to find the elusive Northwest Passage (rumors of which would haunt sailors for another 200 years), he sailed south. Because his ship, the *Golden Hind,* needed major repairs, he hauled her out in a protected bay on the Northern California coast, taking possession for Queen Elizabeth and calling it New Albion (New England) decades before the Pilgrims appropriated the appellation elsewhere.

Drake's descriptions of the bay where he landed are vague, though they make it quite clear that the natives of the region were central California Indians, most likely Coast Miwok, and not tribes to the north or south.

■ SPANISH MISSIONS; RELUCTANT INDIANS

By the 1770s the Viceroy of Mexico, under the direction of the Spanish crown, had embarked on a three-pronged approach to colonize California: missions, military presidios, and pueblos along the coast. The first mission and presidio were established in San Diego in 1769, followed by a mission and presidio at Monterey in 1770. In roughly 50 years, Franciscans built a total of 21 missions, planted grapes for sacramental wine, and introduced olives, corn, and other useful plants. Adventurers and idealists, they believed they were bringing salvation to the heathen, but in the end they converted few and—unwittingly, by carrying contagious diseases—instead contributed to the destruction of the people they meant to help.

Mexico gained its independence from Spain in 1821, and in 1833, the missions were secularized. (When the Americans took over in 1848, they returned many of the churches and cloisters to the Catholic Church.)

In this DeBry etching Indians welcome Sir Francis Drake to California in 1579.
(following spread) A view of what was supposedly California, in 1720.

MAR DE LAS CALIFORNAS Ô CAROLINAS

MARE DE LAS CALIFORNAS Ô CAROLINAS

GRAN QUIVIRA

CALIFORNAS Ô CAROLINAS

Cº Blanco
Cº de S. Sebast.
Tolongo
Cº Mendocino
P.ⁱ de S. Fran.co
P. ͥ Carinto
Pᵗ.ᵈ la Conception
Rio del Coral
Pᵗ. de Sᵗᵃ Lucia
Bᵗᵃ de la Concepcion
Sᵗ Diego
Bᵗᵃ d. Todos Sᵗᵒˢ
Isla d. Sᵗᵃ Catalina
Bᵗᵃ d S. Simo y Judas
Isla d. Sᵗ Clemente
Bᵗᵃ d. las once Virgenes
Cº dl. Engaño
Isla d. Pascaros
Isla Ceniza
Isla d. Cedro
Pᵗᵈ S. Bartholome

MAR DEL SUR

Tropique de Cancer.

TOUOMARICOPAS
Pᵗ de S. Clara
Marcos
Mathro
Rosalia
Virgenes
Sᵗᵃ Thodosia
Los Reyes
S.t Juan
Sᵗ Xaccarias
Sᵗ Tirso
Rio d. S. Thomas
Pᵗ de S. Martin
Pᵗ d.S. Andres
S. Margarita

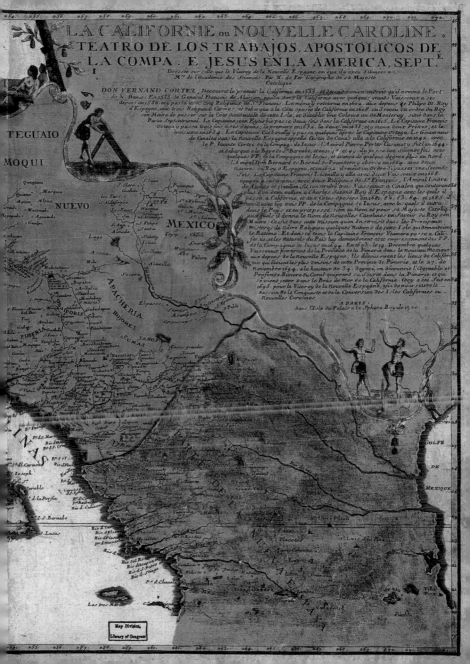

■ RANCHO ERA

After a number of missions, pueblos, and presidios (military forts) had been established, settlers began to make the arduous journey north from Mexico and to spread over coastal hills and plains. The vast grasslands of coastal California (just in from the sea) proved ideal for raising livestock—a Mexican gentleman's preferred way of making a living. Land for the ranchos was obtained by government grant. By the time the United States occupied California, some 8,987,000 acres had been granted. California had become a land of vast cattle ranches (some of them several hundred square miles in area). The cattle needed no feeding and no care, and they were rounded up only for the annual branding of the new calves and for the periodic *matanzas,* or slaughters.

The ranchos had *vaqueros* skilled with rawhide *riatas,* who could subdue the semi-wild cattle with ease and lasso grizzly bears "just for sport" and drag them to town. There were even tales that more than one love-struck swain, distressed that a rival in love was serenading the woman of his heart, caught a grizzly and released it next to the guitar-strumming rival, to chase him off. Such a ploy might have worked or not; the *caballeros* were known to charge the bears with swords as their only weapons.

The garden at Mission Santa Barbara.

California's Rancho Period was idyllic for the Spanish, despite frontier living conditions and few cultural diversions. There were fiestas, dances, weddings, and lengthy visits to friends. These were peaceful times, when travelers could ride the length of El Camino Real, from San Diego north to San Francisco, without having to fear for their safety. Nor did voyagers have to worry about food or lodging, for ranchos and missions alike welcomed all visitors, entertained them free of charge, and even gave them provisions and a fresh horse to continue their journey.

■ YANKEE TRADERS AND AMERICAN SETTLERS

While the Spanish controlled California, settlers could only trade with the mother country and its colonies. Russians established an outpost at Fort Ross (west of modern-day Healdsburg) beyond the reach of the Spanish, but they were not allowed to barter for goods in San Francisco Bay. When Count Nicolai Rezanov sailed through the Golden Gate in 1806, hoping to buy food for the starving Russian settlement at Sitka, he was politely refused by the presidio's *comandante*. However, over the course of many hospitable dinners at the presidio, Rezanov and the comandante's daughter fell in love; while the marriage was deferred, Rezanov did in the end manage to buy the food he needed.

Trade with Americans was carried out through smuggling, by surreptitiously landing goods on the Channel Islands or in hidden coves.

After Mexico gained its independence from Spain, trade was permitted, and Yankee traders, skilled at navigating the turbulent North Pacific in their solidly built, fast ships began to call on the coast at regular intervals.

Bostonian Richard Henry Dana, who shipped out as a common seaman in 1835, wrote in his *Two Years Before the Mast* that his ship supplied:

> Spirits of all kinds (sold by the cask), teas, coffee, sugars, spices, raisins, molasses, hardware, crockeryware, tinware, cutlery, clothing of all kinds, boots and shoes from Lynn, calicoes and cottons from Lowell, crapes, silks; also shawls, scarfs, necklaces, jewelry and combs for the ladies; furniture; and in fact everything that can be imagined, from Chinese fireworks to English cartwheels—of which we had a dozen pairs with their iron rims on.
>
> Things sell on an average at an advance of nearly three hundred percent upon the Boston prices.

The so-called Californios had little money to pay for these goods—what silver they had went into decorating their elaborate saddles and horse trappings—but they had plenty of cowhides, which the Yankees were willing to take in trade. Soon these hides became known as California bank notes.

The loading of the hides onto the ships was done by the sailors because, strange for a people living on the coast, the Californios had no boats—not even at Monterey, the capital and official port of entry. William H. Thomes, who visited the coast in 1843 as a ship's boy, reported, "wonderful as it may seem, the port officers of Monterey did not own a boat for the purpose of boarding vessels that traded with the people." Nor were there piers: all the trade goods, as well as the hides, had to be taken through the surf by ship's boat. This could be wet work, especially in places where the surf was heavy. "The beach at Santa Cruz did not appear inviting, as we surveyed it from aloft. The surf was breaking heavily, and it looked as though some of us would get ducked the next morning, when we landed, and our predictions were true . . . ."

Americans played a prominent role in Mexican California as settlers, rancheros, and even as politicians. Most converted to Catholicism (leaving their conscience at Cape Horn, as a popular saying had it), married the daughters of prominent Californios, and obtained land grants from the government. In 1835, the United States tried to buy California from Mexico but bungled the deal. On October 19, 1842, Comm. Thomas Catesby Jones of the U.S. Navy captured Monterey, believing the U.S. and Mexico were at war. When he learned otherwise, he lowered the American flag, apologized, and sailed south to San Pedro, where he was entertained by the local rancheros.

Four years later, on June 14, 1846, several American settlers proclaimed California's independence, captured the "fortress" of Sonoma, and took military commander Mariano Vallejo captive. This time, as it turned out, the U.S. and Mexico were actually at war. On July 7, Commander John D. Sloat raised the American flag at the Monterey customs house and formally declared California a possession of the United States. The Californios were not that willing to concede, but several months—and skirmishes—later, on January 13, 1847, the Californios capitulated at Rancho Cahuenga in Southern California. Mexico formally ceded California on February 2, 1848, in the Treaty of Guadalupe Hidalgo. On September 9, 1850, President Fillmore signed an act of Congress admitting California as a state into the Union.

■ GOLD, VINEYARDS, AND RAILROADS

Until the Americans acquired California, much of its history happened near the coast, where most of the settlements were. But after gold was found at Sutter's Mill in the Sierra Nevada foothills on January 24, 1848 (nine days before Mexico officially ceded California), the action shifted inland. By 1849, hundreds of sailing ships were bringing prospectors from all over the world up the coast, and the town of San Francisco roared to life as the state's first important city. So many sailors jumped ship in San Francisco between 1849 and the 1880s that trading ships' captains routinely sent out thugs to "shanghai" young men and force them to stick out the trip to China.

After the Gold Rush, California's political and economic focus shifted back to the coast (and has remained within 75 miles of saltwater ever since). As veins of ore gave out, many of the miners turned to other pursuits: they established farms and orchards in coastal valleys, logged the redwood forests, and built boats to exploit the bounty of the sea. Vineyards and orange groves began to replace cattle pastures. William H. Thomes, visiting the coast from 1843 to 1845, talked about eating ripe grapes straight from the vine, and commented in 1884 that California raised "enough grapes to manufacture a sufficient supply of wine and brandy to supply the whole of the United States, and part of Europe."

Northern California's population swelled after railroads connected it with the East Coast in 1869, although Southern California remained largely a backwater until a direct rail connection was established in 1885. By the 1930s, as farmers from the dust bowl came to pick California fruit, the state's population topped five million.

■ MODERN TIMES

During World War II, not only did California become one of the major staging areas for the war in the Pacific, but war-related industries infused the state's largely agricultural economy with manufacturing. Soldiers who had gone through basic training at Ford Ord, Camp Pendleton, Fort Roberts, or one of the other military bases near the coast—or who had been stationed at the naval bases on San Francisco Bay, in Long Beach, or in San Diego—liked what they saw and stayed on after the war. The Cold War spawned massive defense and aerospace production, attracting ever more workers to the Golden State. Coastal towns soon had world-class hotels and restaurants, theaters, opera houses, and museums. The state's

A view north along San Francisco's Golden Gate Bridge during its construction.

early universities were also established near the coast; even today, most campuses of the far-flung state system are within easy driving distance of beaches and surf.

Nor are the modern centers of California far inland. Hollywood and its foster child, Culver City, are an easy drive from the ocean, which provides a frequent movie backdrop; Silicon Valley is but a clam toss from southern San Francisco Bay just over the hills from the laid-back Santa Cruz boardwalk. Coastal pleasures have been unabashedly sybaritic—an outlook on life enhanced by real estate advertisements, the songs of the Beach Boys, a score of surfer movies, and newspaper and magazine gossip columns commenting on the life of the movie stars living on or near the beaches.

A dynamic economy and a mild climate were the engine behind California's population growth. By the end of World War II, San Francisco's population numbered 750,000; L.A.'s more than two million. By 1950 there were 10.5 million people living in California; 35 million at the end of the 20th century.

As California's population continued to grow by leaps and bounds, real estate developers tried their best to get their hands on all of the coast—even some of the parks protecting the most scenic spots. In the 1970s, then-Gov. Ronald Reagan even talked of turning idyllic Leo Carrillo State Park into a coastal Disneyland. In the meantime, housing developments began to appear on once pristine bluffs and the lagoons so essential to migratory birds on the Pacific Flyway were being drained and filled. Actions like this (and fear of runaway development) led to a counter-revolution among environmentally minded Californians, who realized that their greatest treasure, the natural beauty of their coast, was rapidly disappearing under concrete and subdivisions. In November of 1972, California voters passed Proposition 20, the Coastal Initiative, which protected much of the coastline that was as yet undeveloped.

The coast is a beautiful, if unstable place. Beaches and cliffs fall victim to the ever-gnawing surf, while tectonic forces raise old sea bottoms to the height of marine terraces. The works of man, too, have often proved temporary—some 19th-century logging ports and towns, for example, have already reverted to nature, making a landscape once well populated again seem half-empty. Let's hope that, no matter how much the physical appearance of the coast fluctuates, the snowy plover, willets, pelicans, gulls, ospreys, egrets, sea otters, elephant seals, sea lions, and whales will be able to survive, and that we will continue to have an opportunity to enjoy the mysterious power and beauty of marine animals and birds, marshes and lagoons, and wild, surf-washed beaches.

SAN FRANCISCO BAY

The city of San Francisco sits at the head of a peninsula; the surging Pacific Ocean marks its western boundary. Across from San Francisco's northern edge (where most of its historic areas are located) are some of the best places to visit in the Bay Area: Alcatraz and Angel islands, Sausalito, and the southern Sonoma and Napa wine region, Carneros.

Urban pleasures to be enjoyed here include San Francisco's hillside neighborhoods and fine architecture, majestic bridges, good food, and leisurely walks. San Francisco is compact for a city its size. It's possible to walk across town (I've done it), or to walk from the city to Marin County (as novelist Jack Kerouac once did). You'll find it's a great place to take a walk because of its diverse historical and ethnic neighborhoods—and because there are so many parks and hills you'll not only be diverted but also well exercised. If you get tired, hungry, or thirsty, you're always within a few steps of a bar or café where you can rest and refresh yourself with a snack and a drink. Or you can just sit quietly by the bay or the ocean shore and watch the gulls and pelicans fly by.

■ FOG AND FERRY BOATS ON THE BAY

The sky is gray and San Francisco Bay is a bit choppy, with light-gray crests, as we pull away from the ferry dock at Fisherman's Wharf. A sea lion raises its head from the water and stares at the bow of our boat, and executes a smooth dive as we close in on him. A dozen seagulls and two brown pelicans follow in our wake, mistaking us for a party boat.

All of San Francisco Bay's landmarks are clearly visible in the crisp morning air—the Golden Gate Bridge to the west, its paint coat of international orange looking a bit dull this morning. Mount Tamalpais rises to the northwest, high above the Marin Headlands, and the windows of Sausalito beneath it flash like signal mirrors in the early sun. The rock of Alcatraz and bucolic Angel Island lie straight ahead; and to the east, the Bay Bridge glimmers silver above Yerba Buena Island.

As I walked to the pier this morning, the air carried the aromas sent into the morning breeze: crabs boiling in huge outdoor cauldrons; the heart-warming smell of garlic, slowly sautéing in olive oil; the tang of barbecued pork, soy squid, and glazed duck at a Chinese take-out place; the bite of fresh chiles wafting across the

Bicycling down the famously curvy Lombard Street.

street from a neighborhood taqueria; the nose tingling lure of freshly baked sour-dough bread.

This special San Francisco air has been proposed as one of the reasons why San Franciscans are so fond of good food and wine—the air allows them to appreciate their aromas to the fullest. The marine tang increases and the land aromas fade as we run out into the bay, and the boat heels slightly as it feels the impact of the flood current rushing through the Golden Gate.

The Golden Gate marks the dividing line between the two worlds of San Francisco, the world of the Pacific Ocean and the world of the bay, between the chill, windswept ocean side of the peninsula over whose very tip the city spreads, and the calmer and warmer bay shores where most of the city's business, dining, and entertaining takes place.

The bay provides a focal point for the city, much in the same way the Seine does for Paris and the Thames does for London. Yet, in all truth, it's more splendid than either of these famed waterways. Its primal beauty draws me whenever I return to San Francisco. It orients me (as also do the hills) and it ever serves as a resting place

INCIDENT ON THE BAY

The hero of the Jack London novel The Sea-Wolf, *a smug intellectual, is crossing from San Francisco to Sausalito on a ferry doomed to collide in the fog with another ferry. Here are some of his observations just before the crash:*

I fell to dwelling upon the romance of the fog. And romantic it certainly was—the fog, like the gray shadow of infinite mystery, brooding over the whirling speck of earth; and men, mere motes of light and sparkle, cursed with an insane relish for work, riding their steeds of wood and steel through the heart of the mystery, groping their way blindly through the Unseen, and clamoring and clanging in confident speech while their hearts are heavy with incertitude and fear.

■ ■ ■

Then everything happened, and with inconceivable rapidity. The fog seemed to break away as though split by a wedge. . . . I could see the pilot-house and a white-bearded man leaning partly out of it, on his elbows. . . . As he leaned there, he ran a calm and speculative eye over us, as though to determine the precise point of the collision, and took no notice whatever, when our pilot, white with rage, shouted, "Now you've done it!"

—Jack London, *The Sea-Wolf,* 1904

for my eye, reducing the tall office buildings and awesome bridges to a proper perspective. When I look around me—at the rows of houses climbing the steep sides of the bayside hills, and at the old business edifices that survived the 1906 earthquake—I'm reminded that this cosmopolitan city did not grow up along the windy shores of the Pacific, but along the inland shores of a sheltered bay, 50 miles long and several miles wide, rimmed by grassy and wooded hills. It is no gray, chill seaport city but, as the late, great newspaper columnist Herb Caen once observed, a many-splendored Baghdad-by-the-Bay. As you stand atop one of the city's hills and look out over the bay and the cities lining its shore, it can be hard to believe that the Bay Area is indeed populated by more than six million people.

■ ■ ■

On a sunny morning, with the waters of the bay sparkling in the silver light, I board a ferry at the Larkspur Landing in Marin County for a scenic trip to San Francisco. Now, the famous San Francisco fog is creeping in through the Golden

Hiking in the Marin Headlands, by the Golden Gate—San Francisco is in the distance.

Gate. It coils and swirls like a dragon, and covers the bay and the low-lying parts of the city in no time at all.

With the shores veiled in mist—but the islands and hills still rising above the fog—it is almost possible to imagine how this bay must have looked in August of 1775, when the first Spanish mariner to sail through its narrow entrance, Juan Manuel de Ayala, anchored his ship in the Angel Island cove that now bears his name. Around him the shore was lined with small villages, some of them rising on top of huge shell mounds as large as 600 feet long and 30 feet high. Ohlone Indians lived to the east and south; Coast Miwok to the north. The gentle climate made for easy living; the waters of the bay provided abalones, oysters, mussels, and fish, the marshes teemed with ducks and geese.

My ferry is now approaching Pier 41, and though the fog has entered the bay itself, it hesitates at Angel Island. As the boat docks, I watch the city and its hills

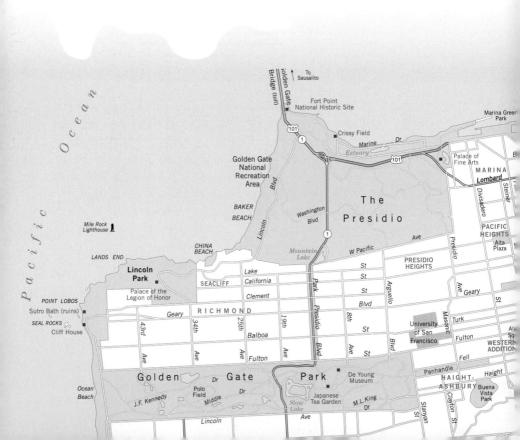

come into focus again. Perhaps no neighborhood is more emblematic of San Francisco's early days than Telegraph Hill, with its wooden, pastel houses, its intimate gardens, its steep slopes and sheer rock faces, and the white column of Coit Tower at the top.

In 1849, the bay lapped at the edges of Telegraph Hill, and ships moored right below it. I can't help but wonder what it must have been like to arrive here aboard the first true Gold Rush ship—the mail boat *California*—which left New York harbor in October of 1848 with seven passengers. Rounding Cape Horn, the ship picked up another 150 passengers off Peru. By the time it reached Panama, news of the California gold strike had been announced by President Polk. Heavily armed Americans demanded to be taken aboard, and 350 passengers soon jammed the decks. When the *California* docked below Telegraph Hill, the crew and everyone else aboard headed for the hills.

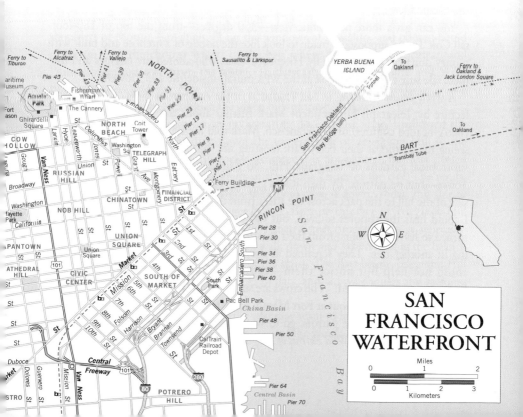

SAN FRANCISCO WATERFRONT

■ NORTH BEACH

The valley nestled between Telegraph Hill and Russian Hill is known as North Beach, but don't look for any waves; the cove and beach were filled in back in the 1870s. Once a thriving Italian immigrant neighborhood, North Beach still has some of its old flavor, although it is no longer, alas, saturated with the heady aromas of fermenting *must* that each fall wafted from the Italian homes. This scent was lovingly described by Margaret Parton in *Laughter on the Hill*:

> As I walked down Union Street toward the streetcar I could smell the
> purple grapes hanging rich and heavy in the hidden arbors behind the
> bare white fronts of the Italian flats. Great wooden barrels, scoured for the
> wine to come, began to appear in front of every doorstep, and one day
> there was the stained old wine press starting its yearly journey from the
> houses at the top of the Hill down to the late harvesters at the bottom.
> Each day as I passed, it would be moved a little further down, its
> heady smell mingling with the warm air from the basement bakeries.

Back in my college days, when friends and I visited the city, we would always make our first stop at poet Lawrence Ferlinghetti's City Lights Bookstore. Located near the intersection of Broadway and Columbus (and set at the southwest corner of North Beach), City Lights remains an important part of San Francisco today. As the nation's first paperback bookstore, City Lights always has a good selection of virtually unknown authors and books from small presses (and is still the best place to stock up on the works of Jack Kerouac and other Beat authors).

I still come here, then head across Columbus and up Grant a few blocks to stop at one of the neighborhood's many Italian bakeries for freshly baked bread. I'll stop at **Washington Square** to enjoy the life of the neighborhood—a big Italian wedding party emerging from Saint Peter and Paul's Church; or the huge groups of middle-aged Chinese practicing tai chi in the morning. Artists set up their paintings for sale, and locals come out of their apartments to sit on the grass and read their newspapers.

Nearby is **Club Fugazi**, where *Beach Blanket Babylon,* one of the funniest revue shows anywhere, has been playing to sell-out audiences for longer than anyone remembers. At Washington and Mason, you'll find the **cable car barn**, where spinning wheels and whirring cables provide the power to drive all of the city's remaining cable cars. For some reason the place has always reminded me of a huge candy factory.

One of my favorite haunts is **Vesuvio Cafe** at 255 Columbus (across the alley from the City Lights Bookstore), one of the classic old bars—and one of poet Dylan Thomas' favorite places in the city. Jack Kerouac got drunk here back in 1960, when he was supposed to be on his way south to meet Henry Miller at Big Sur. He couldn't tear himself away and never got to meet Miller.

Vesuvio is unique. Even though most of the Beat poets are gone, interesting characters still drop in. Perhaps they're lured by the sign that proclaims, "Don't Envy Beatniks . . . Be One!" There are always big, happy crowds here, as well as at Tosca and Specs, both across the street. I remember one night when a patron brought a pet rabbit into Vesuvio, making it the most petted rabbit in the city before the night was old. Just goes to show what a friendly place Vesuvio is. (More recently, a man carrying a knapsack with several rabbits was seen at Specs; he apparently is often found hanging out at one of the local bars.)

Friends and food alfresco near Union Square.

Tosca Cafe, next door to Specs on Columbus, is another old-time hangout, where Bob Dylan was once ousted, along with Allen Ginsberg and Lawrence Ferlinghetti, because a friend they had brought along had misbehaved. The place is still a hangout for writers and musicians, most of whom make a lot more money in a year than most Beat poets made in a lifetime.

■ ■ ■

There's an embarrassment of riches here—so many good and interesting small restaurants, you'll probably want to eat at all of them—Caffe Puccini, Cafe Michelangelo, Caffe Stella, Cafe Greco, Cafe Roma, Rose Pistola.

If you're in need of picnic food, stop by **R. Iacopi & Co. Meats**, 1460 Grant at Union, which has traditionally cured pancetta and prosciutto; **Molinari's** on Columbus, famous for its cheeses and sausages; or the **Liguria Bakery** at 1700 Stockton for focaccia. **The Italian French Baking Co. of San Francisco** at 1501 Grant also has a great selection of baked goods. If you're thinking of getting some wine to go with it, try an Italian chianti classico, or perhaps a California sangiovese or barbera. Molinari's sells wine and North Beach Liquor (Columbus and Union) has a pretty good selection.

■ AMBLING THROUGH CHINATOWN

South of City Lights Bookstore and along Broadway and Grant begins one of San Francisco's most historic—and lively—neighborhoods, Chinatown, which is expanding into North Beach.

The last time I came to San Francisco, I approached Chinatown not from North Beach but from Nob Hill, leaving a friend's apartment at the break of dawn and strolling down California Street toward the bay as the gray towers of the Bay Bridge emerged from the gloom. Turning north on Grant, I wandered into Chinatown just as it was coming alive. Big men unloaded double-parked refrigerator trucks that restock the Chinatown larder: crates of exotic fruits, herbs, and vegetables; fish so fresh they wiggled on the ice; whole hog carcasses; and loads of fresh flowers. Vans brought cages of chickens and chukar partridges, and bins filled with huge green frogs and freshwater turtles. Merchants were just starting to set up crates of produce outside their shop, while cooks started up the barbecue ovens and began to prepare the savory take-out dishes which would be displayed in the shop windows. Soon the delectable tang of barbecued pork, soy squid, and glazed duck wafted down Stockton and Grant, intermingling with the fragrances of flowers and exotic spices.

As the sun rose, I headed east again along Kearny Street, and my pace quickened—out of necessity—as I entered the Financial District, where thousands of people were rushing energetically to work. But I had my eye on the Ferry Building and the newly spruced up Embarcadero.

■ EMBARCADERO

Earthquakes now and then do some good. The last one so destabilized the Embarcadero Freeway (which cut off downtown from the bay) that the structure was demolished and the waterfront is once again integrated into the city. A new wide sidewalk runs along the bay, backed by sycamores and palm trees (which may seem a bit odd to dyed-in-the-wool San Franciscans, but they look nice, and remind the locals that, yes, indeed, they're part of California, despite the frequent fog). There's a great deal of new, architecturally interesting housing here and residents jog and walk along the waterfront, past the old Ferry Building and past the tugboats moored near the Bay Bridge. On Saturdays residents walk down from Telegraph Hill or out of the Embarcadero apartments to shop or eat at the farmers market by the Ferry Building—one of the best such urban markets on the West Coast. Not only is the produce extraordinary, with huge strawberries and thin-stemmed asparagus, but several excellent local restaurants sell prepared food here at booths, and set out tables, chairs, and awnings. The view, while you're sitting there sipping your cappuccino, is of the Bay Bridge, the Tuscan-style Ferry Building, and the tall office towers of the Financial District—plus, of course, Telegraph Hill.

The venerable **Ferry Building** (next to Pier 1), which survived the big 1906 earthquake, was used only as an office building for many years after the bridges replaced the cross-bay ferries. But in recent years commuter demand has brought passenger ferries back to the bay, and the Ferry Building's tall tower once again watches the multitudes clamber onto outgoing ferries and rush off the incoming boats. You can choose from several ferry trips across the bay.

The ferry to **Jack London Square** across the bay in Oakland takes 20 minutes. It passes Yerba Buena Island, which author Henry Richard Dana visited in 1836, and its adjacent landfill, Treasure Island, before gliding between the silver towers of the Bay Bridge. After steering up the Oakland estuary, the ferry docks right

Two women participate in Chinatown's Moon Festival.

people only, and a baseball store selling trivia items for every imaginable team. Sea lions squat on several yacht floats north of the pier. On nearby Jefferson Street is a Ripley's Believe It Or Not and a Guinness Museum of World Records.

To the west, seafood restaurants can be found both on and off the water, and with or without views of the bay and the fishing boats. (Few San Franciscans eat at Fisherman's Wharf, however.) You can also buy a freshly cooked, ready-to-eat crab. While it won't be from San Francisco Bay—most "local" crabs are brought in from Eureka, the Pacific Northwest, and Alaska—it will still be very good. Prepare to pay about $10 per crab; one feeds about two people.

Fishing boats still tie up along the working part of Fisherman's Wharf. On a back pier, half-hidden by waterfront restaurants, is a small chapel catering to the spiritual needs of the rugged men and women who draw their sustenance from the turbulent waters off the Golden Gate.

An early morning walk along the commercial boat docks of Fisherman's Wharf can bring close encounters with brown pelicans, but on one morning in the summer of 2004, black-crowned night-herons and snowy egrets stole the show, perching atop the piers and on a large bait float. Asked if they posed a problem, a worker scooping up bait for waiting fishermen said they did not. The brown pelicans were hanging out with the sea lions at Pier 39.

You should visit the wharf at least once in the gray light of early morning, when it looks like a scene from a French *noir* movie. Brown pelicans have discovered not only that the tops of pilings make for perfect (and very secure) preening places, but that it's perfectly safe to hang out at the ends of the docks as well. Sometimes you can get surprisingly close to these big birds. And don't be startled when something barks at you from the water. Sea lions seem to be everywhere along the San Francisco waterfront.

The Cannery (2801 Leavenworth) was one of the country's first brick factories to be converted into a shopping mall. Like the former chocolate factory at nearby **Ghirardelli Square,** it's had its ups and downs, but there's usually something interesting to see, plus a few good shops and restaurants. After a major makeover in 2004, the square has been renamed Del Monte Square (www.delmontesquare. com), and it now houses a boutique hotel and maritime Museum.

■ ■ ■

Parking at Fisherman's Wharf is unbelievably expensive—about $30 for five hours. Avoid the high cost by walking, parking farther down the Embarcadero, riding a

Cable cars ride among traffic at Union Square.

Muni bus or a cable car, or taking a ferry from Oakland or Marin. The majority of the Wharf's shops and restaurants are located right along the Embarcadero, as are Pier 39 and the ferry dock at Pier 41, from which boats depart for Sausalito, Alcatraz and Angel Island. There are several sailings daily; 415-705-5555.

■ ALCATRAZ ISLAND

You can see the former island fortress-prison, known to prisoners as "The Rock," from almost any point along San Francisco's northern shores and from the north-facing slopes of its hills. The late, much revered San Francisco columnist Herb Caen once called the prison San Francisco's "Chateau D'ifficult." I love taking the short ferry ride from Fisherman's Wharf to Alcatraz, because I think of it less as a prison than as a former citadel. I can walk past the bomb-proof barracks (with 10-foot-thick walls), whose casemates still have the old embrasures and square gun ports designed for muzzle-loading cannons, up the old ramps below the high fortress walls from the 1850s, and through the well-defended 1857 fortress gate (which once had a moat and drawbridge, and still looks like something straight out of a European medieval history book).

Other than Fort Point (see page 56), Alcatraz is San Francisco Bay's only pre–Civil War fortress. Designed as a fortress to protect the entrance of the bay from enemy ships, the island had no human habitations before the first citadel was built here between 1853 and 1859, and was instead the abode of seals, sea lions, and pelicans (*alcatraz* means "pelican" in Spanish). The island's life as a citadel was short; the Rock became, in turn, a prison for locals who sympathized with the Confederacy during the Civil War, a military prison, and a notorious federal penitentiary. Such evildoers as "Machine Gun" Kelly; Al Capone; Alvin "Creepy" Carpis; and Robert Stroud, the Birdman of Alcatraz, were incarcerated in the large cell block on top of the island. Supposedly, men on Alcatraz could hear the voices of party-goers at the San Francisco Yacht Club on quiet evenings—which made their punishment even harder to bear. Alcatraz is now administered as part of the Golden Gate National Recreation Area. Rangers give tours ("interpretive walks" during the day and tours of selected areas during the evening) and tell stories of famous prisoners who tried to escape into the cold water and wild currents of the bay.

Alcatraz is also a strangely beautiful place, with green lawns, trees, and flowers (planted on soil shipped in from the mainland). It's worth the visit just for the spectacular views of the city, the bay, the Golden Gate, and the Marin and Contra Costa shores. Look for seals, sea lions, and sea birds hauled out in the small sandy coves or on the rocks below. The last time I was there I even saw brown pelicans roosting on their eponymous island. A two-and-a-half-hour ferry ride/guided tour leaves daily from Pier 41 on Fisherman's Wharf; *415-705-5555*.

■ ANGEL ISLAND

This beautiful, rocky island rising straight from the blue waters of the bay wears a robe of classic California flora that gives off a rich aroma: a fragrant blend of dry summer grasses, bay trees, and pines. In spring, the island is verdant and covered with wildflowers. Wild white and purple iris bloom on the top of Mount Livermore. If you would like to have a picnic in the country while staying in San Francisco, walk to Fisherman's Wharf and take the ferry to this magical island.

On sunny weekends, hundreds of people disembark with their bikes and picnics at Ayala Cove. From the cove's green lawn and sandy beach you look across Tiburon Strait to the wooded island of Belvedere, the peninsula of Tiburon, and the forested hills rising behind it.

Follow the signs and walk the road that circles the island for marvelous views. In some coves the water is an almost tropical emerald green. As you turn east you'll pass a former immigration and quarantine station, which operated as the "Ellis Island of the West" from 1910 to 1940; it served as an entry point for Asian immigrants. Because they had to prove they were related to an American citizen and carried no communicable diseases, some had to wait here for weeks, even months, before they were allowed to enter the country. The walls of the old dormitory still carry poems scribbled by frustrated detainees. *Island*, by Him Mark Lai, Genny Lim, and Judy Yung gives a good account of this period. One of the interned wrote: "This place is called an island of immortals, when in fact, this mountain wilderness is a prison. Once you see the open net, why throw yourself in? It is only because of empty pockets I can do nothing else." (*Island*, poem 23.)

Angel Island ferry leaves from Pier 41; 415-705-5555. You can avoid paying the high parking fees near the pier—about $30 for five hours—by walking to the wharf, or by driving north across the Golden Gate Bridge to Tiburon and taking the ferry from there.

■ HYDE STREET PIER AND AQUATIC PARK

Hyde Street Pier, just west of Fisherman's Wharf, serves as permanent moorage for a number of historic ships, all of which are open for visiting (although occasionally one or another is closed for restoration). They include: the *Eureka,* a paddle-wheel ferry that made the last run to Sausalito; *C. A. Thayer,* a three-masted lumber schooner—and one of two survivors of the vast schooner fleet that once rode the waters of the Northwest—and the *Balclutha,* a full-rigged ship that once sailed between San Francisco and Britain and later worked the Alaskan fishing trade.

■ ■ ■

Looking across the bay from Aquatic Park, with its sandy beach protected by a curved pier, you can conjure up much of the maritime history of the bay—Spanish navigator Juan Manuel de Ayala's ship coming to anchor in 1775, the steamers and clipper ships carrying passengers to San Francisco during the Gold Rush, the

(following spread) The Golden Gate Bridge across San Francisco Bay.

Italian fishermen in their sleek, Mediterranean-style lateen-rigged fishing boats, the lumber and sealing schooners, and the great ocean liners that once sailed from San Francisco to Hawaii and East Asia. **The San Francisco National Maritime Museum**'s collection of ship models will augment the historic ships you visit at the Hyde Street Pier and will give you a sense of the bay's maritime history. Nearby is the Dolphin Club, whose members come to swim in the icy bay every morning and evening, and to kayak from here around the bay.

The **Golden Gate Promenade,** which you can follow all the way to Fort Point underneath the Golden Gate Bridge, begins here. The path is very popular with joggers, who love the shoreline's beautiful views and bracing breezes.

FORT MASON AND MARINA GREEN

Fort Mason, a former Army bastion, now houses a number of cultural institutions. Greens restaurant serves vegetarian haute cuisine; try the restaurant or pick up food from the to-go counter. Walk out with a delicious chili or soup to sit on the benches by the pier and watch the bay.

Continue along the shore to the Marina Green, a waterfront greensward that has great views of the Golden Gate Bridge and of the yacht harbor. Early in the day women perform tai chi exercises; at other times of the day it's filled with kite-flyers, joggers, and dog walkers. On the city side, the Marina Green is faced by elegant, California-style houses.

The Wave Organ, on a tip of the harbor breakwater, is a sculpture that transmits the sound of bay waters.

The Palace of Fine Arts (a short detour down Baker Street; the parking lot is right off Marina Boulevard) was built for the Panama Pacific International Exposition of 1915 and designed by architect Bernard Maybeck. It's a faux palace with huge stucco pillars topped by female figures dressed in togas, who face away from all viewers. When the fair ended, San Franciscans could not part with this supposedly temporary structure, and in 1962, a Marina resident donated money to have the decaying "palace" restored. It is surrounded by a large reflecting pool and is one of the most popular places in San Francisco to get married. Behind the rotunda is the **Exploratorium,** dubbed the finest science museum in the country.

The Palace of Fine Arts (top left) is a local landmark.

A bridge painter toils at his never-ending task high above the Golden Gate.

■ FORT POINT

This brick and granite pre–Civil War fort is especially impressive on a foggy day, as its tall walls rise into the mist. The huge south arch of the Golden Gate Bridge looms overhead.

Constructed between 1853 and 1861, according to a pattern familiar from such East Coast fortresses as Fort Sumter, this massive citadel is the only defensive structure of its kind on the West Coast. Its guns—three rows of casemated 42- and 32-pound muzzle loaders and a rooftop tier of 8-inch shellguns—have never fired a shot in anger. Fort Winfield Scott, as it is officially known, has an entrance gate constructed of heavy oak. It's large enough for teams of horses to drag through the huge cannons that once armed the fort and protected the Golden Gate.

The passage inside the gate is protected by "murder holes," gun ports through which the defenders of the fort could shoot invaders trapped between the inner and outer doors. Inside, arched casemates open onto a courtyard on the seaward side of the fort, living quarters border the landward side. There's a mysterious air about this citadel, perhaps because its pattern of construction goes back to Elizabethan times, when guns were first used to defend castles. When fog wafts through the courtyard and veils the wide-yawning openings of the casemates, you can imagine all sorts of strange and mysterious happenings taking place here.

Rangers in Civil War garb give tours and lectures and may draft you into a gun crew and teach you how to load and fire a Civil War cannon. From the top gun tier and from the promenade surrounding the fort you can enjoy some truly great views of the Golden Gate and the Marin Headlands.

During a 2004 visit, much of the fort's waterside was blocked off because Golden Gate Bridge earthquake retrofitting overhead created the danger of falling debris. Visiting hours are limited to Friday, Saturday, and Sunday during Golden Gate Bridge seismic retrofitting. Check www.nps.gov/fopo/home.htm for updates.

■ WALKING ACROSS THE GOLDEN GATE BRIDGE

A walk across this bridge (2 miles one way) is a spiritual and bracing experience in any weather, so dress warmly. You can really appreciate the height of the towers, which rise 746 feet above the water, from the pedestrian walkway. Don't worry if the bridge shifts beneath you: it's designed to sway 27.5 feet from east to west in strong winds or earthquakes.

From the bridge deck and from the overlook north of the Golden Gate Bridge, you get a good view of the city, the towers of the Financial District poking their tops above Russian Hill, the Marina District, and the Presidio. And, of course, you can see the bridge itself as it sweeps across the Golden Gate from the Marin Headlands to the green hills of the Presidio.

■ ■ ■

Remembering that the early nautical explorers along this coast missed the entrance to San Francisco Bay for several hundred years, I recently asked a bay tugboat captain at what point, when out on the ocean and looking from his pilot house toward the east, he could tell that he was entering a bay instead of piling up on a rocky shore. He answered that he hadn't thought about it before; he just follows a prescribed course. But without reference to the Golden Gate Bridge and other man-made structures, he said, you had to wait till you got to Land's End before you could tell the opening led into a bay. Which explains perfectly well why the early explorers sailed past the bay without seeing it—Land's End is awfully close to disaster for an old-fashioned galleon, and its crew wouldn't have dared to sail in that close without knowing that the sheer rock walls they saw from their pitching deck would open onto a passage to a safe anchorage.

◼ THE PRESIDIO

The 1,480-acre Presidio, a military reservation until 1995, was founded by the Spanish in 1776. One of four such fortresses established in California, the Presidio served as Northern California's social center during the Spanish period. It was here that Russian Count Nicolai Rezanov arrived on an American ship, the *Juno*, in 1806 hoping to buy food to feed the starving Russian colony in Sitka, Alaska. The Spanish, who had closed their ports to foreigners, did not allow the Russians and Americans to land. Rezanov not only won them over though, he also won the heart of the Presidio comandante's beautiful 15-year-old daughter, Concepcion (Concha) Arguello. The middle-aged widower proposed marriage and was accepted, but, because he was a member of the Russian imperial family, he had to return to Russia to ask the czar's permission. After loading much needed food aboard the *Juno* and dropping it off in Sitka, he set out for St. Petersburg. But he died on the arduous overland journey through Siberia. Concha Arguello waited for him until she learned of his death; then she entered a convent in Benicia, where she lived out her final days.

I did a double take when I visited Crissy Field, a former military air strip, in the summer of 2004. "What a great habitat restoration," I thought. Had I not known that this was a former air field, I would never have guessed it. An elevated walkway leads through the newly created marsh, and across the saltwater lagoon. This restored "natural" shoreline of the Presidio stretches between the Palace of Fine Arts and Fort Point. It consists of 100 acres of restored beach, marsh, lagoon, and wind-swept dunes, plus a picnic area, barbecues, a fishing pier, and the Farallones Marine Sanctuary Visitors Center.

The Community Environmental Center at Crissy Field offers programs that address the convergence of natural and urban environments through community workshops, cultural events, family outdoor adventures, stewardship opportunities, youth leadership initiatives, and educational programs. *For more information, check www.crissyfield.org or call the Crissy Field Hotline at 415-561-4844.*

A view of the Marina district and the bay, from Pacific Heights.

■ Bay to the Pacific

The Presidio's beautiful **Coastal Trail** starts south of the Golden Gate Bridge toll plaza. (If you're coming from the city, take the last exit before the toll plaza and follow signs to the Presidio. This will take you through a tunnel under the bridge approach. Follow signs directing you to the trail and park your car in the dirt parking lot west of the road. If you come from the north, turn right on the first road after the toll plaza.) The Coastal Trail winds its way south along the cliffs through groves of eucalyptus and cypress in the Presidio, past abandoned batteries, and along Lincoln Boulevard and El Camino del Mar.

A great view of the Golden Gate, the bridge, and the Marin Headlands can be had from the crumbling bastions of World War I–era Battery Boutelle on top of the cliffs (just off Merchant Road), especially if you're willing to brave the vertical ladders that take you to the top of the redoubt.

The Presidio is getting to be a pretty wild place: there's now a yellow "coyote crossing" warning sign on Lincoln Boulevard—the main north–south road running above the cliffs on the west side of the Presidio.

Farther west, rising from a Lincoln Park hilltop, is the spectacular **California Palace of the Legion of Honor,** an art museum devoted mainly to Continental, especially French, art. The museum houses a varied collection from the sculptor Rodin, including the original bronze casting of "The Thinker." During the next several years, it will also be the main venue for traveling art exhibits, as its sister institution, the de Young Museum, is brought up to earthquake safety standards.

From **Lincoln Park** the Coastal Trail descends on steps to **Land's End,** the most rugged stretch of shoreline in San Francisco, with some truly great ocean views. Be careful if you leave the main trail, perhaps to take a spur down to little pocket beaches. The surf can be treacherous. There's also been a lot of erosion in recent years, and trails (and even part of El Camino del Mar) have fallen into the ocean.

If you're looking at **Fort Miley** (www.cr.nps.gov/nr/travel/wwIIbayarea/mil. htm) from an offshore boat, you don't see much besides the Veterans Administration Hospital, which rises from a steep, rocky cliff dotted with trees and shrubs, But there are abandoned gun emplacements hidden in the rocks, and trails meander along the bluff tops; one steep trail winds down to a sheltered beach. The fort was part of the seacoast defense of San Francisco Harbor, after America became involved in World War II (though construction of the fort began in 1899). West Fort Miley has a picnic area with restrooms. Sutro Heights Park on San Francisco's Point Lobos and the Cliff House are to the south. The fort is partially administered by the National Park Service.

At the northern end of Ocean Beach stands the **Cliff House**, one of San Francisco's most famous landmarks, and one of the city's first tourist attractions. It was originally built in 1863 by real estate tycoon Charles Butler. In 1881, Adolph Sutro bought the property and turned it into a family resort, bolstering business with a huge bathhouse next door, known as the **Sutro Baths.** That earlier Cliff House burned in 1907; the present incarnation, built in 1909, is a restaurant more popular with tourists than locals. Relaxing in the bar, with its expansive view of the ocean and wildlife on offshore rocks, is a wonderful way to spend a quiet hour or so. Nearby paths lead down to the ruins of the Sutro Baths, which burned in the late 1960s.

A major renovation stripped the 1909 building down to its original, boxy, concrete form, but the harsh lines have been mitigated by a modern, curved addition with lots of windows, which give visitors a better view of the coast, the sea lions, and the Sutro Bath ruins to the north. Inside, the restaurant, bar, bistro, and deli all offer a view with the food. *1090 Point Lobos; 415-386-3330; www.cliffhouse.com.*

■ BEACHES OF SAN FRANCISCO

Baker Beach

In the Presidio, a road winds through the woods down the cliffs to Baker Beach, whose 4-mile-long strand offers views of the Golden Gate Bridge and, across the frothy waters, the rugged, brown cliffs of the Marin Headlands. On rare warm days families from throughout the city set up their picnic lunches on the southern portion of the beach. Towering above are magnificent houses set into the cliffs.

Baker Beach is listed as a "clothing optional" beach (and a gay beach) by many publications, and the far northern end, toward the Golden Gate Bridge, is certainly quite a scene: everyone's naked, and a vigorous volleyball game always seems to be going on. (Closer to the parking lot, everyone wears bathing suits and the beach is filled with families.)

China Beach

China Beach's name is from a Chinese fishing village that once stood here. South of the Presidio, Lincoln Boulevard takes you past the beautiful mansions of the Sea Cliff neighborhood. As the road turns west, it changes its name to El Camino del Mar. (Follow the "49 Mile Scenic Drive" signs.) At a stop sign one block beyond 27th Avenue, look for a sign that says "Public Beach," turn right, and then turn immediately left into Sea Cliff Avenue. Follow this road; there's a parking lot at the end of it. Park and walk down to the beach on the service road. This beach is unusual for San Francisco's oceanfront, because it's safe for swimming. Though the water is abominably cold, many people swim here anyway. Brrr!

Ocean Beach

San Francisco's Ocean Beach (reached by driving through Golden Gate Park) is apt to be a chilly, wind-swept, sandy waste in the summertime, when it is socked in with fog 66 percent of the time. In fall and winter, however, it's clear and clean, and on sunny days it becomes packed with sunbathers. Children laugh as they chase each other and scream as they make mock runs at the surf. Joggers and kite-fliers are out in force. The beach glistens in the sun, and the spindrift sparkles like diamonds. Even the seagulls are smiling. The surf, however, is dangerous.

When the surf is rough at Ocean Beach, there will be surfers at the Taraval Break, often led by Doc Renneker, the "Surf Doc"—made famous by an article in *The New Yorker* magazine. His fellow surfers on this wild break are apt to be local celebrities as well: singer Chris Isaak; Stephan Jenkins, lead singer of the rock band Third Eye Blind; and surf writers Daniel Duane and Matt Warshaw.

If you're looking for a place to stop for hot tea or a meal, drop by the restored Beach Chalet at the west end of Golden Gate Park. It's where the locals come, and it's worth it.

■ GOLDEN GATE PARK

With its 1,017 acres, Golden Gate Park is the largest cultivated park in the country and the only one to border the Pacific Ocean. It was designed by William Hammand Hall in 1871, after he took on the seemingly impossible task of landscaping the largest stretch of sand dune on the California coast.

The western end of the park borders the Great Highway, which runs parallel to Ocean Beach, and this western half is far quieter than the park's busy eastern half. Here, during the week, a stroller on Speedway, Marx, or Lindley meadows or along the Chain of Lakes will meet few passers-by. Holding down the westernmost corners of the park are two windmills from Holland, installed at the turn of the century to irrigate the park. Below the windmills, the Queen Wilhelmina Tulip Garden blooms in spring.

■ SAN FRANCISCO BAY

San Francisco Bay is set inland from the Pacific Coast, stretching north and south some 50 miles and embracing a region of more than 6 million people. The university town of Berkeley and the bustling harbor of Oakland (shielded from gales by Alameda Island) dominate the eastern shore; San Jose and the Silicon Valley lie to the south; eastern Marin County is to the west; and the Carneros Wine Country stretches along the northern shore. Along the shores of the bay are rural islands bordering cities, historic parks, wildlife preserves, and boat harbors.

Almost entirely landlocked, except for the rocky gap of the Golden Gate and the entrance to the Carquinez Strait, San Francisco Bay is a great place for sailing and kayaking. But beware of the tides, which can be very strong, and the sea fogs that roll in through the Golden Gate and shroud both the water and the land in impenetrable whiteness. The north, east, and south shores of the bay are often warmer

Japanese Tea Garden, Golden Gate Park.

China Camp, sunbathers lie shoulder to shoulder on the narrow beach like sardines in a can, while children splash in the warm water of the cove. Rock music drifts from the family picnics on the low bluffs, often with lyrics in Cantonese. Fifteen miles of hiking trails wind through grasslands and oak groves; the campground has 25 campsites tucked into the oak woods above the shore, plus restrooms, showers, and a group campsite that can accommodate as many as 200 people. *For information, call 415-456-0766. For camping reservations, call 800-444-7275.*

The best time to visit **Olompali State Historic Park** is in spring, when wildflowers are in bloom beneath the native oaks and the lower slopes of 1,558-foot Mt. Burdell—which stretches east to the Petaluma River, a navigable slough running north from San Pablo Bay—are unobstructed by fog or smog. "Olompali" was the name of a Miwok village that stood here for several thousand years before the first Europeans arrived. Its last chief, Camillo Ynitia, received the land as a grant from the Mexicans and was the only Native American to hold on to his grant after the Americans took over.

When the motley band of adventurers who raised the Bear Flag in 1846 and proclaimed California's independence in Sonoma's plaza marched west, they fought a battle with the rancheros at Olompali. During the next century and a half, the land changed hands several times. (It was owned by the rock band The Grateful Dead in 1966.) A mansion was burned when a hippie commune occupied the place, but pieces of an adobe once owned by Ynitia survive. The site was eventually bought by the state for a park. The calla lilies blooming along the creek for much of the year are not native but remnants of the ranch garden. (Three miles north of Novato. Access only from southbound U.S. 101; for information, call 415-892-3383.)

■ CARNEROS WINERY TOUR

The Carneros district, an American Viticultural Appellation established in 1983, stretches across the cool, lower reaches of Sonoma and Napa counties at the northern reaches of San Francisco Bay (the area known as San Pablo Bay). Grapes were planted here before Prohibition, but the Carneros wine boom did not take off until the 1970s and 1980s, when winemakers discovered that the relatively cool climate of these often foggy vineyards put complex flavors into the grapes and gave the wines character and backbone. The local wine industry experienced a major

Spring wildflowers carpet the Marin Headlands.

expansion in the 1990s, as more and more cattle and sheep pastures were plowed up and planted with vines. Some recently planted vineyards come so close to tidewater you can almost pick grapes from a boat.

The wines made from Carneros grapes are unique. They have better acids and more subtle fruit than the grapes grown in Napa and Sonoma's warmer valleys. Even warm-climate grapes like cabernet sauvignon and merlot ripen well in favored locations. Yet zinfandel may not ripen at all, and chardonnay needs shelter. Surprisingly, the fickle pinot noir fares well on exposed, windy slopes, making excellent wine of great complexity and depth. While chardonnay and pinot noir are generally considered the area's top grapes—both also make superb sparkling wine—merlot and cabernet sauvignon from Carneros vineyards are also excellent.

The Carneros district is the wine region most easily reached from San Francisco, less than an hour's drive from the city. Head north on U.S. 101, turn east onto CA 37 in Novato, and then turn north on CA 121 (Carneros Highway) at the Sears Point Raceway.

As you drive along CA 121, a two-lane highway that sometimes carries an astonishing amount of traffic through the rolling green hills north of San Pablo Bay, you'll soon begin to spot wineries. Some of my favorites are listed on the following pages, in the order they appear along the highway as you drive north.

Cline Cellars

You can really feel the famous Carneros winds, with their ocean chill, at the grounds of Cline Cellars. As you taste the wines you will encounter some unusual but very pleasing flavors. The marsanne tastes quite unlike any other California white, and the mourvèdre is quite different from the more familiar cabernet sauvignon. Be sure to taste the Cotes d'Oakley, a blend of red Rhône grapes, as well as the vin gris, a white wine made with red mourvèdre grapes. There are also semillon and zinfandel for more traditional palates. *24737 Arnold Dr. /Hwy. 121, Sonoma; 707-935-4310.*

Gloria Ferrer

As you drive north from Cline, look for a winery to your left, up against the gentle slopes of the hills, looking sunny even on a gray Carneros day. This is Gloria Ferrer Champagne Caves, built in 1982 by the Spanish sparkling-winemaker Freixenet. The winery is named for the wife of José Ferrer, the company president. The sparkling wines made here under the direction of winemaker Bob Iantosca are truly superb, but also be sure to taste the chardonnay and pinot noir made by

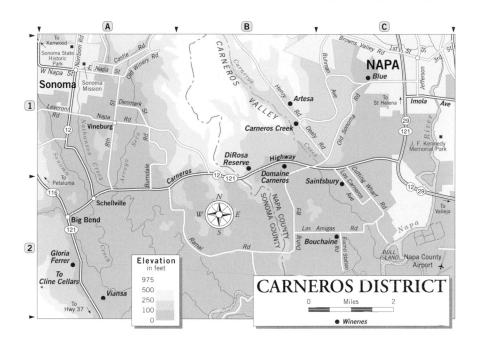

Iantosca. Both have that elusive Burgundian quality California winemakers often strive for but seldom achieve.

Sitting on the deck at Gloria Ferrer on a warm, sunny afternoon, sipping sparkling wine as you look out over the vineyards and listen to the birds sing, is one of Wine Country's happiest experiences. *23555 Hwy 121, Sonoma; 707-996-7256.*

Domaine Carneros

After Big Bend, the Carneros Highway runs west, passing through a landscape of fields, pastures, and dairy farms before coming to the next winery, on the Napa side of the district. A large French chateau to the right side of the highway is Domaine Carneros, established in 1987 by the champagne house Taittinger and American partners. The sparkling wines made here are very austere, the perfect accompaniment for fresh Tomales Bay or Point Reyes oysters, or for caviar from farm-raised Sacramento Valley sturgeon.

There's a reason why Domaine Carneros looks like an authentic French chateau: it is a copy of the Château de la Marquetterie, an 18th-century mansion owned by the Taittinger family in Champagne. *1240 Duhig Rd., Napa; 707-257-0101.*

Saintsbury

You'll have to call ahead and make an appointment to visit Saintsbury, a small winery that has gained renown for the quality of its pinot noir, but it's worth the effort. *1500 Los Carneros Ave., Napa; 707-252-0592.*

Carneros Creek Winery

To visit a truly pioneering winery, drop in at Francis Mahoney's Carneros Creek Wincry, a bit up the hill off Old Sonoma Road. While other wineries—most notably Louis Martini—established earlier Carneros vineyards, it was Mahoney's winery, opened in 1972, which proved that cool-climate pinot noir could be very complex indeed. *1285 Dealy Ln., Napa; 707-253-9463.*

Artesa Winery

This ultra-modern hilltop winery was built in 1991 as Cordoniu Napa, a Spanish-owned sparkling wine facility. In a major turnaround in 1999, it changed its name and winemaking style to make "still" wines. Ever since, Artesa has produced some of the Valley's best cabernet sauvignon, sauvignon blanc, chardonnay, and pinot noir. Artesa has a small wine museum and rotating art exhibits in its visitors center, plus tours and tastings. *1345 Henry Rd., Napa; 707-224-1668.*

Truchard Vineyards

Not only chardonnay and pinot noir grow well here; Truchard Vineyards has amply proved that merlot planted here can reach surprising complexity as well. Be sure to call ahead for an appointment at this small winery, whose pinot noir is also in a class by itself. (And don't miss the zinfandel and cabernet sauvignon.) *3234 Old Sonoma Rd., Napa; 707-252-8864.*

Bouchaine Vineyards

Bouchaine Vineyards, on the south side of the Carneros Highway, is rather close to tidewater, between Carneros and Huichica creeks and the tidal sloughs of San Pablo Bay. The alternately breezy and foggy weather has a special effect on the fermenting wine. Call ahead and make an appointment to taste the chardonnay and pinot noir, which are surprisingly Burgundian, as well as the gewürztraminer, which has a definite Alsatian character. *1075 Buchli Station Rd., Napa; 707-252-9065.*

Di Rosa Preserve

Part of a former vineyard (Winery Lake), this 217-acre art and nature preserve has a lake, meadows, oaks, 150-year-old olive trees, a 130-year-old stone winery (serving

Carneros Creek Winery is home to the cool-climate pinot noir.

as a residence), and some 2,000 works of art by 800 artists; some of it suspended from trees. Admission is by reservation only. *5200 Carneros Hwy, Napa; 707-226-5991; www.dirosapreserve.org.*

For other Carneros wineries and for wineries in the Napa and Sonoma valleys, see the Compass Guide to the *California Wine Country.*

■ BAY AREA PARKS & RESERVES

■ SOUTH OF SAN FRANCISCO

Jutting eastward into San Francisco Bay, **Candlestick Point State Recreation Area** has great views, both from the shore and from its two fishing piers. Facilities include trails, a wind-sheltered picnic area with barbecues, and a fitness course for seniors. It's very windy here, so windsurfers love this area. Wind harps and chimes are permanently set up on Windharp Hill, where they make music in the lightest breeze. Tide pools are exposed at low tide. There are two stories about how the park got its name: one claims that it was named after a rocky pinnacle that once

Don Edwards San Francisco National Wildlife Refuge

The waters overflow the flatlands and form the Delta because tidal waters pushing up through Carquinez Strait hold them in check, allowing for only a slow outflow. The resulting maze of river beds, sloughs, and channels—several thousand miles of them—winds through a fascinating mix of marshes (both fresh and salt), dense willow thickets, jungle-like riparian woodland, valley grassland (green in spring, golden from summer through winter), and Central California oak woodland. Above it all rise the strange black walnuts of the Delta, their upper branches often dead and bleached, reaching for the sky like gnarled hands. Islands protected by levees are often marked by a sheath of riprap rocks (broken-stone foundations) on the water sides; unprotected islands, called "berm islands," are covered with lush growth—some of which may be covered by water at the highest tides. Trees with broad canopies often grow above the riprap, making for shady picnic sites with a view.

The Delta can get very hot in summer, though fogs drifting in from the ocean often cool it down. In winter, cold, thick tule fogs may rise from the marshes and, during freezing weather, turn the roads into skating rinks. But cold spells rarely last long, nor do temperatures drop far below freezing. (After all, oranges ripen here.)

Pear orchards, vineyards, corn, and sorghum fields grow on the fertile lands protected by the levees; century-old mansions hide in dense groves of shade trees. Fig trees, gone wild, often cover the sides of the levees near farms and settlements.

Three Delta towns—Courtland, Locke, and Walnut Grove—have escaped the advance of progress largely unscathed and still look pretty much the same as they did in the early 20th century. There isn't much to Courtland—tree-shaded homes, an old neo-classic post office building on Main Street below the levee, and a grocery store on top of the levee, overlooking the Sacramento River. In fact, there isn't much to any of these towns, but visitors can stroll their streets, look at the old buildings (some of them dating back to the late 19th century), and succumb to that pleasant state of mind the locals call Delta Time. Some visitors fish, some come by boat, but all succumb to the Delta's laid-back feeling. One Courtland restaurant, **Al the Wop's,** has been a regional favorite for its steaks and cocktails for several decades.

Locke was built in 1915 as a bedroom town for Chinese farm workers (the only town in the U.S. built by the Chinese exclusively for Chinese residents) after the Chinatown in Walnut Grove, just down the river, burned. During a recent visit I noticed that Locke's current inhabitants were mostly Hispanic, though the shops sported Chinese signs.

Walnut Grove, just downriver, has an old Chinatown and is more prosperous, but has maintained its Delta character in the face of progress. Walnut Grove dates back to 1850, but most of its houses were built later in the 19th and in the early 20th centuries. The town's buildings have changed little since 1920, though its oldest building—a former produce shipping warehouse—now serves as a boathouse. The second oldest, erected in 1912 as a beer hall, houses the **Chinese Garden Restaurant** (River Road; 916-776-2100). It has outdoor as well as indoor dining, but you can also get a take-out meal to bring to a grassy picnic spot on a levee.

Walking-tour guides are available on the town's website (www.walnutgrove.com). Main Street is still lined with false-fronted buildings, and part of town is still separated into Chinese and Japanese quarters. (At one time, Walnut Grove had the West Coast's largest Chinatown outside San Francisco.) The **Dai Loy Museum** (Main Street; 916-776-1611) displays Chinese artifacts and gives guided tours of the town. Walnut Grove's favorite restaurant, **Giusti's** (14743 Walnut-Grove Thornton Road; 916-776-1808), serves steaks, pasta, and spirits. **Ernie's Saloon**, father down the river in Isleton, is known for its big platters of crayfish. You may feel like you've been transported to a different, more famous delta farther southeast.

MARIN COAST

The shoreline from the Golden Gate north to Bodega Bay in Sonoma County is one of the most scenic stretches on the West Coast. It is a landscape of great variety: rocky shores alternate with sandy beaches; reedy inlets and estuaries are over-towered by tall cliffs. Deep river canyons, where sea fog lingers even on hot summer days, shelter groves of tall redwoods.

Hills are brown and gold in summer and fall, and thick with green grass and wildflowers in the late winter and spring. Trees—mostly oaks, California bays, Bishop pines, and Douglas firs—stand straight and robust along the ridgetops or hug the bottom of small valleys where creeks run in the wintertime.

■ HEADING NORTH FROM SAN FRANCISCO

When I have enough time to spend several days ambling along the shores and uplands of this beautiful coast, I like to leave San Francisco early in the morning and cross the Golden Gate Bridge just as the sun clears the Berkeley hills to the east, casting long slants of light westward, and lighting up the bay in a silvery, almost translucent blue. As commuters wind slowly south, I leave U.S. 101 and drive west on CA 1, through Mill Valley up to a spur of Mount Tamalpais and then down the coastal slopes to Muir Beach. Near the top of the ridge a road leads north to Muir Woods (a grove of ancient redwoods in a deep creek canyon some 3 miles from here) and continues to Stinson Beach. Another road runs north to **Mount Tamalpais** (2,571 feet), with its miles of hiking trails and grand views of bay and ocean.

The winding road to Muir Beach (CA 1) leads down a steep-sloped valley of low treeless hills toward a blue Pacific Ocean. The road turns and twists till it comes upon a eucalyptus grove and a turnoff for Green Gulch Farm run by the San Francisco Zen Center. This retreat has a small Japanese-style inn, where people interested in attending lectures or meditations spend the night, drink tea, and wander through the beautiful farm and gardens down to Muir Beach. At the bottom of the hill, the road reaches the pastures of a horse farm and a spur road turns toward the beach.

At the entrance to this road stands the **Pelican Inn,** a perfect re-creation of an English pub, with flowers and a green lawn out front. Here you can warm yourself with a hearty meal, enhanced by a pint of stout ale.

The very end of the Point Reyes Peninsula.

■ MUIR BEACH *map page 85*

Several unmarked trails lead from the paved parking lot through a marsh to a beach of dark sand, past ducks dabbling in the waters of the tidal lagoon. You may see a great blue heron waiting for the movement of a minnow or amphibian. The pocket beach is quite small, even for a North Coast beach, hemmed in as it is by steep headlands. It usually has a somber, lonely, and bracing quality to it, but on some days can get warm, shielded by the cliffs from the chilly northwesterly breeze.

■ ■ ■

North of Muir Beach, a vista point just off the highway has a splendid view of the ocean, with the headlands of the Point Reyes Peninsula jutting into the sea to the northwest and the Farallon Islands, prime haven for breeding seabirds, looming up on the western horizon. To the south spreads glimmering San Francisco. Note that CA 1 is very curvy here; one switchback bears the ominous name "Sports Car Cliff Diving Curve."

A road sign pointing to **Muir Woods** will lead you to one of the most glorious stands of redwood trees on the West Coast. Nestled in a valley of the coastal mountains, this small national monument protects magnificent, thousand-year-old red giants that tower up to 280 feet above the trails. On a sunny day, narrow shafts of light filter through the high branches; when the fog swirls through the trees, the effect is mystical. Clear-running Redwood Creek, along which silver salmon and steelhead migrate in the winter, winds through the forest.

■ STINSON BEACH *map page 85*

Over a ridge and a few switchbacks to the north of Muir Beach, and at the base of the west flank of Mount Tamalpais, sits Stinson Beach, one of the finest beaches in Northern California. Many of the facing village's beach houses are supported in the sand by short stilts. Traffic slows to a halt along the two-block-long main street, where there's a kayak rental and, not surprisingly, a surf shop, as well as

a few small restaurants. The Parkside Cafe, just off the main drag, is the popular local hangout (the menu is augmented by hamburgers from a takeout stand in summer). There's also a good market uphill from the Coast Highway; over the years the shop has evolved from a country store to a place where you can buy local wines, roasted chickens, imported cheeses, fresh breads—everything you need for a picnic. Stinson

Ron Kauk, rock climber par excellence, tackles "Endless Bummer," an overhang at Stinson Beach.

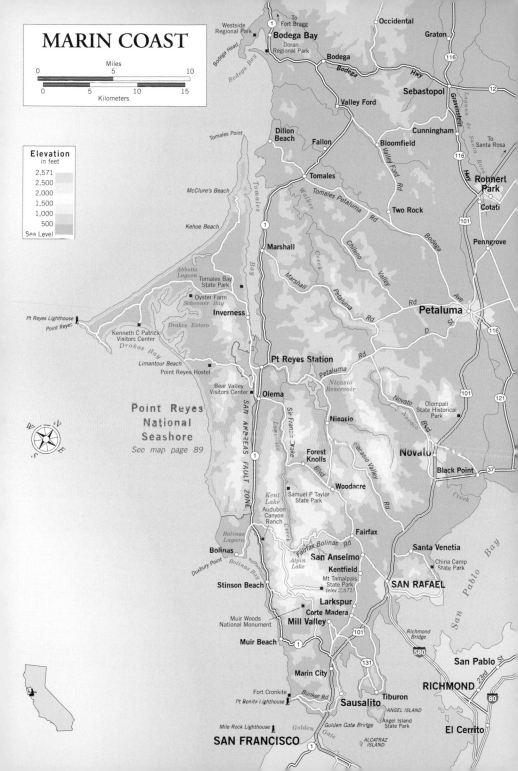

Beach Books (half a block north) advertises itself as the only bookstore located directly on the San Andreas Fault.

Facing south and shielded by Point Reyes from the northwesterly sea winds and much of the fog, this beach gets quite toasty. This is a wonderful place for a long barefoot walk through white sand. Mornings and evenings the ocean is often calm and reflects the colors of the sunrise or sunset. Birds are everywhere—marbled godwits and dunlins probe deep in the wet sand for edible invertebrates. Sanderlings rush about in busy groups, first following the receding waves, then running from the surf wash, snatching up any morsels dislodged by the swirling waters. These tiny shorebirds move their legs so quickly they look like mechanical toys on wheels. Willets probe more deliberately. They look like washed-out, plain gray birds until they are disturbed and flash dramatically black-and-white wings during take-off.

Even though the ocean here has dangerous riptides and can be quite cold, some people swim at Stinson. (If you can rent a wet suit at the surf shop, do it.) It is also a popular surfing spot. On the Fourth of July surfers have a famous bonfire, then pray to the god of surfing, asking for a good year.

■ BOLINAS LAGOON AND BOLINAS *map page 85*

Just beyond Stinson Beach, the two-lane Coast Highway runs along the eastern shore of Bolinas Lagoon, a tidal inlet that is in the process of becoming a salt marsh. The silted-up channels are a paradise for shorebirds, who congregate here in great numbers in fall, winter, and spring. Great blue herons, egrets, and cormorants can be seen at all seasons. Harbor seals and their pups haul out on a sandbank near the eastern shore. Bolinas Lagoon harbors the greatest concentration of great (white) egrets on the California Coast—more than 60 have been counted on the mudflats at one time. Monarch butterflies overwinter in local trees.

■ AUDUBON CANYON RANCH

A bit farther north, east of the highway, is a bird refuge with a heron and egret rookery in one of its redwood canyons. Visit in February and March, when the great blue heron and snowy egret chicks hatch in nests high up on top of the redwood trees. From a trailside viewing platform with stationary binoculars, you can look down upon the nests and watch the chicks wait for their parents to return with minnows or frogs from Bolinas Lagoon. *415-868-9244.*

■ Bolinas

Unless you look carefully, you can easily miss the turnoff to the village of Bolinas—which remains unmarked because residents tear down any direction signs the state or county put up. The center of the village is composed of two narrow streets, with side roads leading to houses tucked away into craggy nooks above the ocean and all along the Bolinas plateau. Both commercial streets dead-end on narrow beaches; parking spots by the beach itself are almost non-existent. From the westernmost of these beaches, you can walk to the tide pools of Duxbury Reef, which are very popular with marine biologists because of their varied intertidal marine life. Bolinas's main road runs down to the outlet to the Bolinas Lagoon and has a few docks for boats. The channel is so shallow that boats loll on the mud at low tide.

Bolinas no longer has a gas station; there is one farther north in Point Reyes Station. To learn more about the village and its history, visit the Bolinas Museum on Wharf Road. Bolinas folk tend to be wary of strangers, but less so if those strangers walk rather than drive.

An egret pauses in the glow of a Marin coastal sunset.

Just up the road from the museum lies Smiley's Schooner Saloon, considered the longest continually operating tavern in the United States, a relic from the days when schooners carried redwood lumber from the Bolinas wharf to San Francisco. William Tecumseh Sherman, of Civil War fame, was once shipwrecked on Duxbury Reef, walked to Bolinas and took a schooner bound for San Francisco, but the ship foundered in the high swells of the Golden Gate. After being rescued for the second time in 24 hours, Sherman finally reached San Francisco by rowboat.

Today, the high cliffs above the Bolinas beaches are slowly slipping into the sea, as are the houses precariously perched above them. The cliff-houses are visible from Stinson Beach, but not from the center of the village.

■ POINT REYES NATIONAL SEASHORE *map page 89*

The crown jewel of this coast is Point Reyes, the large, roughly triangular peninsula jutting out from the beautiful coast north of San Francisco. It has been called an "Island in Time," because it is part of a landmass that has moved north over the millennia. It is separated from the mainland by a narrow rift valley that's filled with water at Bolinas Lagoon to the south and Tomales Bay to the north.

The rocks and vegetation of Point Reyes differ from that of the mainland, and give this National Seashore a special magic. Time seems to have stood still in Point Reyes—and, in many ways, it has. Little has changed here since the National Seashore was established decades ago. Most of the land has been preserved in its natural state, which bestows a timeless aura on its cliffs and beaches, meadows and forests, valleys and hills, and saltwater inlets.

A tree or two may fall down, others will grow up, a pasture will be taken over by brush, but the changes take place so slowly that you'll hardly notice them. Even the burned pine woods below Inverness Ridge are growing back and will soon have regained their timeless serenity.

■ BEAR VALLEY ENTRANCE

From the Bear Valley Road at Olema, you enter the central section of the National Seashore. Don't let the landscape confuse you. You cannot see the ocean from any point in this narrow valley, because Douglas fir–clad Inverness Ridge to the west blocks the view. Stop at the **visitors center** to pick up a detailed map of the seashore and get a quick update on what's happening.

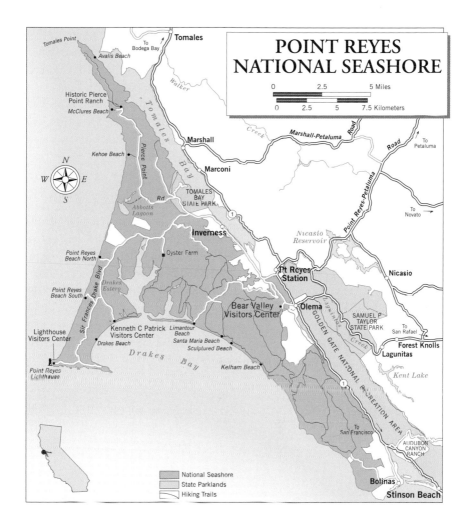

POINT REYES
NATIONAL SEASHORE

National Seashore
State Parklands
Hiking Trails

Kule Loklo

You might want to take the short but beautiful walk to Kule Loklo, a meadow where the bark-slab houses, sweathouse, and shade ramadas (open shelters with thatched roofs) of a reconstructed Coast Miwok village rise from the dewy grass. Look for the red-capped, black-and-white acorn woodpeckers—they chatter noisily on the fence posts that part the trail from the meadow where the rangers pasture their Morgan horses. The village looks alive, when fog drifts in and out among the trees and slab houses, or as the sun heats the grass and water vapors rise like smoke from native campfires.

The short earthquake trail begins on the east side of the parking lot (look for a prominent marker). This trail straddles the San Andreas Fault, which is explained by markers with photos, rock samples, and plaques. You can see the spot where the peninsula moved 16 feet north in the 1906 earthquake and where a cow was said to have been swallowed whole, leaving only its tail protruding from the crack.

Bear Valley Trail

This 4.1-mile-long trail is well graded and mostly level, with a slight rise near Divide Meadow. The trail runs through laurel, oak, Douglas fir, and alder woods along the banks of creeks to the coast and has a sea arch where Coast Creek enters the ocean. The trail has many rustic benches (cut from huge logs) for weary travelers to rest their legs, as well as a picnic area in Divide Meadow. Odd trees and flowers growing along the trail and in the meadow remain from when the area held old cabins and a former hunting lodge. The latter was also responsible for the herds of exotic Asian axis and European fallow deer. The axis deer are reddish brown and have whitish spots (only the fawns of native black-tailed deer have spots); the fallow deer come in a variety of colors, including pure white.

GETTING TO POINT REYES FROM SAN FRANCISCO

There are two ways to reach Point Reyes from San Francisco; whether you're planning a day trip or an overnight stay in the area, you may want to make the journey in a loop.

Option 1: From San Francisco along scenic Highway 1, take the Stinson Beach exit from U.S. 101 and follow the signs north.

Option 2: Take U.S. 101 north to Lucas Valley Road and travel west to the town of Point Reyes Station. (See map opposite.)

No entry or day use fees are charged at Point Reyes National Seashore. Camping is permitted only in four hike-in campgrounds; fee. Call *415-663-1092*, Monday–Friday, 9:00 A.M. to noon, for reservations.

■ Limantour Beach

Farther north on the Bear Valley Road you reach the turnoff for Limantour Road, which winds over the spine of the peninsula to Limantour Spit, Estero, and Beach. West of Inverness Ridge, where many of the magnificent native Douglas fir forests fell victim to the great fire of 1995, blackened tree trunks still rise against the skyline. The area's non-woody vegetation has recovered quickly, however. The Bishop pine forest has undergone a remarkable regeneration—the seedlings have been helped along by beneficial soil fungi. The ridge now has many more species of plants than it had before the fire. In the spring, wildflowers densely cover the burned slopes; white-headed cow parsnips and multi-colored lupines grow 5 feet tall. The **Point Reyes Hostel** charges the most reasonable lodging rates in the region. In spring the ground around the hostel, a former farmhouse, is dense with yellow daffodils.

The road ends, almost with a question mark, in a rather rough parking lot on a gentle slope above the lagoon. From here an easily walkable paved trail leads down the slope to a causeway across Limantour Estero, which here consists of a series of ponds and marshes connected by sluggish creek channels. To the east of the causeway upstream is a pond where coots and their odd-looking black-and-red chicks putter in spring. Listen for the piping calls of a black rail from a reedy thicket on the far shore.

Bird-Watching Along Limantour Spit

At different seasons, you can watch dowitchers probe the shallow mud as they walk along in tightly packed flocks, moving their heads up and down in unison in a stitching motion; or you can watch long-billed curlews daintily stepping across the marshy ground as they reach forward with their long, downward-curved bills, picking unsuspecting insects off reed and grass culms. You might come across a yellowlegs rapidly stalking through the shallow water of the marsh, jabbing at animals on or below the surface of the water. Then again, you might hear the high-pitched trill from a flock of least sandpipers emerging from the salicornia (pickleweed) margin of the marsh, picking and probing for tiny crustaceans among the fleshy joints of the succulent plants. These sparrow-sized least sandpipers are the world's smallest shorebirds, yet they often crouch to get closer to their prey, getting their legs and belly feathers quite muddy in the process.

You can't miss the white egrets (both "snowy" and "great"). They may be standing quietly in marshy nooks, flying overhead, or racing through the shallow water to chase a frog, fish, or garter snake. Merlins look for prey on the wing by slipping low over the edge of a bluff, then soaring high on an updraft before dropping down to repeat the maneuver. Turkey vultures gently rock their wings as they soar overhead.

The estero is a shallow fresh- and saltwater lagoon that spreads between the bluffs of the peninsula and the sand dunes and beach of sandy Limantour Spit. The path ends on the western shore of the estero, but the low dunes are easily crossed on informal trails.

Beyond the dunes, a wide, sandy beach beckons. In spring, harbor seals haul out here with their pups, but stay clear: it is illegal to disturb the seals or the pups. At all seasons, even in summer when they're supposed to be breeding in the arctic or on the shores of upland lakes, shorebirds probe the wet margin of the sand. World-weary willets poke their beaks listlessly into the sand, while dunlins, startled by a human intruder, will dash into the air, where they twist and turn, alternately exposing their grayish-brown backs and wings and their white bellies. At one moment they flash like a bright signal, the next moment they seem to have vanished from the air as they blend into the dun background color of the bluffs; then the flock suddenly turns and flashes another white signal. Back on the beach, the dunlins settle down to the serious business of extricating worms and crustaceans from the mud of the estuary and the wet sand of the beach; moving as a solid phalanx, head down, they probe the ground.

As you approach a flock of sanderlings resting above the high-water line, watch their curious behavior. Like other shore birds, sanderlings puff up their feathers and pull up one leg under the warm covers to preserve body heat. As you come closer, the whole flock may hop away from you—instead of flying off—on one leg. It seems that sanderlings can hop around on one leg as easily as they can on two, so why waste any extra motion.

If you visit coastal beaches and marshes in winter, you may wonder why most of the birds appear to be sleeping through the day instead of foraging actively. That's because in winter the lowest tides—the ones during which the birds gather most of their food—occur at night.

Arch Rock, at the end of Bear Valley Trail, in the Point Reyes National Seashore.

SONOMA & MENDOCINO

This rugged, wild-looking coast of scenic, surf-splashed headlands, sandy beaches, and quiet coves can be surprisingly solitary, but it's not at all uncivilized. Away from the sea, lovely valleys hide foggy redwood dells, sunny vineyards, and fragrant apple orchards—many of them perfect for picnics or strolls. Restaurants and inns in the small villages dotting the shore are among California's best.

■ SONOMA COAST BEACHES

North of Bodega Harbor, Highway 1 winds from Bodega Bay to the mouth of the Russian River and beyond. The beaches along the way are very popular, but they are rarely crowded, and the majority of visitors come for only a few hours, to lie in the sun or watch the surf. There are more than 40 parking areas with beach access along Highway 1 (most of them free).

The best of these beaches is **Goat Rock,** just south of the Russian River mouth, which is connected to the shore by a low spit (which is, unfortunately, topped with a parking lot). Sweeping views up and down the coast more than make up for the uninspired shore facilities. Murrelets, cormorants, and gulls coast above the surf and seals haul out on sandbars. Arch Rock, a few hundred yards offshore, supports a colony of cormorants, gulls, and other seabirds. Even though the gray-green water is considered unsafe for swimming, on warm summer days many intrepid folk of all ages (and not all in wet suits) brave the surf. Perhaps they're inspired by the way those tiny murrelets and auklets roll with the breaks.

■ BODEGA AND BODEGA BAY

The small country town of **Bodega** (not to be confused with Bodega Bay), just north of Highway 1 as it crosses into Sonoma County, was the setting for Alfred Hitchcock's 1963 thriller *The Birds*. (The schoolyard scene was shot in Bodega, but the harbor and cafe are actually in Bodega Bay.)

The highway returns to the coast at **Bodega Bay,** just south of Doran Spit, which protects the harbor from the southeasterly gales of winter. The narrow strip of land between the highway and the tideflats is lined with fishing boat docks, marine supply shops, fish processing plants, and restaurants. The most popular of

A gorgeous day to walk along Bluff Coast Trail.

Father Aurelio blesses the grapes during the Wine Harvest Festival, at Sonoma Mission.

these is Lucas Wharf, which also has a seafood market that sells freshly caught local fish. Lots of fresh seafood is landed at Bodega Harbor, which is the largest fishing port between San Francisco and Eureka.

A hundred years ago, Bodega Bay was known less for its fish than for its red potatoes—which, along with other produce grown in the hinterland, helped keep Gold Rush San Francisco supplied with fresh food. Agriculture in Bodega Bay was started by Russian fur traders who settled here in 1812, 5 years before the Spanish founded Mission San Rafael north of the Golden Gate and more than a decade before Padre Jose Altmira established Sonoma Mission (1823). The Russians raised cattle and hogs on the coastal slopes, as well as vegetables. They grew grain inland, in the Freestone Valley. But the Russians were hunters and traders, not farmers, and their farms did not prosper.

I've spent the night in Bodega Bay at the Inn at the Tides, and enjoyed a simple meal while looking across the bay at Bodega Head. I'd driven up from Marin that day, so my meal consisted of bread from the bakery in Tomales; a Camembert from the Marin French Cheese Company (707-762-6001) on the Red Hill/Petaluma–Point Reyes Road; sweet sheep's milk cheese from Bellwether Farms, a local sheep dairy; and a bottle of Russian River pinot noir that I bought at Gourmet au Bay (913 CA 1; 707-875-9875), an excellent little wine shop in town on Highway 1 just north of Tide's Wharf.

Bodega Head

Bodega Head, a rocky promontory jutting out into the Pacific Ocean, is even more windswept and bleakly beautiful than Point Reyes, perhaps because it does not have as many visitors crowding its trails.

Narrow dirt trails lead to headlands, hidden coves, and vast stretches of sand dunes. Chaparral-covered Bodega Head is a great place for watching both sea and land birds, the sea lions that hang out on offshore rocks, and the fishing and pleasure boats winding their way through the mudflats of the harbor on a narrow channel.

■ JENNER

The village of Jenner clings to the cliffs of the north bank of the Russian River. Once a bustling bedroom community for local loggers, Jenner is best known today for its cliffside restaurants and inns. East of Jenner, Highway 116 and River Road lead to the vineyards

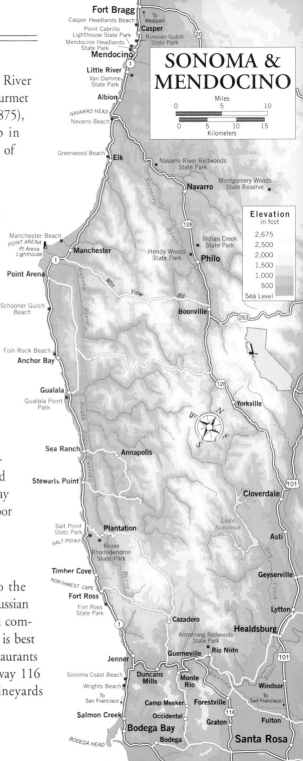

SONOMA & MENDOCINO

Miles
0   5   10

0   5   10   15
Kilometers

Elevation
in feet
2,675
2,500
2,000
1,500
1,000
500
Sea Level

If you're planning to have a picnic, the deli counter at Speer's Market has all the fixings you'd ever want, plus a great selection of local wines. *A few blocks off River Road, Forestville, at 7891 Mirabel Rd.; 707-887-2024.*

Also consider stopping for a meal at the Farmhouse Inn and Restaurant, on the west side of the highway at the junction of River and Wohler roads. *7871 River Rd., Forestville; 707-887-3300; www.farmhouseinn.com*

Cut across the valley (and Russian River) on Wohler Road, turn right on Westside Road, and drive north until you come to Hop Kiln Winery on your right. (If you want to visit Russian River Valley Wineries farther upstream, consult the Compass Guide to the *California Wine Country*.)

Hop Kiln

A unique feature of this small winery, founded in 1973 by Dr. Marty Griffin, is that it was built in and around a historic hop kiln without destroying any of the kiln's equipment. Thus you'll find wine stored in the old ovens (kept cool by their thick stone walls) and strange pipes and railroad tracks running through the winery. The wines are mostly estate grown and include such rare varietals as valdiguié and verveux. Your best bet for a picnic on the winery's sunny grounds is a wine appropriately called Marty Griffin's Big Red. *6050 Westside Rd., Healdsburg; 707-433-6491.*

Rochioli Vineyards & Winery

After visiting Hop Kiln, retrace your route on Westside Road to Rochioli; its small parking lot is immediately west of Hop Kiln, on the same side of the road. The Rochioli family became winegrowers in 1933, when they took over vineyards planted in the 19th century and planted new vines of their own on gravelly benchlands above the Russian River. After decades of selling their grapes to local wineries, the Rochiolis started making their own wine in 1982. Production is small, but the wines are worth stopping for. Considering the family's farm background, it is not surprising that Joe and Tom Rochioli believe in letting the vineyard determine the quality of the wine. Because of the cool growing conditions, the flavors of their pinot noir, cabernet sauvignon, chardonnay, and old-vine sauvignon blanc are intense and complex. The tasting room patio, shaded by roses, is a great place to sip wine and enjoy the view across the Russian River vineyards. *6192 Westside Rd., Healdsburg; 707-433-2305.*

Cabernet Sauvignon grapes on the vine.

■ ALBION   *map page 107*

There's little that remains today to suggest that this hamlet was a major mill town during the height of the redwood timber boom. The Albion River Inn, north of the river on the ocean side of the highway, has great food and great views, as it did in the old days, but it's a safe bet that it has a lot less excitement than it did in those rowdy times of steam schooner skippers and loggers with caulked boots.

Most folks driving up or down the coast on CA 1 notice the Albion River just in passing, because it is spanned by a high trestle bridge. Most of the homes, and even the inns and restaurants are on top, to take advantage of the view, but there's a pretty stretch of river at the foot of the cliffs, plus boating facilities. You'll also find a narrow sandy beach west of the trestle, and a couple of campgrounds and marinas in the final river bend—as well as great fishing. This small port has not been developed into a full-fledged marina, because the river can get very shallow at its mouth when the tide runs out, but kayakers can explore rock gardens, tide pools, and sea caves, with seals, ravens, ospreys, and kingfishers to keep them company.

The view from the Albion River Inn extends out over the coast.

■ **VAN DAMME STATE PARK** *map page 107*

This small, sandy cove, where the Little River (one of several coastal rivers with that name) empties into the ocean, once had several shipyards where coastal schooners were turned out in assembly-line fashion right on the beach. Now there are campgrounds and miles of hiking trails up the creek, where a large lumber mill once stood. No traces remain of this 19th-century industrial glory, except for a mooring bolt in an offshore rock. This beach is very popular with scuba divers and has an annual abalone festival. *For information call the Van Damme State Park visitors center at 707-937-4016.*

■ **ANDERSON VALLEY WINERY TOUR**

The mouth of the Navarro River—flanked by tall, grassy bluffs dotted with pine woods, and almost closed off from the ocean by a wide sandbank—looks much like the other rivers on this coast. But a few miles upstream, the grasslands give way to redwood forests, which open to pastures and fields as the valley widens. Here, where the coastal fogs are conquered by sunshine, is where some of California's best wines are made.

The redwoods along this stretch of river are all second-growth (the original trees were cut long ago and floated downstream to waiting schooners), but that doesn't make them less striking. The trees have had time to grow up, and the forest cover—dense carpets of green and golden mosses, dark-green clumps of sword ferns, and emerald-green willows—carpets the open spaces between the big trees and lines the streamsides. Look for kingfishers and ospreys in riverside boughs. In season, when silver salmon and steelhead run upstream, the river may be thronged with fishermen.

By now you're close to the magnificent giants of **Navarro River Redwoods State Park** (see map page 125) The **Paul Dimmick Wayside Campground** is in a redwood grove bordering the Navarro River. It's not only a good place for summer camping (it floods in winter) but it also has some good picnic spots. If you want to walk in the shade of more impressive redwoods, head south to the virgin redwoods of **Hendy Woods State Park**. They seem like an anomaly here, because this is a warm part of the valley, but the same fog that cools the valley enough to put flavor and complexity into grapes also creeps upriver to sustain these majestic trees. Ask the rangers to point out the locally famous fallen redwood stump where an eccentric known as the Boonville Hermit used to live.

■ **MENDOCINO** *map page 107*

Whenever I approach this clifftop village, I'm freshly impressed by the views: the bridge over the river set off by a wall of dark conifers and the broad sandy beach at the mouth of the Big River. Above the flower-bedecked bluffs spread the green meadows of the headlands, over which towers a finely crafted white church with a pointed steeple. (The headlands, with their meadows and cliff-edge trails, are quite definitely the place to go for a long, thoughtful stroll.) On one side stands the large "goat lady's" house, where well into the 1970s a local woman lived and kept a flock of goats. Behind the church are the false-fronted business houses of Main Street. They look out to sea across an expanse of wildflowers, past cliffs where gnarled Bishop pines appear to rise straight from the sea.

Mendocino was founded in 1852 as a lumber town, but after the local mill closed down in the 1930s, Mendocino fell into an economic slumber, which helped preserve its old buildings and water towers. It was rediscovered in the 1950s by artists looking for pretty scenery and low housing prices. By the 1960s and 1970s, the village was being invaded by weekend travelers, many of whom liked the community so much they wanted to settle down. This new generation of "locals," worried about exchanging their newly discovered rustic lifestyle for yet another Sea Ranch–style version of exurbia, then forestalled a major development on the headlands by having the meadows and bluffs surrounding the village turned into a state park. Since its establishment in 1974, **Mendocino Headlands State Park** has attracted almost a million visitors a year. Even so, its miles of cliffside trails are rarely crowded. Wildflowers cover the bluffs in spring; gray whales swim past the headlands in spring and fall, on their annual migration; and the bird-watching is great year-round. Several small but high offshore islands serve as refuges for cliff-dwelling shore- and seabirds, including cormorants, murres, murrelets, storm-petrels, oystercatchers, turnstones, and gulls.

I have fond memories of Mendocino, because I showed my artwork at galleries here back in the early 1970s, when I sketched most of the village's venerable pine trees, cypresses, and homes. What attracts artists is not only the scenery but also the quality of the light. The color of the water can be extraordinary, ranging from indigo and turquoise to silver, slate-gray, and even brown; the headlands can change from golden to dark purple to deep red to pale ash almost in the blink of the eye. Only the black oystercatchers and their bright scarlet bills never change—

The quaint town of Mendocino is a favorite weekend getaway spot.

they look the same whether they probe dark beach rocks for mussels and limpets, or whether they are sitting out a particularly vicious high tide on the upper edges of the headlands cliffs.

I have been visiting Mendocino on and off for almost 40 years, and the village hasn't changed much. It's the kind of place where you read a good book in a comfortable inn, and then pull on a heavy coat and wander the bluffs. On a clear night, you can sit at the edge of a meadow and admire the brilliance of the stars. Even in the fall, when the grass on the headlands is a silvery brown and blows back and forth in the wind like ruffled bear fur, you can still find a flower or two blooming in its hidden depths.

Mendocino is truly timeless. In the summer of 2004, it seemed like the town was going through a crisis, with several well-established inns, including MacCallum House and Whitegate Inn, up for sale. But the inns were immediately snatched up by new innkeepers, and the MacCallum House is now even better than it was before. **Patterson's Pub**, where the locals hang out, is still very busy and boisterous at night, proof that the town is alive and well. Up the coast, at the

north end of town, the cottages at Agate Cove Inn are still popular with visitors, and the resident osprey still perches outside the dining room window as it checks the cove for potential prey. The nicest place in town also nestles at the north end, above the steep cliffs of Agate Cove: the **Sea Rock Inn** has been refurbished by its owners and now sports cozy rooms, paneled with carefully selected knotty pine. Each room comes with a fireplace, a private deck, and a view of the ocean. Best of all, the inn has its own power generator, assuring that the cabins keep their lights when winter storms plunge the town into darkness.

While many of the artists who made Mendocino famous have escaped the steady crush of visitors by moving south to Point Arena or north to Fort Bragg, the **Artists Co-op of Mendocino** (on Main, near Woodward) is still the best place for buying local art. The workshops and classes taught at the **Mendocino Art Center** are also very popular. *45200 Little Lake Street; 707-937-5818.*

■ ■ ■

Many of the old homes here have been converted into B&Bs, with varying degrees of luxury and with generally great breakfasts. Most local inns have their own coffee blends, put together by a local roaster. And all of the inns are within easy walking distance of the village's shops and restaurants. There are some great restaurants here—Café Beaujolais, the Mendocino Hotel, and MacCallum House may be the best known—but the Mendocino Cafe and the Bay View Cafe are the local favorites.

Along the quiet streets are a number of historic buildings: the **Temple of Kwan Ti** (1852), the oldest Chinese temple on the North Coast; the **Kelley House** (1861), now a museum (45007 Albion Street); the **Ford House** (1854) on Main Street, which now houses the Headlands park headquarters and a historical museum; the **Masonic Lodge** (1866), topped by a sculpture of "time and the maiden" carved from a single redwood log; and the **Mendocino Presbyterian Church** (1868), whose spire rises above the cliffs of the cove, a Mendocino landmark. Trails lead from the back of the church down to Big River Beach, which on sunny days is popular with sunbathers and volleyball players.

Mosaic sculpture New Mother *by the local artist Ron Belt.*

■ RUSSIAN GULCH AND JUGHANDLE RESERVE
map page 107

A few miles north of Mendocino is **Russian Gulch State Park,** known for the blowhole through which seawater blasts skyward during storms. It also has wild-flower-covered bluffs, a cliffside picnic area, and a sandy beach in a rocky cove. Trails lead into the redwood forests of the shady canyon. *2 miles north of Mendocino on CA 1; 707-937-5804; www.parks.ca.gov.*

About a mile north of Russian Gulch State Park, on a side road (but well marked by signs), is one of California's newest and most pleasant state parks. Opened in 2001, the **Point Cabrillo Lighthouse State Park** is a terrific bet for hikers, wildflower aficionados, bird lovers, and lighthouse cognoscenti. *1 mile north of Caspar on Cabrillo Point Rd.; Mendocino; 707-937-5804; www.parks.ca.gov.*

The lighthouse, which dates back to shortly after the turn of the 20th century, was built after the San Francisco earthquake to provide an extra measure of security for lumber schooners. Its outbuildings are more or less complete and intact—only a barn is missing—and are being restored; one of them will become an inn to support the efforts of the volunteers maintaining the light station. The tower, which is off-limits to visitors, has a working Fresnel lens.

Besides the lighthouse and parking lot, which are situated a half-mile apart, the reservation consists of steep, surf-beaten cliffs, a large meadow dotted with mounds of coyote brush (which smells sweet, like honey, when it blooms in late summer/autumn), clumps of wind-sculpted California wax myrtle, and a few stands of cypress.

■ ■ ■

A few miles to the north you'll find **Jughandle State Reserve,** a largely unspoiled slice of coast and mountain. I always enjoy walking out onto the headlands, where wildflowers hang over the edge of the bluffs, and cormorants can be seen nesting on an offshore sea stack. Gnarled spruces, pines, and Douglas firs lie at odd angles, broken apart by winter storms. A steep trail leads down to a small beach and another leads up the hill into a landscape known as an "ecological staircase"—a series of five marine terraces that have uplifted over the millennia. There's a surprisingly even spacing of about 100,000 years between each uplift, making the lowest terrace—the one with the wildflower meadow and the cliffs—some 100,000 years

Redwood logs are transported from the woods using the Excelsior Redwood Company railroad in 1892, near Mendocino.

old and the highest terrace, about 650 feet above sea level, about 500,000 years old. The trail ends at a **pygmy forest,** a dense stand of trees dwarfed by highly acidic soils. Among the unusual trees growing here is the endemic Bolander pine. A 2-foot-tall Bolander pine with a trunk 1 inch in diameter may be 40 or 50 years old; ancient trees may top out at a height of only 5 or 6 feet. Carry water when going on this hike—all that uphill climbing makes for a mighty thirst. *Hwy. 1, 1 mile north of Caspar; Mendocino; 707-937-5804; www.parks.ca.gov .*

■ FORT BRAGG *map page 107*

Rising above beautifully sculpted sea cliffs, this small town began as the headquarters of the short-lived Mendocino Indian Reservation and was, until recently, a major mill town. By the 1990s, Fort Bragg had become a haven for artists, writers, and retirees. It began when the huge Georgia Pacific lumber mill, by far the largest employer in town (and with other businesses dependent on it), began to close down and many mill workers left. Entrepreneurs, catering to the rising tourist trade, bought up shop buildings and homes, and installed boutiques, galleries, and restaurants here. (Because its downtown is compact and fairly level, Fort Bragg is a town made for walking.) Retirees, who bought up old homes, also supported the new enterprises. A new concrete bridge over Noyo River has replaced the narrow old iron span over the gulch at the south end of town. Several historic homes have been converted into inns, and at the north end of town, motels have sprung up east of the former Haul Road—which, now that's it's part of MacKerricher State Park, allows access to beaches and bluffs.

On the western shores of Fort Bragg is the unusual **Glass Beach**, a former (1950 to 1967) city dump. The state bought the beach as an addition to MacKerricher State Park in 2003, and hauled away large metal objects and other trash, but bottle glass was left behind. Rounded by the surf (some ground as fine as sand) the glass pieces paint the beach in strange, multi-faceted colors that glisten in the fog and sparkle in the sun. Despite frequent promises, there still is no pedestrian access to the Pudding Creek trestle that connects the park bluffs to Glass Beach and the town of Fort Bragg. **Noyo,** the fishing port on the banks of the Noyo River at the south end of town (turn right after the bridge), is about as authentic a gunkhole port as you'll find anywhere. It's all business, with little space devoted to visitor amenities. A couple of seafood restaurants and a motel overlook the river and the docks. Charter boats cater to fishermen. I often stop at a seafood shop here to stock up on the excellent smoked sablefish, salmon, and albacore.

Skunk Train

At the foot of Laurel Street, one block west of Main and a short walk from the North Coast pub, is the terminal for the California Western Railroad "Skunk" Train. It got its name from a smelly gasoline car used in the early years of operation; today the train has a steam locomotive and an open excursion car. The tracks wind inland above Pudding Creek and the Noyo River, above marshes and through meadows and redwood forests. It's an exhilarating, scenic ride. There's a stop at North Spur, where the engine is switched to the other end of the train and fills its water tank at an old-fashioned railroad water tower. Here you can catch the train across the mountains to Willits or get some drinks and snacks. *707-964-6371.*

■ MacKerricher State Park

In its heyday, the local lumber company had a private haul road that ran from the mill north to the Ten Mile River. This road, as well as the eight miles of cliffs, meadows, and beaches lying between it and the ocean, is now part of the state park, whose main entrance and campgrounds are about 3 miles north of Fort Bragg. The road now serves as a foot and bicycle trail. I like to walk it from the beach beneath the old Pudding Creek trestle on the north end of town. This sandy beach borders the favorite local swimming hole, where the shallow waters of the creek get quite warm by afternoon. If I have time, I wander along the bluffs to Laguna Creek, where trails lead down from a series of low cliffs to tide pools and small sandy beaches.

During one visit, I stood watching oystercatchers perform their courtship flights, and I let a killdeer believe that I was fooled by its feigned injury. I looked carefully where I trod, because killdeer eggs look so much like rocks that it's easy to accidentally step on them. Birds were everywhere that evening. As I dawdled along, the sun began to set. Soon the entire landscape was clothed in pure gold—the bluffs, the surf, the pines, and the birds. But I could still distinguish the species by their shapes and songs: black oystercatchers on the rocks and on the sand of a pocket beach, little killdeer running along the surf line, mourning doves on the trail, and white-crowned sparrows in the shrubbery. A hawk circled overhead before gliding off to a copse of tall cypress trees. At Laguna Point, even the harbor seals had taken on a golden sheen. I took the raised wooden boardwalk (which makes the Point wheelchair accessible) to the parking lot and walked back to my lodgings in the deepening glow of the sunset.

A sandy beach stretches north from Laguna Point toward the Ten Mile River. Here and there, the broad strand is interrupted by rocky outcroppings and backed by sand dunes. Harbor seals and their pups loll on the rocks, utterly unafraid of the presence of man. Step carefully: this is a harbor seal pupping area. The seals are colonizing more offshore rocks; I'm assuming that means the herd is expanding.

The Old Haul Road, which is partly eroded in places, is continually washed out north of the state park campgrounds, but a trail bypasses the washout. (Or you can just walk along the beach.) Sometimes the sand covering the washed-out road is strewn with bleached driftwood logs—and they usually remain there until they rot.

As you walk north along the beach from the main entrance to the state park, you'll come upon a small lake and marsh above the beach: these are Sand Hill Lake and Inglenook Fen in the park's Ten Mile Dunes Preserve (just south of CA 1 and Simpson Road). The creek that winds through the dunes preserve and across the wide, sandy beach is cut off from the ocean by a sand bar during most of the year. (This is also true for the mouth of the Ten Mile River, except during very wet rainy seasons.) The chunky sea stack at the mouth of the Ten Mile (north bank) is called Guardian Rock.

The pretty **Seaside Beach** is one ridge north of the Ten Mile River, where CA 1 dips down to a sandy cove hemmed in by cliffs. Several dramatically pointed "sea stacks" rise from the sand and the surf. Such formations, common on the rocky coasts of central and northern California, are formed over time, as the force of the surf cuts holes into rocks. When the hole gets large enough, the rock becomes known as an arch or natural bridge. Eventually the top of the arch collapses and creates a pair of sea stacks.

In summer, when sand blocks the mouth of the Ten Mile to the south, you can walk all the way to the MacKerricher State Park dunes and beaches. The beach, which is extremely popular with locals, has only shoulder parking, plus a couple of tiny dirt parking lots. There is no sign identifying the beach, and no rules are posted.

Drive just a little north and you'll reach **Pacific Star Winery** (look for a large sign just off the highway to the west.) This winery would be a great place to visit even if it didn't make (and sell) first-class wine, because it sits above a dramatically sculpted cliff and the tasting room staff is very visitor-friendly. The north side of the winery is very close to a surf-washed cut in the cliff. Here the low cliffs reach out like the fingers of a knobby hand trying to grasp the surf. *33000 N. Hwy. 1, Fort Bragg; 707-964-1155.*

On CA 1 north of the winery is a parking area with fabulous views of the ocean and cliffs (it's on the west side of CA 1, with a trail leading to the cliff edges). This is the **Kibesillah Gulch View Area**. There is no easy descent to the shore here but divers and fishermen manage to scramble down. (Beware: In the summer of 2004, one of these divers was killed by a great white shark.) A little farther north is **Bruhel Point,** which also allows splendid views of the ocean, the rocky shore, and steep cliffs and mountains. Just beyond it is **Chadbourne Gulch**, which has an access trail to a mile-long beach popular with surf fishermen. And just before you reach Westport you'll see **Elephant Rock**, a big sea stack with a natural bridge hole.

Rhododendrons grow in the midst of an old-growth redwood forest.

REDWOOD COAST

Only a few towns brave the wildness of this lonely stretch of steep coastal mountains and sandy shores. Along the great rivers that flow into the ocean here grow the world's tallest trees—the magnificent California redwoods. The silent woods are perfect for contemplative walks; the beaches teem with clams, free for the digging; and small towns and villages like Shelter Cove, Ferndale, and Trinidad invite you to relax while, perhaps, catching a few fish. Humboldt Bay, California's second-largest estuary, is ideal for bird-watching from the shore or from a canoe or kayak.

■ LAND OF MIST AND WILD SCENERY

Seagulls cry as they wheel above the surf, which seems to have the consistency and color of thick cream on this calm morning. The sun, muted by the shroud of fog clinging to the jagged ridge of the coastal hills to the east, lightens up the shore and sea with deeply golden rays, making the gulls and the surf spray look almost supernaturally bright against the dull indigo of the ocean. To the south, coastal terraces and low hills spread as far as the eye can see; to the north, steep cliffs and tall mountains—their seaward side still cloaked in gloom—rise straight from the Pacific. The piercing cries of black oystercatchers rise from the tidal rocks below my vantage point, as the scarlet-billed birds probe the rough, kelp-swathed surface for mussels and limpets.

I have pulled off the road to look at the spectacular scenery where CA 1, the Coast Highway, turns inland, away from the shore. Fog swirls past rocky outcroppings and precariously poised patches of trees, alternately veiling and baring the mysterious faces of the rugged sea cliffs. Looking north along the rocky escarpment, it's easy to see why, so far, no more than a narrow dirt road has penetrated the wilderness ahead. The mountains are too steep, and the cliffs, their bases constantly gnawed by the surf, are too unstable.

This coast looks like a different land from the gentle coastal terraces and river bottoms of the Mendocino Riviera, which stretches from the Navarro River north to Fort Bragg. It looks like a lost world—and in many ways it is.

Called the Lost Coast because it is so remote and difficult to access, the 100-mile stretch of shore between Rockport and the mouth of the Eel River is the

A crab fisherman at Shelter Cove, on the Lost Coast.

loneliest stretch of coast in California. It is bypassed by both U.S. 101 and CA 1 and is touched by paved roads in only a few places: at Shelter Cove; at the mouth of the Mattole River; along a 4-mile stretch of beach south of Cape Mendocino; and at Centerville Park west of Ferndale.

Don't, by the way, look for "Rockport" on your map. The place no longer exists, but persists on maps because it conveniently marks where the Coast Highway leaves the shore.

■ LOST COAST

The northern Mendocino County coast, from Rockport to just south of Shelter Cove, is a beautiful, albeit almost impenetrable, wilderness of steep-sided gorges, roaring creeks, burbling brooks, dense forests, razorback ridges, sheer cliffs, and quiet sandy and rocky beaches.

The 7,312-acre stretch from Usal Creek north to Whale Gulch, the former fishing and hunting ground of the Sinkyone Indians, has been set aside as the Sinkyone Wilderness State Park.

A **hiking trail** runs from the mouth of Usal Creek, through very rough country, north along the 16.7-mile strip of park land to Orchard Creek, where it connects with the King Range National Conservation Area trail system (call the BLM at 707-986-7731 for information), and with Black Sands Beach, near Shelter Cove, which stretches north to the mouth of the Mattole River. You will need a wilderness permit to hike in these areas. Call the Sinkyone Wilderness State Park (707-986-7711) in Whitethorn for permit, campground, and road information.

Other trails cross the King Range. Hiking through the region, you feel at times like you're on an archaeological expedition as you stumble upon house foundations and bits and pieces of abandoned pilings, and perhaps a weather-beaten shack or two. During the heyday of local logging, this region was much more heavily settled than it is now. When the logging companies left, they not only took the mill machinery with them, but sometimes the company towns as well. Today, the back-country is sparsely settled, the coast virtually not at all. For a good insight into the region, read Ray Raphael's *An Everyday History of Somewhere.*

The southern end and western edge of this wilderness are accessible from CA 1 via the unpaved Usal Road (No. 431), which turns north near Rockport at milepost 90.88. (Slow down here; the sign is hard to see and there's a sharp uphill turn.) Jack London and his wife took this road back in 1911 in the conveyance best adapted to its ruggedness—a team and wagon. The road is passable for automobiles to the campground at the mouth of Usal Creek for most of the year, and to the north in the dry season. It connects with the Briceland Road (No. 435) near the north end of the Sinkyone Wilderness. If you can get through, you can drive from here, via Chemise Mountain Road, to Shelter Cove. If not, you have to return and take CA 1 to U.S. 101, head north and take the (marked) road from Redway to Shelter Cove. The road into Shelter Cove is very steep and puts tremendous strain on brakes. Use low gear.

■ SHELTER COVE

This is one of those odd places that has a lot of charm in spite of itself. First developed as a community of fancy getaway homes for Southern Californians with airplanes of their own, this isolated seaside community of 300 people has never really taken off. But, because of the spectacular scenery and the good fishing, it has attracted families with summer homes and a small population of year-round residents—retirees, fishermen, and artists.

The coast south of **Point Delgada** (about the center of town) has tide pools where you can watch sea anemones try to snag small fish, hermit crabs scurry about, and tiny fronds of kelp wave in the current. If you're lucky, you may see a small abalone crawl among the limpets, mussels, and sea snails. Watch oystercatchers pry open mussels with their flat beaks, and look for black turnstones—the black-and-white birds that turn over rocks as well as all sorts of flotsam and jetsam washed up by the tide—as they gobble up crabs and other small animals hiding underneath (and not fast enough to make a quick getaway). The tidal rocks are also very popular with poke polers (see page 115). The sandy beaches north of Point Delgada are great for long walks and hikes and for beachcombing.

The main cove in "downtown" Shelter Cove (at the end of Machi Road) has a public boat launch where you can also rent a boat or go on salmon charters if there are salmon—increasingly uncertain, as their population has been eroded by overharvesting and environmental damage. Hikers take note: Access to Black Sands Beach—the southern trailhead for the hike north—is washed out. You can still scramble down to the beach, but there is limited parking on the access road.

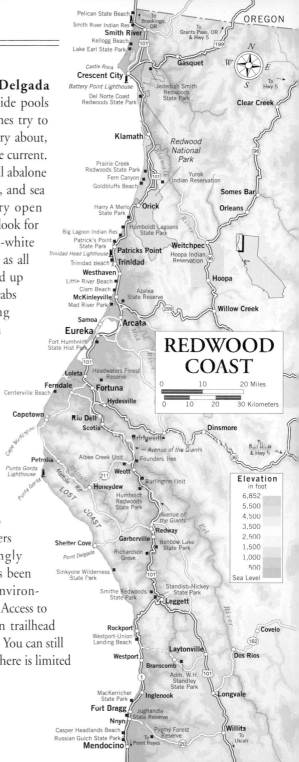

REDWOOD COAST

| 0 | 10 | 20 Miles |

| 0 | 10 | 20 | 30 Kilometers |

Elevation
in foot

| 6,852 |
| 5,500 |
| 4,500 |
| 3,500 |
| 2,500 |
| 1,500 |
| 1,000 |
| 500 |
| Sea Level |

Shelter Cove doesn't have fancy restaurants (the ones that open here periodically seem to vanish quickly), but you can get good food from the **Shelter Cove Campground Store** (492 Machi Rd.; 707-986-7474), near the boat ramp. While you eat, strike up a conversation with the owner, who has lived here for a long time, or with other residents who come for their daily coffee and chat. I learned over lunch one day (some of the best fish 'n' chips I've had anywhere) that one reason the place didn't take off is because the airport is fogged in for much of the year. But never mind the fog, the beaches are particularly beautiful on gray days, capturing your imagination with their stillness, the heightened sound of the sea, the indiscernible shapes looming in the mist.

■ SHELTER COVE TO MATTOLE RIVER HIGHWAY

The Kings Peak and Wilder Ridge roads, which connect Shelter Cove to the Mattole River Highway at Honeydew, are paved, but that does not at all make them easy to drive—they are narrow and they wind their way in and out of steep-sided canyons on countless switchbacks. (I had blisters on my hands by the time I got back to U.S. 101.) But the scenery is wildly handsome and makes the drive well worthwhile, even though you're miles from the ocean. In spring, the meadows are red, white, blue, and golden with wildflowers; in summer the roadway may be all but covered with the cream-colored flowers that have dropped from red-trunked madrone trees overhanging the road, and at all times of the year, a deer or cougar may step from the roadside woods. California quail forage for seeds along the banks, goldfinches flit across thistle patches, and golden eagles soar overhead.

■ HUMBOLDT REDWOODS *map page 141*

While there are small groves of redwood trees tucked away in the canyons of the Lost Coast, chances are you will not see them unless you plan to do some major hiking. Even so, these trees are not comparable to the giant redwoods of the Eel River Valley and of the forests north of Humboldt Bay. You will already have driven beneath giant redwoods near Redway, if you took the road from U.S. 101 to Shelter Cove. If you continue north toward Eureka, you will shortly come to signs directing you to the "Avenue of the Giants." This scenic 31-mile two-lane highway

Starfish and octopus cling to tide-pool rocks during the lowest tide of the month.
(following spread) Surfers at Black Sand Beach in Shelter Cove, on the Lost Coast.

Rockefeller Grove in Humboldt Redwoods State Park.

through the redwoods is an alternative to the busy U.S. 101 freeway. The road runs through tall stands of redwoods, skirts the Eel River in places, and allows access to the trees via many well-marked trails. It seems amazing that some of the biggest redwoods are so easily accessible, but some of California's tallest trees are just short walks from the parking areas.

On a hot, sunny summer day, the redwoods lack the mystic light of a foggy day, but they are still enjoyable, minus the shady coolness you have come to expect. Beware the poison oak that grows here as both a ground cover and a vine clambering up the redwood trunks—I have found myself standing in it.

Near Dyerville lie the remains of the "Dyerville Giant." Once considered the world's championship redwood, it reached 370 feet (as tall as a 30-story building) before it fell on March 24,1991.

You'll find plenty of other redwoods to marvel at in the **Big Tree Area,** on Old Mattole Road. It's 4 miles west of Avenue of the Giants (follow signs leading to the Rockefeller Forest). Hiking distance: 100 yards. Time: 10 minutes each; easy. Here you'll find the following: **Tall Tree of the Rockefeller Forest,** 359 feet high, 42 feet in circumference, 13 feet in diameter, last measured in 1957; **The Giant Tree,**

The wilder areas of Humboldt County are home to many black bears.

363 feet tall, 53 feet in circumference, 17 feet in diameter, designated "Champion Coast Redwood" by the American Forestry Association in November 1991; and **Founder's Grove**, just off the Avenue of the Giants (mile marker 20.6). All this is an easy half-mile, half-hour loop trail.

Farther south on U.S. 101, the **Montgomery Woods State Reserve**—about 11 miles west of Ukiah on the Orr Springs Road—are several large redwoods, including one giant towering at more than 360 feet. **Headwaters Forest Reserve**, the center of protracted controversy over logging of old-growth redwoods, is finally open to the public—it's on the Elk River Road via U.S. 101 south of Eureka.

■ MATTOLE RIVER ROAD AND BEACH *map page 141*

CA 211 is a state highway, but this scenic road isn't much wider or straighter than the roads you've taken north from Shelter Cove. But never mind that. You have lots of time, and the mountain landscape is even lovelier here than it was to the south. The valley of the Mattole is stunning.

From **Honeydew,** the road winds its way slowly downriver toward the coast, passing through a river valley that's green even at the height of a hot and dry summer. There are very few homes, farms, or ranches on this narrow road, which winds and twists its way through these fractured mountains. But little birds—warblers, flycatchers, sparrows—keep you company as they flit through the roadside shrubbery, catch insects on the wing, or scratch for seeds by the side of the road.

Unless you're into serious hiking—and if you don't want to get your car dinged on gravel roads or stuck in muddy bottoms, and you don't want to burn out your brakes on steep hills—the best way to experience the Lost Coast is to take the narrow but paved **Mattole Road** that runs from the Founders Grove on U.S. 101 through Honeydew and Petrolia to Ferndale (with perhaps a short side trip to the mouth of the Mattole River).

If all you want to see is some pretty scenery, plus a few rugged beaches, the beach at the mouth of the Mattole and the coastal strip south of Cape Mendocino should more than satisfy you. If you want more beaches, you'll need to hike. (The King Range trails are accessible via Mattole Road.)

The Mattole Road that leads to Honeydew is not well marked. (It is the only road that crosses the mountains at this point, but it's known locally as the "Honeydew Road" from the Avenue of the Giants to Honeydew.) If you get confused, look for signs directing you to the Rockefeller Forest. Continuing on this road takes you through the Rockefeller Forest and up the mountainside to Panther Gap and the Mattole River (and Valley). The distance from U.S. 101 to Ferndale via Mattole Road is about 60 miles.

For the first 5 miles, Mattole Road winds through groves of tall virgin redwoods and is quite narrow (so built to preserve as many of the big trees as possible). After you leave the redwoods, the road widens and you'll start climbing all the way to Panther Gap at 2,744 feet. After that you drop down to the Mattole Valley, where your lowest point, Petrolia, is a mere 250 feet above sea level.

This stretch of road may look familiar, by the way. Apparently many car commercials are taped in this area.

The Mattole is not a large river, though it widens out in places. It purls over gravel banks and sinks into deep pools, where trout like to hide; it winds lazily through sunny meadows and gurgles in the deep shade of alders, cottonwoods, and willows where wood ducks build their nests in hollow trees. It reaches the ocean in a shallow bay framed by sand dunes and sheltered by wooded cliffs. Mattole Road meanders alongside the river for large stretches and crosses it on several one-lane bridges. Grassy, tree-shaded **A.W. Way County Park,** just off the highway and near the river, has camping.

The main highway (Mattole Highway) leaves the river and turns right (north) across the Mattole River over a bridge just before you get to Petrolia. If you continue straight downriver on Lighthouse Road, toward the wild and lonely beach at the mouth of the Mattole, you'll reach a sandy strand cowering beneath steep bluffs. Beyond the marsh and low dunes to the north you can just make out the bulky mass of Cape Mendocino. The primitive campsites at the mouth of the Mattole River (south of the small lagoon at the river's mouth and just above the sandy beach) are shielded from the sea wind by huge driftwood logs. You can park your car here (or camp) and walk south 3 miles along the beach to the abandoned lighthouse at Punta Gorda. Or you can hike along the beach all the way to Shelter Cove (about 24 miles one way).

■ ■ ■

You reach **Petrolia** by driving back to the intersection with CA 211 and turning north. The village got its peculiar name when oil was discovered here in the 1860s, leading to California's first commercial exploitation of the sticky black liquid. But the boom quickly proved a bust, and Petrolia has been snoozing ever since. During one visit, things were so quiet in mid-morning that I spotted a covey of California quail who were strolling down Mattole Road in downtown Petrolia—and didn't mind posing for a photo.

■ CAPE MENDOCINO *map page 141*

Coming in from the southeast, after climbing the ridge beyond Petrolia (watch for stray cattle), Mattole Road touches the coast at McNutt Gulch Beach (public access near the first bridge over a seashore creek), runs north along the shore, then turns inland just before Cape Mendocino. On a sunny day, the beach is gorgeous. Most of it is rocky, with just a few patches of sand, but it's great for surf- and storm-watching. You'll find shoulder parking (unmarked) in several places with easy to moderately difficult access to the water. Offshore are several beautiful sea stacks (like most California sea stacks, in the drought year of 2004 their tops were whitened by guano). In late summer, golden-flowered grindelia blooms by the wayside. The coast here is fabulous enough for you to sit in your car on a wet, stormy day and watch the ferocious battle between the land and the sea while staying snug and dry—just make sure you don't get swept away by a rogue wave.

You can't miss the big bulk of Cape Mendocino rising to the north. This sizeable hunk of rock poking into the Pacific is not, as guidebooks often claim, the westernmost point in the contiguous United States. (Check your atlas: Cape Flattery, Washington, is at W 124 degrees, 43 minutes, 90 seconds; Cape Blanco, Oregon—another place for which the westernmost claim is often made—is at W 124 degrees 34 minutes, and Cape Mendocino is at W 124 degrees 24 minutes, 55 seconds.) But the cape is a spectacular sight no matter how far west it stands.

For centuries, this cape has been an important landmark for mariners—it got its name in the 16th century, when the Spanish Manila–Acapulco galleons used it as a marker to tell them when it was time to turn south and catch a ride home on the California Current. It is also an important weather divide. North of here, chances are that you'll get rain instead of fog (even in summer); south of here summer fogs prevail.

It is an immensely scenic spot where the surf seems to be charged with special potency. Sea birds and Steller sea lions breed on Sugarloaf Island and Steamboat Rock just offshore. If you feel the earth move, it's likely an earthquake, not the impact of the pounding surf; the cape lies near the junction of three very active tectonic plates.

■ ■ ■

Capetown, at the mouth of the Bear River, has a couple of houses and barns and that's all. Bear River got its name when a member of the 1850 Gregg party was mangled here by a wounded grizzly bear. (Bear Gulch and Bear River are not the same; Bear Gulch is north of False Cape.)

Beyond the Bear River Valley, the road climbs over an 1,800-foot-high ridge and winds through rugged mountains before dropping back to sea level at Ferndale. The landscape is exquisite—a series of high, soft-shouldered green-grass ridges where wild roses bloom in roadside thickets and goldfinches flit across the road. Pull out before you reach the first ridge and look back. Below you, west of the pastures and whitewashed farm buildings of the Bear River Valley, you can see the surf break on a sandy beach through a narrow gap in the green hills.

As you continue on this very narrow, winding road, keep your eyes on the pavement and away from the deer browsing on roadside brush. The vista opens to truly spectacular scenery, but the road's shoulder drops over a ridge.

Dairy farms in Ferndale.

■ FERNDALE *map page 141*

Mattole Road drops quite literally from the mountains into Ferndale on a series of very steep switchbacks. Ferndale, a pleasant, well-preserved 19th-century village, is known for its Eastlake and Queen Anne–style Victorian houses, which have stood virtually unchanged since the 1890s, except for a bit of earthquake damage now and then. The town is, in fact, so well preserved it's on the National Register of Historic Places. If you're into Victoriana, this is a good place to stop and browse in the shops. Ferndale does have old Victorians, but other than that, it's not an exciting town. Unless you're a dedicated connoisseur of Victorian architecture and want to take more time to study the opulent wooden mansions known locally as "butterfat palaces," the place is worth only a few hours. A side trip along Centerville Road, from Ferndale, takes you to a sandy beach south of the Eel River mouth.

At **Fernbridge**, on the Eel River, a rather plain roadside hamlet overlooks a distinguished bridge. Dating back to 1911, this graceful, multi-arched bridge is the oldest reinforced concrete bridge in the world. Until this bridge was built, traffic to and from the rich dairy region of Ferndale had to cross the Eel River by ferry—a highly risky enterprise during wintertime downpours.

■ Eel River Delta

North of Ferndale, the road runs through the flat Eel River Delta. To the north and northeast, the delta is separated from lower Humboldt Bay by a low ridge that starts at Table Bluff on the ocean and curves southwest, past Loleta to the river.

The land between the ridge and the river is taken up by green pastures. Here, placid cows contentedly munch on lush grasses and transform them into first-class milk. Many delta farms were settled by mid-19th-century Portuguese whalers who gave up the hazardous hunt for the giant mammals, but enjoyed a view of the sea from the parlors of their farmhouses. Near the ocean, freshwater sloughs teem with ducks and other bird life.

Many roads run through the delta and cross the sloughs on bridges. You can scout the sandy and sedgy edge of the **Eel River Slough,** a long, much-branched lagoon and marsh, by walking north along the sandy beach from Centerville Park or south from Table Bluff. There's also a parking lot and an unimproved county park at the end of Cannibal Island Road, west of Loleta, from which you can hike north along the sandy edge of a slough.

■ Loleta *map page 141*

Loleta is a small, very pleasant dairy town, where time seems to have stood still. It sits high on a slope above the Eel River Delta, whose pastures provide the town with its economic sustenance.

Besides homes and stores, Loleta has a creamery and the **Loleta Cheese Factory,** at 252 Loleta Drive. The factory makes some truly great cheddar and jack cheese, as well as several specialty cheeses. The cheese-tasting room has a garden out back.

To reach **Table Bluff** from Loleta, take Copenhagen Road west to Table Bluff Road, then turn left. The beach at the foot of the bluff runs south to the mouth of the Eel River (tides permitting) and north for several miles along the south spit of Humboldt Bay to the south jetty of the bay entrance. The rough waters near Table Bluff are very popular with local surfers. To return to U.S. 101, just follow Table Bluff Road north past the Humboldt Bay National Wildlife Refuge (where there's more great bird-watching in the bayshore marshes) to the freeway.

From Loleta to Eureka, U.S. 101 runs between a bluff and the bay and through dairy pastures on low, gently undulating slopes.

A madrone tree stands sentinel over Eel River country in Humboldt County.

■ EUREKA *map page 141*

You can't miss Eureka; it's the largest town on the North Coast. You know you're getting near when the four-lane highway suddenly sprouts stoplights and shopping malls. The town is known for its elaborate Victorians—of which the Carson mansion, a private club that looks like a giant wooden fruitcake, is the most ostentatious.

A bit too grimy for its beautiful setting, Eureka wears smudges on its potentially pretty face. Ugly malls along the waterfront have not helped. Downtown has a working waterfront and oyster plant, and a couple of decent restaurants. But Eureka is changing its image. In 1860, local settlers massacred the women, children and elders of a Wiyot tribe in their village on Indian Island. As a result of a scathing editorial he wrote about this event, writer Bret Harte lost his job at the local newspaper (then based in Arcata) and was run out of town. In June 2004, the City of Eureka returned much of Indian Island (now one of the supports for the Samoa Bridge) to the tribe. It marked an important step in the town's change from a logging and fishing fortress into a liberal arts community.

Eureka has also spiffed up both its waterfront (First and Second at E and F; west of U.S. 101) and its old downtown (E to K, east of U.S. 101), restoring and cleaning up the old buildings. There's a new museum for local art in the old Carnegie Library downtown; it's named after artist Morris Graves. *Morris Graves Museum of Art, 636 F Street; 707-442-0278; www.humboldtart.org .*

Daily from June to September, you can take a 75-minute harbor tour, operated by the Humboldt Bay Maritime Museum, on the *M.V. Makadet,* the oldest operating passenger ship on the West Coast. *Adorni Center, foot of L Street; 707-445-1910.*

The rocky breakwater at the southern tip of the **Eureka/Samoa Spit** is a great place for watching surfbirds, rock sandpipers, and oystercatchers. Just to the north is a bayside picnic area shaded by Monterey cypresses.

■ HUMBOLDT BAY

Humboldt Bay, a large estuary, is California's second-largest enclosed bay, after San Francisco Bay. It is divided into two sections: South Bay south of Eureka, and Arcata Bay to the north. Humboldt Bay is separated from the ocean by two long, sandy spits, aptly called South and North Spit. North Spit has been heavily industrialized for more than a hundred years and is still covered with pulp mills and other lumber-related plants. The long spit running from Arcata south to **Samoa** became one of California's earliest industrial sites. Samoa's claim to fame today is the Samoa Cookhouse, which once catered to loggers and mill workers and their giant appetites. It's the only cookhouse in the West that's still operating, and still serving up the same kind of hearty food it offered a hundred years ago. Eureka is doing its share of wetland rehabilitation of Humboldt Bay by restoring a wetland behind the Bayshore Mall.

■ ARCATA *map page 141*

Arcata was founded in the 1850s as a supply point for the northern mines but was soon overtaken by Eureka, which has the bay's deepwater harbor. Arcata has an industrial past, like other bayshore communities, but is doing its best to clean up its ill effects. Locals have done a great job with cleaning up the upper bay (today, commercial oyster farms once again prosper—Arcata Bay supplies about 45 percent of California's oysters). They have restored a formerly degraded 65-acre salt marsh by cleaning it up and replanting it with native vegetation. The **Arcata Marsh and Wildlife Sanctuary** now has more than 150 species of birds and all kinds of fish, from angel sharks to sting rays to surfperches, and the Audubon Society (707-826-6918) sponsors nature walks. Arcata exhibits a rare integration of

Eureka in 1895.

a town and its natural surroundings—but has done so in part by pushing off motels and malls to McKinleyville, a few miles north on U.S. 101.

Humboldt State University, in Arcata, is a wholesome and funky campus—there's a pretty plaza surrounded by beautiful old buildings. Here you'll find health food shops, organic grocery stores, and stores selling driftwood lamps. There are fine old Victorian mansions up on the hill. Plenty of surfers congregate here, too, inhabiting vans parked along streets. And, of course, there are the usual dreadlock-wearing college kids (though mostly white).

East of downtown, Redwood Park has picnic tables, lawns, and 600 acres of redwoods. The great event of the year is the annual **Great Arcata to Ferndale Cross-Country Kinetic Sculpture Race,** held on Memorial Day. The "sculpture" should be weird enough to please the crowds and must be able to float across Humboldt Bay. *Information: 707-839-3231.*

■ ■ ■

The coast north of Arcata looks more like the Pacific Northwest than California. The first major beach you get to is called **Clam Beach**—it actually has clams free for the digging. (You do, however, need a license. I always check with a local tackle or bait shop to see what licenses I need, what limits or seasons apply, and where in the sands clams have most recently been spouting.) The beach is a county park and a great place to stop, even though it looks at times like an RV parking lot.

■ TRINIDAD *map page 141*

One of the prettiest villages on the California coast, Trinidad has come a long way since 1939, when the WPA guide to California described it as a place where "small straggling homes, windows broken and boarded, fringe the empty offices, refineries, and vats of the California Sea Products Company, a whaling firm." Trinidad Head, which shields the harbor from storms, rises above a rocky coastline and pocket beaches. Trinidad was founded in 1850 as a supply point for the gold mines of the interior, and it once had a population of more than 3,000 people. It was the North Coast's first "American" settlement.

But before the first white men arrived, Trinidad was the site of the southernmost Yurok village, a settlement more than 5,000 years old. (The Yurok were culturally the most advanced of northwestern California's native tribes.) Perhaps it was the

Yurok's warlike nature and natural reticence that kept them alive as a tribe. Today the Yurok are among the few California natives to still occupy many of their original village sites. But while the Yurok people have survived as a nation for more than 5,000 years, their remaining village sites are now on the Klamath River, the heartland of their territory, and no longer on the coast. The Yurok are a very private people and their villages are off-limits to visitors.

Trinidad is also the place where European explorers first set foot on the far northern shore, when the Spanish explorers Heceta and Bodega erected a cross here in 1775. Peter Corney, a Northwest Company trader, came by in 1817 and described the Yurok people he met there as warlike. They seemed a bit surprised when the ship's crew took the sort of precautions they'd learned on the Northwest Coast, tricing up boarding nets and disarming anyone coming aboard to trade. Corney sadly reported that this was "the only place on the coast where we could not induce the females to visit the ship"—even though the crewmen offered them blankets and axes.

The **Trinidad Museum** (529 B Trinity Street; 707-677-0716) has whaling and logging photos as well as exhibits of native artifacts.

Trinidad State Beach, a small park north of town, has a woodsy picnic area and a little, sandy beach tucked behind a sea stack. Follow signs from U.S. 101 to town, then look for a road on the right, marked with a sign. Take an immediate left (unmarked) and you will get to the parking lot (a sign welcomes you to the beach right after you make the turn). The trail to the beach is rough and steep; you can also reach the beach from Trinidad harbor to the south and from the adjacent Humboldt State University marine research center.

Trinidad's small harbor occupies a rock-girt cove. The surrounding cliffs are topped by evergreen trees, and numerous wave-sculpted sea stacks rise offshore. Only one road runs from the cliff down into the cove, but a trail crosses from the harbor to the sandy beach at Trinidad State Park to the north. If you come at lunchtime, try **Seascapes**, a delightful place where the seafood is very fresh and the smoked fish is delicious.

Note: Because the budget crunch continues in California on the municipal, county, and state levels, not all parks and beaches are maintained as well as they were in the past. In general, those that are well and properly signed are usually also well maintained.

■ PATRICK'S POINT STATE PARK *map page 141*

A back road runs from Trinidad to Patrick's Point State Park (also directly accessible from U.S. 101), another one of the truly great places on the California coast. Patrick's Point has it all: forests, meadows, bluffs, sandy beach, rocky shores, tide pools, and great campsites. It's also home to a very special place, a reconstructed Yurok village.

■ ■ ■

The Patrick's Point **Yurok Village** is a reconstruction, but a very authentic one. Houses of redwood planks, fronted by stone platforms, are partially set into the ground; only low walls and the heavy redwood slab roofs rise above a meadow in which strawberries and daisies are in full bloom. There is also a sweat house and a few finished and half-finished canoes lying next to the houses, just as they might in a real village.

This rocky promontory was not inhabited during aboriginal times, but was celebrated in Yurok myth and song as the abode of the immortals, who left the world after the Yurok arrived, but still linger here. These immortals took on various forms, the most important being dolphins, who are considered even now by the Yurok to be people rather than animals.

You can take a long, pleasant walk on the beach from Agate Beach at Patrick's Point to the Big Lagoon Park beach—between 2 and 4 miles one way.

■ LAGOON COAST

Right after Patrick's Point, as you drive north on U.S. 101, you pass **Big Lagoon,** the first of several bodies of fresh water separated from the ocean by spits of sand. To the north, the park at **Dry Lagoon** includes a marshy lake rapidly turning into a meadow, and the spit separating **Stone Lagoon** from the ocean, with one of the best walking beaches on this coast. At Stone Lagoon, U.S. 101 turns away from the coast for a short stretch. **Freshwater Lagoon** is a beautiful sandy driftwood beach popular with surf fishermen. All of the beaches fronting the lagoons are great for long, meditative walks. (The lagoons are truly gorgeous, even on those days on which it is too foggy to see beyond the beaches and trees.) The shores of the lagoons held several important Yurok villages in pre-contact times (before the natives were "contacted" by white Americans in the 1850s).

There's a vast parking area strip on the southbound (ocean-side) shoulder of U.S. 101 south of the Redwood National Park Visitors Center. It has chem-pit toilets, and RV camping is allowed. (Sign up for spaces at the Redwood National Park Visitors Center.)

At the beach just north of Freshwater Lagoon (and west of U.S. 101) is the **Redwood Creek Beach Picnic Area** and **Redwood National Park Visitors Center**. The national park itself stretches along this coast for miles. The visitors center has a great bookstore and friendly rangers. This may well be the most user-friendly place of its kind on the entire California coast. Pick up one of the limited permits issued each day for seeing the world's tallest tree, a redwood almost 368 feet tall and 14 feet in diameter.

North of the visitors center, U.S. 101, which has reverted from a freeway back into a rural two-lane highway, turns inland to Orick, an odd little town in the

Butch Marks holding up his latest catch.

redwoods with a mixture of tourism savvy and backwoods orneriness. Both sides of U.S. 101 are lined with redwood sculptures, for Orick is the chainsaw redwood sculpture capital of the world. (Now, if they'd just import a few artists and show them how to use a chainsaw . . .) If you can't afford one of the large sculptures, or have no room, you can console yourself with a redwood burl, as Orick is also the redwood burl capital of the world.

Orick derives its name from the Yurok village of *Oreg,* the main settlement on this part of the coast. The village was one of five settlements in Yurok territory in which the Jumping Dance might be held. For this ritual dance, which was designed to renew or preserve the world, dancers wore a buckskin band lined with 50 large woodpecker scalps and bordered with strips of white fur from a deer's belly plus other feathers. The dance was accompanied by a long recitation of sacred texts and might last 10 or more days.

Redwood Creek flows through town, splitting it in two. On a recent visit, Orick looked a tad less seedy, but also a tad subdued: there are fewer big, boisterous chainsaw carvings for sale and more small wooden windmills.

■ PRAIRIE CREEK REDWOODS STATE PARK *map page 141*

A few miles north of Orick, look for the turnoff to Davidson Road on the west side of the highway, which runs across the coastal mountains to **Gold Bluffs Beach** and **Fern Canyon**, within Prairie Creek Redwoods State Park. Also look for elk. During one recent visit, there was a traffic jam at this intersection, because several elk were grazing in a roadside meadow and visitors had pulled their cars off the road to take photos.

The clay-dirt road from Berry Glen to the ocean can be very slick; along the beach beneath the towering Gold Bluffs it may be cut by creeks in several places. Be prepared, in wet or dry weather, to ford several creeks en route to Fern Canyon. You should make it, with a bit of sliding and much splashing—and if you don't, there's likely to be a fellow traveler or ranger to come along and pull you out.

A short trail leads from the Big Tree Wayside—off Newton B. Drury Scenic Parkway, 6 miles north of Orick—to the most massive coast redwood (304 feet tall, 21 feet in diameter). It's accompanied by several huge California bay trees (known locally as "pepperwoods").

■ ■ ■

Fern Canyon is one of the most serenely beautiful places in the West, with row upon row of five-finger ferns reaching out from the steep 50-foot vertical walls, wafting to and fro in the sea breeze. Lady ferns, deer ferns, and chain ferns add variety to the texture of this natural tapestry.

Because Fern Canyon is narrow and steep-walled, and the creek meanders back and forth between the cliffs, rangers install foot bridges during the summer. But don't expect bridges in the off-season. Be prepared to get your feet wet, or bring rubber boots or waders.

■ ■ ■

If you walk onto the beach, watch out for Roosevelt elk. Males have huge racks of antlers, stand more than 5 feet high at the shoulder, and can weigh as much as a thousand pounds. Even the smaller females look about the size of a Jersey cow. Elk should more properly be called wapiti, since the English term originally referred to the European moose, with its shovel-like antlers. The creatures are now considered to be the same species as the European red deer—the stag hunted by royalty as well as by Robin Hood and his Merry Men.

After you return to U.S. 101, the road once again assumes freeway status. Look for the exit to Newton B. Drury Scenic Drive. (It's the first exit after U.S. 101 becomes a freeway and is actually the old U.S. 101, which wound through the redwoods before the freeway was built.) It was once slow going, especially when large tractor trailer rigs clogged the road, but now it's a pleasant bypass with many pull-outs where you can park to explore and admire the giant trees. This road takes you through a thick redwood grove, a beautiful drive that at times seems like a narrow canyon road—except that the road is not hemmed in by cliffs but by huge trees, some of them more than 300 feet tall. A large fenced meadow near the park headquarters usually holds a herd of elk, allowing you to take a good look at the size and majesty of these magnificent beasts.

Ask the rangers to point you to the trail running along the banks of Redwood Creek—it's one of the most peaceful walks anywhere in the West.

A lot of things magically come together in the Prairie Creek redwood forest to make this such an amazing place: a wide, clear stream, meadows with wildflowers in season, elk that are singularly unafraid of human visitors, huge redwoods, and lanky rhododendrons blooming in the understory. Here, where the redwoods stand on fairly level, easily accessible ground, you recognize what magnificent trees they are.

From "SONG OF THE REDWOOD TREE"

A California Song

Farewell my brethren,
Farewell O earth and sky, farewell you neighboring waters,
My time is ended, my time has come.
Along the northern coast,
Just back from the rock-bound shore and the caves,
In the saline air from the sea in the Mendocino country,
With the surge for base and accompaniment low and hoarse,
With crackling blows of axes sounding musically driven by strong arms,
Riven deep by the sharp tongues of the axes, there in the redwood forest
    dense,
I heard the mighty tree its death-chant chanting;
The choppers heard not, the camp shanties echoed not,
The quick-ear'd teamsters and chain and jack-screw men heard not,
As the wood-spirits came from their haunts of a thousand years to join the
    refrain,
But in my soul I plainly heard.

        —Walt Whitman, *Leaves of Grass,* 1882

■ THE MAGIC OF THE REDWOODS

Redwoods are the tallest trees known. The tallest redwood has been measured at a height of 367.8 feet, and there are hundreds of trees more than 300 feet tall, although the average height is about 200 feet. Trunks can reach a diameter of 15 to 21 feet at (human) chest level. The bark contains no resin and may be as thick as 12 inches. Redwoods have surprisingly shallow roots for such huge trees—they go only about 4 to 6 feet down—but the extensive systems may spread as far as 80 to 100 feet from the trunk. Redwoods live to an age of several thousand years. The oldest redwood has been authenticated at 2,200 years old, meaning it was a seedling when the Great Wall of China was built, when Hannibal marched on

Rome, and when Central America's Mayan civilization began its meteoric rise. Redwoods also may be the only immortal beings, since a cut or fallen tree will send up sprouts that are genetically identical to the parent. Early American settlers did, however, manage to kill redwoods by burning the stumps and killing the shoots. Little direct light can penetrate the dense foliage of a redwood grove, but plant life thrives in clearings left by fallen trees and along rivers and creeks.

Continue north on Old U.S. 101 to the U.S. 101 freeway, which is uncommonly scenic for such a high-speed highway—it runs north through alder, oak, and redwood forests and along hillside wildflower meadows, which sparkle in the sun. Look for the turnoff to scenic, 8-mile-long Coastal Drive in Redwood National Park, a clifftop road that extends north to the mouth of the Klamath River. Caution: the road is deteriorating severely in places, with large potholes and abrupt dips. The Carruther's Cove Trail leads from the southern end of the drive to secluded Carruther's Beach.

■ KLAMATH RIVER AND KLAMATH *map page 141*

You can't miss the Klamath; the bridge entrances are marked by gold-painted sculptures of bears. Here ends the last and northernmost strip of the U.S. 101 freeway in California. The Klamath is California's second-largest river (after the Sacramento), and once had great runs of salmon, but stocks have lately suffered from overfishing. The days when fishing boats were packed so tightly next to each other that you could cross the river on them are long gone. Local smokehouses still sell smoked salmon —commonly made with salmon imported from Alaska, since commercial fishing is not allowed on the river.

A spur road leads to **Requa Overlook** on the northern cliffs above the mouth of the Klamath River. The overlook has picnic tables, interpretive plaques, and great views of the Lower Klamath River valley and the coastline. The 4-mile Coastal Trail runs north along the cliffs to Lagoon Creek (see Yurok Loop Trail, following).

You can now take a jet boat tour up the Klamath. *Klamath River Jet Boat Tours, 17635 Highway 101 South, Klamath; 707-482-7775 or 800-887-JETS (5387); www.jetboattours.com. Daily, May 1 through September 30, weather permitting.*

(Following pages) A grove of redwoods at Prairie Creek State Park, where the trees stand 200 to 300 feet tall.

■ LAGOON CREEK AND YUROK LOOP TRAIL

U.S. 101 descends to the ocean at **Lagoon Creek Fishing Access** near False Klamath Rock. There's a pond here, stocked with rainbow trout and brightened by yellow water lilies. Look for ducks, herons, egrets, and river otters. The self-guided half-mile Yurok Loop Trail winds through willows, alders, and over bluffs with some truly spectacularly sculpted Sitka spruces. The "look" of this landscape is one that Chinese landscape painters of the past would have found familiar.

■ ■ ■

I've set up my easel on the cliffs at the seaward side of the trail several times in the past, but one visit was especially memorable. It was one of those special, quiet, soft mornings when the air was filled with the chirping of sparrows, with the distant roar of the surf, and with the delicate, yet surprisingly audible, tingling sounds water makes as it drips off leaves. The water came from fog, not rain. The day promised to be dazzling; the sun was just beginning to pierce the curtain of fog.

As I looked down onto the beach north of the trail, I tried to imagine what it was like when a Yurok village stood here, before white men came to this coast. As a ribbon of fog swirled across the sand and through the trees, it was easy for my mind's eye to turn driftwood logs into redwood-planked lodges (like the ones at Patrick's Point; see page 158) and hand-carved canoes. Sea stacks, barely visible in the mist, loomed offshore, just as they did in the old days, when every one of these monoliths was owned by a family that had inherited rights to the bounty of their intertidal zones—to the mussels, barnacles, and algae growing on the rock, and to the sea snails, limpets, abalones, and sea cucumbers crawling over their rough surfaces or hiding in their crevices.

I took the half-mile trail uphill, through an alder and willow thicket, and past tall grasses and ferns. Where the trail curves to the south, I stood high up on a cliff, above the breakers roiling in from the far reaches of the open Pacific. Suddenly, without warning, a dark specter loomed supernaturally large on the offshore fog bank. Had I trespassed on sacred ground and raised a spirit? Of course not. The sun broke through the low clouds, throwing the shadow of a gnarled Sitka spruce onto the wall of white fog.

I did, however, wonder how a Yurok would have reacted to the apparition. The Yurok believed that the material world is closely intertwined with the spiritual, and that all places and objects, even this humble trail, had their spirits. Therefore, a

Yurok, walking where I had just trod, might have asked permission of the local spirits to trespass. And he might have rested his load and waited until he felt sure that it was all right to go on.

Seeing or imagining spirits is easy on this wet coast, where the land and the sea, the shore, and the tall redwood trees bleed into each other in the misty air. The spirit of the Indians who first settled on this coast is still very much alive today.

The Yurok still hold their traditional Jumping Dance—but the time and place are guarded as a religious secret, and babbling about it to outsiders is seen as a source of bad luck. The daughter of friends of mine, however, recently put on a traditional flower dance than had not been performed for more than a hundred years.

■ NORTH TO CRESCENT CITY

North of Lagoon Creek, the highway runs along sandy Wilson Creek Beach for a short stretch before climbing up along the sheer sides of the cliffs. Soon giant redwoods crowd in on all sides at Del Norte Coast Redwoods State Park, and the road narrows. In almost no time you will be deep in a primeval forest of ancient redwood trees. Pull over at one of the many turnouts and take a short walk into this cathedral of trees, where green huckleberry leaves, pink-flowered native rhododendrons in full bloom, and patches of blue sky provide an illusion of stained glass windows suspended from the boughs. Don't be afraid to gawk—everybody does in the presence of such natural majesty. Occasionally, through gaps between the tall tree trunks, you can spot patches of dark blue or gray ocean.

As the road leaves the forest, it drops down to a sandy crescent of beach, Crescent Beach in Redwood National Park. After leaving the redwoods, look for the road leading to Crescent Beach on the west side of the highway. The beach has a grassy picnic area. That road, an old section of U.S. 101, continues to Enderts Beach and to the **Crescent Beach Overlook**, a parking area on a bluff above Enderts Beach. The Coastal Trail continues south from here.

■ CRESCENT CITY *map page 141*

Crescent City was founded in 1852 as a supply depot for the Trinity River mines; the following year, its first lumber mill began cutting beams and planks from local redwood trees. Today, Crescent City is a small, pleasant harbor at the northwest

end of the long, sandy beach. The downtown doesn't look its age, because much of the old business district was washed away in April 1964 by a tsunami generated by the big Alaskan earthquake. Today, a breakwater of more than 1,600 concrete tetrapods, weighing 25 tons each, appears to be doing a good job of protecting the port during storms.

You can drive onto the southern breakwater on Anchor Way, park, and walk along shore to watch see birds, sea lions, and the bustle of the commercial fishing harbor. The far end has two boat ramps and a Coast Guard station. The road ends at Whaler's Island, a former sea stack now connected to the land by the breakwater. A somewhat rough (but negotiable) dirt and rock trail winds to the top of the rocky outcropping, which is covered with sprawling manzanita and coyote brush and a few straggly conifers; here you'll get views of the harbor, Crescent City, the ocean, and, on a clear day, of the redwood coast to the south. Sea lions hang out on net floats and floating docks in the harbor.

Crescent City shows two faces to the world: a public, not particularly appealing face along the U.S. 101 business strip, and a private face that is among the most beautiful on the California coast. The "private face" starts west of the harbor, and north of the lighthouse, which sits on an island and is, with its museum, only accessible at low tide. You can reach the pretty seaside promenade by driving straight west where U.S. 101 turns north.

This waterfront park, called Beach Front Park, and contiguous Fred Endert Park are about as pleasant as seaside parks without a beach can get. They house the town's visitors center, the public (indoor) swimming pool, and the Northcoast Marine Mammal Center. A fishing pier (called the B Street Pier) is at the end of B Street, just inside the northwest breakwater. You can park in a small roundabout at the end of a short causeway leading to the foot of the pier or in a dirt lot at the foot of the causeway.

A new **Hampton Inn & Suites Redwood Oceanfront Resort** resides on the bluff west of the park—it's the best lodging in town.

The **Redwood National Park/State Park Headquarters** visitors center, downtown, is a required stop. The staff is friendly and helpful and will tell you about all sorts of attractions you might otherwise miss. *1111 Second Street, Crescent City; 707-464-6101; camping reservations, 800-444-7275; www.nps.gov/redw*

The snow-covered Siskiyou Mountains form a backdrop for this aerial view of Crescent City.

The **Rumiano Cheese Company** features, among other cheeses made here, a great dry monterey jack, every bit as rich and nutty as the famed dry Sonoma jack. *9th & E streets, Crescent City; 707-465-1535.*

Castle Rock, northwest of town, has the second-largest breeding population of seabirds on the California coast; only South Farallon Island, off San Francisco, has more. Occasionally, you can spot Cassin's auklets, Leach's petrels, pigeon guillemots, and tufted puffins. You can always count on seeing a few fork-tailed storm petrels fluttering above the surf, and pairs of black oystercatchers working over mussel clusters.

Halfway up the shore is a monument and memorial park dedicated to the drowned crewmen and passengers of the sidewheel-steamer *Brother Jonathan,* which sank in 1865 on St. George reef, 7 miles offshore. Rumors have been widespread that the steamer was carrying a fat payroll up to Portland. In the 1960s, a team of treasure hunters were scouring the sea floor for the gold when, overnight, the crew and ship disappeared without a trace. Many locals believe they found what they were after, and promptly split with the booty.

If you follow the road along the bluffs, as it winds north, you'll come to Point St. George, a grassy promontory that looks like a place straight out of a Scottish or Irish tourism brochure. As you walk out toward the cliffs on the greensward in spring, you will be surrounded by wildflowers; in summer, you may be serenaded by the band-tailed pigeons that appear here in great numbers; in fall, expect to stir up flocks of sandpipers. On a clear day, you can just make out the faint shape of the St. George reef lighthouse, seven miles offshore.

Howland Hill Road is an old stage road that winds from Crescent City east into the most magnificent groves of **Jedediah Smith Redwoods State Park.** It's a slow road, little improved since the days of stagecoaches, and it's very narrow in places, with barely enough space between the giant trees to let a pickup truck squeeze through. These timeless redwood forests still look much the way they did centuries ago. A short trail leads to **Stout Grove,** whose trees are among the tallest in the world (the Stout Tree is 345 feet tall). The road crosses the rocky canyon of the Smith River and connects to U.S. 199 2 miles east of Hiouchi, crossing a covered bridge en route.

■ LAKE EARL AND POINTS NORTH *map page 141*

Unlike the wide-open headland of St. George, nearby Lake Earl is a mystical place. Drive to the parking area at the end of Lakeview Drive, park your car, and sit quietly on a snag. Meadow-like patches of reeds grow far out into the shallow lake. Blending with the morning mists, they obscure the boundaries between land and water, and land and sky, blending all into a marriage of the solid, the liquid, and the ethereal. During the fall and spring migrations, Lake Earl is home to more than 250 species of birds; at all times of the year, look for deer, brush rabbits, river otters, red-tailed hawks, ospreys, peregrine falcons, and an occasional bald eagle.

■ ■ ■

North of Crescent City along U.S. 101, the forests recede from the coast and dairy pastures spread across the lowlands. A short detour will take you to the section of Jedediah Smith Redwoods State Park in the lower valley of the Smith River along U.S. 199 (the two-lane highway running from the coast east to Grants Pass, Oregon).

Pelican State Beach, California's northernmost beach, has no coastal access sign. (Perhaps the locals remove them.) Don't worry, though; this is one beach that's not worth searching out.

■ TRAVEL BASICS

U.S. 101 changes its format as it winds north, sometimes a two- or four-lane highway and occasionally a freeway. Where CA 1 joins U.S. 101 at Leggett, the road is a two-lane highway. It remains so past the Confusion Hill landslide area and through Richardson Grove State Park. A little to the north, it becomes a freeway and then a four-lane highway (with traffic lights in Eureka) until just north of Trinidad. It again becomes a freeway from the southern end of Prairie Creek to the Klamath River. (The scenic drive through Richardson Grove State Park is old U.S. 101.) North of the Klamath it is once again reduced to two lanes (with cross-traffic) to Crescent City. As the highway enters Crescent City, it follows city roads, which have traffic lights at important intersections. After U.S. 101 leaves Crescent City, it once again becomes a freeway, but that lasts only for a few miles, until the start of U.S. 199 (which runs from U.S. 101 northeast to Grants Pass, Oregon). After that, U.S. 101 once again becomes a two-line highway (with passing lines to the Oregon state line and through Oregon up the coast all the way to Washington).

U.S. 101 touches the area known as the Redwood Shore in only a few places: at Humboldt Bay; at Clam Beach; south of the Redwood National Park Visitors Center, at Wilson Creek; and south of Crescent City, but there are many roads and trails leading from U.S. 101 to the water's edge.

Climate

Rainfall along this section of the coast averages from just under 40 inches per year at Fort Bragg and Eureka to almost 80 inches near the Oregon border and along the Lost Coast near Shelter Cove. Summers are generally foggy and cold—the temperature has rarely exceeded 75 degrees during July in Fort Bragg and Eureka. Fall is the clearest and warmest season, but the rains begin sooner and end later than they do below Mendocino, and even October and May can be very rainy months. Tremendous winter gales lash the coastline between November and April. **Water temperatures** are cool year-round (45–60 degrees).

A University of Chicago Field Ecology class breaks for lunch in the Eel River Redwoods.

Food and Lodging

California's northwestern corner is blessed with a bountiful supply of local foods. You can buy fresh rockfish, salmon, shrimp, and Dungeness crab from bay and ocean waterfront seafood markets in Eureka, Humboldt, Trinidad, or Crescent City. Cultivated oysters from Arcata Bay are for sale along the Eureka waterfront.

The land, too, will tempt you with its seasonal bounty: strawberries in spring; blackberries, raspberries, and huckleberries in summer; cranberries and apples in autumn. Wild hazelnuts grow in streamside thickets and moist woods. Mushrooms are plentiful in the woods in the wet seasons, but leave the picking to the experts. Many poisonous varieties are difficult to discern from edibles, and it's better to buy them at a local farmers market than to be sorry.

Cows munch contentedly on the lush green pastures of the Eel and Mad River estuaries—this makes their milk uncommonly rich and puts an extra morsel of flavor into the cheeses produced locally at the Loleta Cheese Factory. Goats, too, thrive in the mild coastal climate, as the tangy goat milk cheeses from Cypress Grove in McKinleyville amply prove.

All of the small and large towns of the region have bakeries where you can buy fresh bread to go with your fruit, cheese, or seafood. Many restaurants have a knack for preparing the best and freshest of the region's foods.

Lodgings in this region tend to be comfortable rather than luxurious (though this coast, too, has plenty of overstuffed B&Bs). But what you lose in luxury you more than make up for in spectacular views and in quiet walks through the woods. Camping is also popular here, and you'll find plenty of places to pitch a tent, park an RV, or sleep under the stars. **Lodging and restaurant listings** by town in alphabetical order begin on page 362.

GOLDEN GATE
TO SAN SIMEON

South of San Francisco, the suburbs and malls give way to rolling hills, wide open spaces, and unobstructed views of the blue Pacific. Along the spine of San Francisco's peninsula, the rugged Santa Cruz Mountains raise their stony shoulders to the sky from marine terraces dropping off sharply to the ocean in cliffs and bluffs.

Along Monterey Bay large stretches of the sandy shores are preserved as public beaches. At the southern end of the bay, spurs of the Santa Lucia Mountains encroach on the beaches, forming the Monterey Peninsula, with its spectacular rocky headlands, sandy coves, and turquoise and indigo sea.

South of Carmel, mountains edge up to the sea, and the pines and cypresses of Monterey give way to grassy slopes. The mountains drop into the surf at an even steeper angle south of the Big Sur River and do not give way to gentler shores until the mountains recede from the coast south of Gorda.

The cities along this coast are small urban microcosms, providing all the amenities of metropolitan areas with a fraction of the urban sprawl and congestion.

■ OVERVIEW OF A RURAL COASTLINE

From San Francisco's Ocean Beach (see page 61) south, suburbs and sprawl line the coast road for about 20 miles, but once the highway passes Pacifica, one of the prettiest pastoral landscapes in California begins. Hillside meadows alternate with groves of wind-twisted pines, sandy beaches give way to steep-sided bluffs, and in places, tall mountains push right up to the edge of the sea. Lichen-covered fences line the spring-green pastures, and weathered old barns raise their frayed roofs from seaside draws. On clear spring days the colors are bright enough to dazzle an impressionist painter: a translucent sky arches over a steely-blue ocean pounding the pale shores with creamy surf; darkly green pines and cypresses make the brightness of the green grass appear even brighter; and fields of golden-yellow mustard flowers are offset by the spiky gray-green fronds of artichoke plants. All of this is swathed in a light mist, which makes distant headlands seem near and causes rocky coves beneath your feet to vanish in a wisp of fog. Above all hangs the constant hum of the surf, punctuated by the chirping of white-crowned sparrows and the trill of meadowlarks and red-winged blackbirds.

■ PACIFICA

In October of 1957, the residents of the coastal communities of Pedro Point, Linda Mar, Rockaway Beach, Vallemar, Fairway Park, Sharp Park, Edgemar, and Westview voted to combine into a new city to be called Pacifica, directly south of San Francisco's Ocean Beach. As a result, Pacifica looks a bit like a group of villages loosely strung together by the Coast Highway, CA 1. Most new development has happened on sea terraces in the north of town and in the gently sloping valleys running from Linda Mar Beach into the folds of Montara Mountain.

As you head south from Daly City, at first you'll be hard pressed to note when you've crossed the line into Pacifica, because the layout of neighborhoods and construction style of homes exhibits a similar urban sprawl. But the look changes as you progress to where the wild mountains of the peninsula spine reach to the coast with sharp-ridged spurs. Some of these sections, most notably Rockaway and Linda Mar, have sandy beaches; others edge up to the sheer escarpments of

A young surfer on a bicycle.

cliffs; Sharp Park has a **fishing pier** (follow signs from CA 1; on-street parking only). On my last visit fishermen were catching mostly small shiner surfperch but, in the proper season, they have been known to catch salmon.

Pacifica has several narrow beaches, one of the most popular being the southern-most, **San Pedro Beach**, called Linda Mar by the locals because it's at the end of Linda Mar Boulevard. The grungy parking lot (immediately to the west of the highway) is usually full of young men and women getting in and out of wet suits—so many, so often, that the city of Pacifica has passed an anti-nudity law.

Unlike other surfer beaches, this is a generally friendly beach, and very democratic—local beach bums mix with young, professional San Franciscans trying desperately to learn to surf. This is *the* learners' spot. Boogie boarders (a boogie board is a short Styrofoam board that you ride flat on your belly) ride the whitewater. Surfers near the shore can find themselves riding the waves between a hydrophilic dog and a curious seal checking out the human scene. People walk their dogs along the strand, beachcomb, sunbathe, and drop by an old wooden house on the beach with a Taco

In winter, landslides often close the Coast Highway just south of Pacifica along a stretch of road known as Devil's Slide.

Bell inside. If the tide isn't too high, walk along the upper edge of the beach, toward San Pedro Point. The brown pelicans put on a spectacular show here, flying low over the water in a loose skein and, one by one, suddenly plunging into the water. Others soar high before diving headfirst into the sea. Their eyes must be able to penetrate the surface glare of the waves, for they get their fish every time.

From November through February, when gray whales migrate south to their calving grounds in Baja California lagoons, they can be easily watched from Pacifica, because they pass within half a mile of the shore.

■ ■ ■

Walking this beach, I often find myself thinking of a Spanish exploratory expedition that struggled through this area more than 200 years ago. Under the command of Capt. Juan Gaspar de Portola and acting on orders from the Viceroy of Mexico, a small party of soldiers arrived here in 1769 after they traveled by foot and horseback from San Diego. Looking for Monterey Bay—as described in the ship's logs of Spanish navigator Sebastian Vizcaino—the party had passed beside Monterey but not recognized it as such, and had continued north

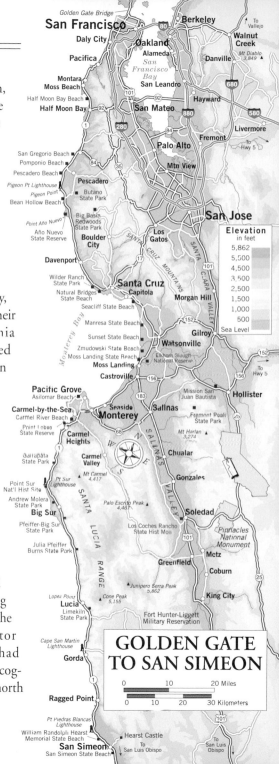

along the coast, plodding through ravines, along surf-swept beaches, and across rocky ridges until they wearily stopped at one of Pacifica's beaches. A party of hunters set out looking for game, and reaching the ridgetops looked east and saw before them a vast body of water. Jose Francisco de Ortega, later to become the first comandante of the presidio of Santa Barbara, is said to have been the first of the party to see San Francisco Bay.

The Portola party was too tired to press further, and they returned to San Diego. The first European settlements of this peninsula, the presidio and mission of San Francisco, were not established for another seven years.

■ ■ ■

Southeast of San Pedro Point, the Coast Highway climbs over a shoulder of Montara Mountain and, after a switchback, emerges high above the sea. The view is breathtaking, but keep your eyes on the road, because there's a sheer dropoff to the right—straight down to the surf. This cliff and stretch of highway certainly deserve their name: "Devil's Slide." Odd pieces of concrete sticking up from the steep and highly unstable slopes are remnants of WW II coastal bunkers.

On the way to Half Moon Bay you'll pass three more beaches worth exploring. They are **Gray Whale Cove State Beach, Montara State Beach,** and **West Beach Trail at Pillar Point Harbor.** Three-mile-long **James Fitzgerald Marine Reserve** at Moss Beach is known for its tide pools. The bluff tops above the reserve were acquired by a conservancy group in 2004, and will be opened once trails are built.

■ HALF MOON BAY *map page 177*

A small Portuguese fishing and farming village just 30 years ago, and a popular hideaway for San Franciscans during Prohibition, Half Moon Bay is now on its way to becoming just another generic suburb. The setting, however, is superb. In summer, flower farms reach far up into the canyons; in autumn, lowland fields are dotted with the orange globes of pumpkins, as families come from all over the Bay Area to pick their favorite jack-o-lanterns. To the west, the small town of **Princeton-by-the-Sea,** with its Pillar Point Harbor, remains largely unspoiled.

While suburban sprawl and beachfront developments have conquered much of Half Moon Bay, pumpkin patches still rule the southern edge of town and merge into fields and pastures that set the tone for the landscape all the way south to Santa Cruz. When you consider how great the pressure has been to develop this coast, it's truly amazing how little the seaboard between Half Moon Bay and Santa

An artist's beach house on Half Moon Bay.

Cruz has changed since the 1970s. Conservation easements obtained in the early 2000s may keep this landscape preserved long into the future.

The coastal bluffs south of Half Moon Bay are covered with flowers and wild strawberries in spring, and artichokes and brussels sprouts grow in the fields. The view from the coast road turns rustic. Slopes to the east are covered with grasses and scrub, offset by copses of pines and oaks and by eucalyptus windbreaks. Roads across the mountains are narrow and twisted—one of the reasons this coast is still largely rural. In late winter and early spring, wildflowers turn the mountain slopes yellow, orange, and blue. Some of this landscape has not changed much since the days when Spanish padres sought converts among the natives and *vaqueros* rode the range.

■ NEAR SAN GREGORIO AND POMPONIO *map page 177*

Along this stretch of road, several attractive, sandy beaches lie to the immediate west of the highway. San Gregorio has a sandy stretch and rocky shore right off the highway (the beach is a good place for watching plovers in winter). Pomponio and Pescadero have beaches of soft sand that can be warm and sunny in summer (and

are therefore very popular and often crowded on weekends). All three have picnic areas with splendid views of the ocean and of the seals, dolphins, and whales that occasionally swim by. San Gregorio and Pomponio are two of my favorite beaches along this coast.

The inviting **San Gregorio General Store,** a mile inland on Highway 84, sells all sorts of books, clothing, and housewares; it also has a comfortable bar, with live music on weekends.

At Pescadero State Beach, a sandy trail to the beach through the dunes has remnants of a wooden boardwalk that was covered with several inches of sand during my last visit (the same wind that covered it may uncover it again, however). I noticed something interesting about the ubiquitous Heerman's gulls: they run through the surf line like sandpipers, hoping to snatch prey.

After you leave the beach, turn left onto Pescadero Road. To the left is the **Pescadero Marsh Natural Preserve.** This miles-long marsh running inland along Pescadero Creek is a prime bird habitat. White egrets are a common sight here, flying low over the water with slow, deliberate wing beats. Red-winged blackbirds sing in the reeds, sparrows flit through the roadside willows, and turkey vultures soar over the golden grasses of the hills, scouring the ground with their dispassionate eyes.

■ TOWN OF PESCADERO *map page 177*

Pescadero is a small, trim village at the head of Pescadero Marsh, surrounded by grassy hills where contented cattle graze. This is a hamlet of a few shops and a bar-restaurant strung out along a main street, plus a few whitewashed houses surrounded by well-tended gardens and orchards. Of course, the place and the setting have been compared to New England, like so many pretty places along the California coast. Pescadero not only has the best food, but also the only gas station for miles around. At the gas station is a small Mexican market and taqueria that sells great tamales, Mexican hats, and even a few medicinal herbs.

Duarte's Tavern, a former stagecoach stop, was opened in 1894 by a Portuguese bartender and barber whose family has run it ever since. You can stop here for artichoke or green chile soup (and you can even get them to go). The most prominent place on Pescadero's short main street, Duarte's is a very friendly, homey place that

Pigeon Point Lighthouse on the Pescadero Coast.

serves excellent seafood and is deservedly popular. The abalone is cooked to tender perfection and the artichoke soup is rich and flavorful. This normally means long waits; reservations are advised on weekends. (Also see page 379).

From Pescadero, you can follow signs inland, directing you to **Butano State Park.** The approach from the north (Pescadero) is much easier than the narrow windy road from the south, but is very narrow and twisty nonetheless, because it runs up a narrow, steep-walled redwood canyon (the redwoods don't look all that old, however, and aren't all that big). There is almost no parking except for a few narrow turnouts in the redwoods, the Año Nuevo trailhead, and the campground. The park has wooden warning signs admonishing you to drive slowly: "Caution! Slow newts!"

■ PIGEON POINT *map page 177*

Back on Highway 1, you'll see flat, windswept Pigeon Point off to the west, and on it the second-tallest lighthouse on the California coast (115 feet high; open Sundays). The beach has some good hiking and tide-pool exploring, and there's a youth hostel in the former keeper's quarters (650-879-0633). Unfortunately, a motel now mars this uniquely beautiful place.

■ AÑO NUEVO STATE RESERVE *map page 177*

Back on January 3, 1603, Spanish mariner Sebastian Vizcaino sailed past a low rocky island and point on the California coast, which a padre accompanying the expedition named Año Nuevo, for the New Year's Day on which they had first spotted it. The chaparral-covered headland looked as unappealing to later settlers as it looked to the Spanish explorers. Today, almost 400 years later, it has changed so little that Vizcaino would have no problems recognizing it.

Año Nuevo is protected as a state reserve because its unspoiled cape and offshore island appeal to a variety of wild animals—pelicans, sea lions, and, most notably, elephant seals. The popularity of high-quality "sea elephant" oil drove the creatures to the brink of extinction—only one small colony survived on islands off Baja California—but they have made a strong comeback since they were fully protected, and have expanded their range to as far north as Cape Blanco, Oregon.

Male elephant seals, the largest marine mammals to haul out on land, can grow to a length of 16 feet and a weight of three tons. They are so enormous that they occasionally kill their mates by falling asleep on top of them.

Bull elephant seals joust for dominance at Año Nuevo State Reserve. Researchers have marked the seal on the left for identification purposes.

The Año Nuevo colony is strictly protected, and admission during the winter is by reservation only, though you can often walk in at other times of the year. Even at the height of the season there are two daily walk-in tours, but you have to get to the reserve by 8 A.M., because these tours usually fill up by 8:30. *Call 650-879-2025 for questions about schedules. For reservations, call 800-444-4445.*

The elephant seal colony is on the beach at Point Año Nuevo, north of the entrance road and parking lot of the reserve. (I walked from the parking lot about a mile north on a trail to the reserve check-in station and about another half-mile north from the station to a beach where a guide took me to the elephant seals.)

If you cannot get in during the height of the seal breeding season, don't give up. The point is stunning at all times of the year, especially in spring and summer when its low-growing shrubs—which look like exquisite bonsai miniatures—are interspersed with wildflowers. Chances are you'll see a few straggler seals lolling on the beach, and you can watch brown pelicans soar along the bluffs.

South of Año Nuevo (and south of the Santa Cruz County line), you touch the western margin of **Big Basin Redwoods State Park** (established in 1902), California's oldest state park, which touches the coast at Ranch del Oso (Waddell

Santa Cruz surfing club, 1941.

The town's liberal epicenter, by the way, is up the hill on the campus of the University of California at Santa Cruz, though its professors and students live all over town.

At **Natural Bridges State Beach,** a sheltered beach at the north end of West Cliff Drive, brown pelicans like to preen by a scenic sea arch. Picnic tables are perched on a slope above the beach in a eucalyptus and pine forest; there's also a visitors center with natural history and Monarch butterfly displays, a Monarch butterfly reserve with a small milkweed garden for the butterflies, and the Monarch Trail—a boardwalk that winds into a grove of eucalyptus trees where the butterflies overwinter. Beware: it's heavily infested with poison oak. During my last visit I got a pleasant surprise at the small lagoon at the north side of the beach: a flock of Wilson's phalaropes swimming in circles, catching bugs. (Phalaropes are odd sandpipers that prefer swimming to walking. While swimming, they stir up aquatic insects with their long legs.) **West Cliff Drive** itself has a bicycle/pedestrian path between the road and the edge.

■ SURF CAPITAL

The reliable waves here have brought surfers, making Santa Cruz a surfing capital. Surfing also fosters a special, laid-back lifestyle—it's less a form of recreation than a way of life. Daniel Duane describes a "surf session" in his book, *Caught Inside,* as "a small occurrence outside the linear march of time," and explains that:

> One often hears surfing compared to sex; quite a stretch, except perhaps in the unselfconscious participation in a pattern of energy, in a constant physical response to a changing medium—at its best, emptying your mind of past and future.

You see the cars and pickup trucks of surfers parked all along the coast, from Montara south to Santa Cruz, and you can watch surfers, dark as sea lions in their wet suits, riding every major break, including the huge and dangerous ones farther north at Mavericks (just north of Pillar Point).

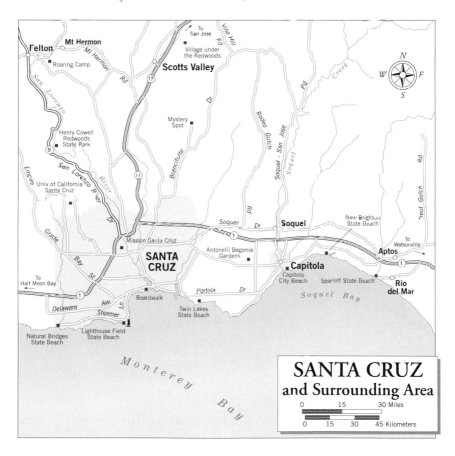

SANTA CRUZ
and Surrounding Area

0   15   30 Miles

0   15   30   45 Kilometers

■ Santa Cruz Sites

Signs from Highway 1 lead down commercial streets to the interesting parts of town, including a lively downtown and many woodsy neighborhoods filled with gracious houses. Attractive old buildings have been refurbished, and along Pacific Avenue you'll find a great bookstore-cafe, flower sellers, and locally owned shops. It's a cool town to be in, with a real sense of place. If you need to re-energize yourself, you can take your pick of several first-rate coffee and espresso shops, and on a sunny day, head out to Lighthouse Point, to look at the surfers zooming down Steamer Lane.

Pacific Avenue also leads to one of the coast's earliest amusement parks: the Boardwalk, erected at the turn of the 19th century. If you're in the mood for a roller-coaster ride, cotton candy, and a corn dog, this is the place to come. The unmistakable Giant Dipper is the only wooden roller coaster left on the West Coast. **Santa Cruz City Beach**, directly in front of the boardwalk, is the perfect spot for observing the local wildlife of the human kind—you'll see more bikini-clad Lolitas, more teenagers, more punks, and more vacationers in short-shorts than anywhere else on the coast.

The **Municipal Wharf,** a few feet up the bay, served primarily as a commercial fishing wharf until about 1960, when it was converted to restaurants and shops.

The Boardwalk parking lots are expensive ($10-$15), but there is metered on-street parking at the eastern end of Beach Street (near the roller coaster), when the road curves and becomes Third Street.

From the Boardwalk drive north to West Cliff Drive and find your way to **Lighthouse Point**—one of the best places anywhere to watch surfing. Backed by a grassy park-like area with big trees, the bluff-top sidewalk is a great place for a stroll, or to sit on one of the benches and read the Sunday paper. Off the cliffs is Steamer Lane, where a large contingent of Northern California's best surfers can be found any day the surf is up. It's best in the wintertime, and the biggest surf begins way out at the end of the point. An expert surfer will begin out there and cruise in toward the beach. In summer the surf is low, and you'll see surfers cutting up little waves close to shore. There's also a sort of temple of surfing, the **Santa Cruz Surfing Museum,** in the lighthouse replica on West Cliff Drive.

The Giant Dipper at the Boardwalk.

THAT SPECIAL SANTA CRUZ LIFESTYLE

Santa Cruz may have the most alternative lifestyles on the coast, but that's nothing unusual. The special Santa Cruz lifestyle dates as far back as 1797.

Six years after Mission Santa Cruz was founded, a civilian settlement was established by decree of the Viceroy of Mexico on the east bank of the San Lorenzo River and named Villa de Branciforte after him. Since the viceroy couldn't find any volunteers to populate his new town, he rounded up the sort of folk the government couldn't get along with and shipped them up the coast. The mission priests couldn't get along with them either, even though a river separated them, and they clashed right from the beginning, and constantly thereafter. The first real crisis came in 1818, when the privateer Hippolyte de Bouchard sacked Monterey. He was expected to sack Santa Cruz, too, so the Spanish governor gave orders to abandon the mission and town. The priests fled, instructing the Brancifortians to take care of the mission goods. The civilians were said to be especially happy when they discovered the padres' stash of *aguardiente*, or brandy.

Had Bouchard actually arrived, he could probably have shanghaied the entire town without an iota of resistance. When the padres returned, they wanted their goods back, but the Brancifortians replied with the Spanish-colonial equivalent of "tough luck."

Then, as now, Santa Crucians did not give much of a hoot about religion. After the Mexicans secularized the mission in 1834, it melted away. It was the town of Branciforte that prevailed, taking on the older name. The place soon became a hangout for whalers and loggers out for a good night on the town. By the 1860s, the first summer cottages, hotels, and bathhouses popped up. Going to the beaches became popular: since Santa Cruz faces south, the town's water was (and still is) warm enough for swimming.

Santa Cruz has many comfortable Victorian-era houses. The downtown, damaged in the Loma Prieta earthquake of 1989, is now rebuilt and very inviting. Tourists have been mainly local—people from San Jose, the farming valleys, or the peninsula towns.

A few rich people built mansions on the bluffs. One of these, James D. Phelan, opened his home to writers and artists like Gertrude Atherton, Ambrose Bierce, Isadora Duncan, Jack London, and Joaquin Miller. It set the tone for things to come.

Even though Santa Cruz has some of the highest home prices in the nation, the town is still somewhat grungy compared to its southern suburbs. But the locals like it that way—though Santa Cruz has grown to more than 55,000 people, the residents seem unwilling acknowledge the size: traffic patterns are confused, streets can get jammed, and signs make it easier to get from CA 1 to the beach than from the beach back to CA 1.

■ SOUTH OF SANTA CRUZ ON MONTEREY BAY

Other pleasant, sandy, and often sunny beaches in the Santa Cruz area include **Seabright Beach, Capitola City Beach** (backed by shops), **New Brighton State Beach, Sunset State Beach,** and **Palm Beach.**

Capitola, the first resort built on the coast (back in the late 1800s) still draws the crowds. It turns out to be a very pleasant place that's attractive without being cloying. In other words, Capitola works as the sort of seaside village it is trying to be, even though parking can be tight and enforcement is strict. There's a bay with a sandy beach sheltered by steep cliffs, plus a pier, a waterfront park and promenade, a creek, creekside and beachside restaurants and inns, and kite shops. Oddly, Capitola has the only large shopping mall in Santa Cruz County (but it's up the hill, away from the waterfront and out of sight).

South of Capitola, different beaches stretch all the way south to Monterey County. Some have odd names: Beer Can Beach, locally known by surfers as "The Can"; Pot Belly Beach; and Palm Beach (where I saw no palms).

Monterey Bay is home to hundreds of playful sea otters.

At **Aptos,** east of Santa Cruz, is **Seacliff State Beach,** with the oddest pier on the coast: it ends at a World War I cement ship—not a ship built to carry cement but built from reinforced concrete. It was a revolutionary way of construction at the time, but the war ended before the ship, the *Palo Alto*, saw service. It was towed to Seacliff and moored at the end of the pier as a maritime dance hall. As it deteriorated with time and erosion, it first became a fishing hulk, and later a craggy hangout for pelicans and cormorants, who love it. A visitors center (at the entrance to the day-use parking lot) is open year round (Wednesday to Sunday). The park has RV campsites at edge of the beach (reservations essential). *For park information, call 831-429-2850; for camping reservations call 800-444-7275).*

You can get to **Sunset State Beach/Palm Beach** (together they form one long, continuous public state beach) via an access road that winds through hillsides covered with chaparral and topped with pine and cypress woods. The campsites are in the woods, a long hike from the beach. (The campground is usually full, so make reservations.) This is one of the wildest beaches in Santa Cruz County south of Santa Cruz—almost as wild as some of the north county beaches—but the view is somewhat marred by condominiums at the far south (Palm Beach) end. There's also a boardwalk through the dunes to Sunset Beach at the end of the parking lot. You get to Palm Beach by a road along the Pajaro River. (Follow signs from CA 1.) You can also reach it by walking down the coast from Sunset Beach, but that's a 7-mile hike.

Past the cluster of beachfront villages south of Santa Cruz, the road traverses a rustic landscape of dairy farms and artichoke fields.

Moss Landing State Beach is essentially a strip of dunes and beach reached by a narrow access road that crosses the far northern end of the Moss Landing/Elkhorn Slough harbor basin. On a recent visit, harbor seals were sprawled out on a sand bank at the park side of the slough. I stopped on my way out to take pictures of little peeps (small sandpipers) at the tidal margin and came upon an awesome trio: an egret, a cormorant, and a sea lion hanging out together on culvert pipes. The beach runs south to the mouth of Elkhorn Slough and north to the Pajaro River.

Marked by a tall-stacked power plant are Moss Landing and **Elkhorn Slough**. The latter is a great place to go birding in a canoe or kayak.

Little has changed at **Moss Landing** over the years: the basin is still filled with boats and the shore teems with birds. Even on a cloudy off-season day in midweek you'll find plenty of visitors. The **Moss Landing Café** still serves good food; I had an excellent open-faced crab sandwich with a side of artichoke for lunch there.

Just beyond Moss Landing, pull off at a roadside stand and stock up on fresh produce. This is the lower Salinas Valley, the very heartland of American artichoke production; a short side road leads into **Castroville**, known as the artichoke capital of the world. Today, the lower Salinas Valley not only grows artichokes, but is also the lettuce bowl of the nation, supporting a $2 billion annual agricultural economy. The artichoke fields end where the sand dunes start, and while the dunes are beautiful in themselves, they hide much of the shore from the road.

On the northern edge of the former Fort Ord Military Reservation, **Marina**, once a grimy service town, has undergone a transformation since the base closed—motels and a resort in the dunes; hang gliders at **Marina State Beach**; and shopping near Del Monte and Reservation roads.

Marina State Beach has a wood boardwalk through the dunes, which is supposed to be wheelchair- and bicycle-accessible. However, the wooden boards are covered with blown sand in many places, and several planks are loose or missing (often in critical spots). The dunes of the state beach are popular with hang gliders (who look eerie when they glide low over the dunes in the fog). In case you're wondering why there's a water treatment plant in the dunes north of the state beach parking lot: it's not a wastewater treatment plant, but a desalination facility that turns sea water into drinking water.

This part of Monterey Bay has miles and miles of firm sandy beach—walk north to the mouth of the Salinas River/Moss Landing, or south to Monterey through the not-yet-opened but accessible Fort Ord Dunes State Park. (Given the state of California's budget, it's unclear when these 4 miles of sandy beach, just south of Marina State Beach, will be officially open.)

■ MONTEREY PENINSULA

Monterey Bay is impressive both from the land, as you look south or north along the vast crescent of sandy shore, and from the window of an airplane, which allows you to see the gorgeous, gleaming sweep in one glance. Sandy beaches and dunes dominate the shore between Santa Cruz and Monterey, but at Monterey, at the southern end of the bay, spurs of the Santa Lucia Mountains encroach on the beaches, forming the spectacular rocky headlands of the Monterey Peninsula.

■ ■ ■

In the autumn of 1769, a ragtag band of Spanish soldiers and missionaries invaded this area. It was Don Juan Gaspar de Portola and his men, who had traveled north to take possession of the land for the King of Spain. They meant to find Monterey Bay but missed it, so they plodded onwards until from a lookout point above modern-day Pacifica, they saw San Francisco Bay. But they returned to Monterey in the spring of 1770 to found a presidio and mission. Monterey served as the capital of California from 1775 until the American occupation of California in 1848.

There are several ways to reach the Monterey Peninsula. You can drive south from San Francisco on Highway 1, following the route laid out in the previous pages of this chapter, or you can travel from U.S. 101 near Salinas and cross west on CA 68 (until it intersects with Highway 1; *see maps on pages 177 and 195*). The southernmost Monterey exit leads to Cannery Row and the Monterey Bay Aquarium. Just follow the signs. For easy access to Monterey's historic downtown and the waterfront, you might want to park your car at centrally located Fisherman's Wharf, which has ample pay parking.

■ MONTEREY'S FISHERMAN'S WHARF *map page 195*

Monterey's historic Fisherman's Wharf has been spruced up in recent years, but somehow it still works. You'll see more visitors than fishermen, however (to see the latter, go across the harbor to Municipal Wharf No. 2). Seafood restaurants are tucked between fish markets and seashell, T-shirt, and knickknack shops—most of them with spectacular views of the rocky shore, the harbor, or the ocean. Sea lions hang out beneath the piers; brown pelicans may perch on the roofs. (They can be seen roosting on rocks near shore for most of the year.) The restaurants offer decent seafood salads, fresh fish, or deep-fried squid with a view of sea otters frolicking in the kelp. You can also order deep-fried artichokes, or bowls of clam chowder accompanied by chunks of French bread, at one of several take-out places.

Fisherman's Wharf sits more or less right in the center of Monterey harbor, a breakwater-protected embayment on the east shore of the peninsula. Its northern end is marked by the Coast Guard Pier; its southern end by Municipal Wharf No. 2, which is where the warehouses are and where boats unload sand dabs, sole, squid, shrimp, salmon, rockfish, anchovies, herring, and sardines (you can drive onto the pier from the south end of the parking lot).

■ ■ ■

During Spanish and Mexican times, passengers and goods were landed by surf boat in the small sandy cove below the harbor's customs house. It got its first pier in 1870. Local fisheries got their start from Chinese fishermen who harvested abalone and squid, then Sicilian fishermen who conquered the huge schools of sardines coursing along the shores.

Carmel poet Robinson Jeffers described the sardine fishery as a beautiful and terrible scene, with the fish caught in the seine wildly beating "from one wall to the other of their closing destiny the phosphorescent water to a pool of flame, each beautiful slender body sheeted with flame, like a live rocket, a comet's tail wake of yellow flame."

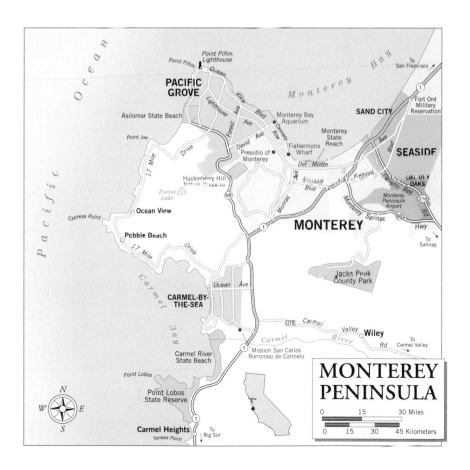

■ CANNERY ROW *map page 195*

In the mid 1940s, John Steinbeck wrote:

> Cannery Row in Monterey in California is a poem, a stink, a grating
> noise, a quality of light, a tone, a habit, a nostalgia, a dream.
> Cannery Row is the gathered and scattered, tin and iron and rust and
> splintered wood, chipped pavement and weedy lots and junk heaps,
> sardine canneries of corrugated iron, honky tonks, restaurants and
> whore houses, and little crowded groceries, and laboratories and
> flophouses. Its inhabitants are, as the man once said, "whores, pimps,
> gamblers, and sons of bitches," by which he meant Everybody. Had
> the man looked through another peephole he might have said,
> "saints and angels and martyrs and holy men," and he would have
> meant the same thing.

Once sardines are caught in great numbers, there has to be a way to process, store, and market them. Monterey's canneries, which were built to package the local salmon, were soon converted into sardine canneries and fish reduction plants, creating the effect Steinbeck so aptly described above in his novel *Cannery Row* as a poem and a stink.

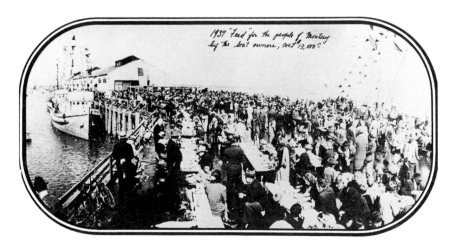

Boat owners of Cannery Row provide food and beer at this 1937 Sardine Week Celebration.

Many of Monterey's citizens failed to recognize the "poetic" aspect of the canneries, noting only the noise and the stink. Tom Mangelsdorf, in *A History of Steinbeck's Cannery Row*, gives a good synopsis of the battles between citizens, fishermen, and cannery owners. These fights lasted until the sardines, which had been overfished for decades, ran out in the early 1950s. By strange coincidence, the heavily insured canneries began to burn down almost as soon as the fish ran out. But the waterfront was too pretty to be left to rot. In the 1970s and 1980s, new restaurants and hotels sprang up.

To those of us who have read and enjoyed John Steinbeck's novel, the "new" Cannery Row seems like another gussied up "historic" mall. There's none of the old aura (and fortunately none of the old aroma) left. But the removal of canneries has opened up the shoreline, with its rocks, seabirds, tide pools, and offshore kelp beds where sea otters hang out and where you can, at times, watch white egrets stand *on* the floating kelp, waiting for fish to swim by. (It's a curious sight, since egrets, unlike gulls, pelicans, and cormorants, do *not* swim.)

■ ■ ■

Now, not even the return of the sardines can bring back the canneries of old—although, strange to say, the sardines are indeed returning. This brings us to an ironic footnote: because canned Monterey sardines were not tasty enough to attract willing buyers, the canneries often made more money from fish reduced to fish oil and meal; but fresh Monterey sardines, prepared by a competent chef, are truly excellent.

Today, sardines have made such a comeback they are the second-most valuable seafood landed by California fishermen, right after squid.

■ Monterey Bay Aquarium

The main reason for visiting Cannery Row today is the Monterey Bay Aquarium, which is partly tucked into the old shell of the Pioneer Hovden Cannery (immortalized by John Steinbeck as the "Hediondo," i.e., "Stinking Cannery"). This huge aquarium complex, which first opened its doors in October of 1984, is one of the most exciting places to visit on the coast. You'll get an idea of the vastness of the place when you step into the entry hall and see a full-sized *lampara* boat (a Sicilian lateen-rigged fishing boat that pioneered the Monterey sardine fishery) suspended from the ceiling. A group of life-sized cetacean sculptures—a gray whale, orca, and other whales and dolphins—are suspended from the ceiling a bit up the hall, and dwarfed by the cavernous interior.

There's nothing small about this aquarium, not even the tanks. One—a full-sized, multiple-story re-creation of a kelp forest—is so big that a scuba diver drops into the tank to feed the fish. In several of the big tanks, the huge swirling mass of fish conveys with vivid immediacy the energy of the ocean.

Monterey Canyon, just offshore, is one of the world's richest marine habitats, and the aquarium allows you to share in the bounty, by bringing fish, shellfish, and sea mammals up close to you, where you can watch them in an almost natural habitat. If the viewing windows of the sea otter tank inside are too crowded, which they often are, just step outside and look for sea otters in the kelp. Free spotting scopes (mounted on columns) bring them very close.

One room has an artificial beach were you can take a long, leisurely look at shorebirds like sanderlings, snowy plovers, black-necked stilts, and phalaropes.

There's even a petting tank for rays and other "touchable" fish. In short, this aquarium gets you as close to the energy and beauty of marine ecology as you'll ever get without donning scuba gear. Because it is *very* popular, plan to visit in the off-season or in midweek; *call 831-648-4888.*

■ **PACIFIC GROVE** *map pages 177 and 185*

Pacific Grove starts on the other side of the aquarium and old Cannery Row. This pleasant town spreads over the northern tip of the peninsula, from Monterey all the way to Point Piños, with its 1855 lighthouse—the oldest continuously operating lighthouse on the West Coast—and on to Asilomar Beach.

Lighthouse Avenue runs right through Pacific Grove, from Monterey's Cannery Row all the way to the end of Point Piños. It is one of the most pleasant, old-fashioned main streets on the coast, with small shops, bookstores, and no tourist hubbub. Side roads lead to Lover's Point and other headlands and beaches on the eastern shore of the peninsula.

Several pleasant inns make it possible for you to stay near Point Piños, with its low rocky cliffs, dunes, and sandy beaches—all washed by a white surf and a turquoise- and indigo-colored sea. You can reach Lover's Point, with its jagged

Visitors watch jellyfish swim around in a large tank at the Monterey Bay Aquarium.

CARMEL MISSION, 1786

French navigator Jean Franc[cd]ois de La Pe[ac]rouse visited Monterey Bay in September of 1786, as commander of L'Astrolabe *and* La Boussole, *the first foreign vessels to visit Spain's California colonies. Ordered and outfitted by King Louis [sc]xvi[esc] of France, the ships were to spend four years at sea exploring new lands.*

La Pérouse was well received by the priests at Carmel Mission. Following are excerpts from his diaries describing his visit, which occurred two years after the death of the mission's founder, Father Junipero Serra.

It is with the most pleasing satisfaction that I speak of the pious and prudent conduct of these religious men, which so perfectly agrees with the goal of their institution. I shall not conceal what I conceived to be reprehensible in their internal administration, but I must affirm that, by being individually good and humane, they temper by their mildness and charity the austerity of the rules which have been prescribed by their superiors.

■ ■ ■

Mission San Carlos Borromeo de Carmel *by Edwin Deakin, 1895.*

Indians of Monterey *by José Cardero, 1791.*

The president of the missions, in his ceremonial vestments and with his holy water sprinkle in his hand, awaited us at the gate of the church, which was illuminated in the same manner as on the greatest feast days. . . .

Before we entered the church, we had passed through a square in which the Indians of both sexes were ranged in a line. They exhibited no marks of surprise in their countenance, and left us in doubt whether we should be the subject of their conversation for the rest of the day.

■ ■ ■

The color of these Indians, which is that of Negroes; the house of the missionaries; their storehouses, which are built of brick and plastered; the appearance of the ground on which the grain is trodden out; the cattle, the horses—everything in short—brought to our recollection a plantation at Santo Domingo or any other West Indian island. The men and women are collected by the sound of a bell; a missionary leads them to work, to the church, and to all their exercises. We observed with concern that the resemblance is so perfect that we have seen both men and women in irons, and others in the stocks. Lastly, the noise of the whip might have struck our ears, this punishment also being administered, though with little severity.

—Jean François de La Pérouse, Journals, 1786,
excerpts from *Life in a California Mission,* Heyday Books

in the early 1900s, when such well-known writers as Jack London, George Sterling, Lincoln Steffens, and Mary Austin lived in the seaside woods, as close to nature as they could manage. At times their lives appeared more like staged productions than a slice of reality. According to the *Carmel Pine-Cone:*

> Picnics such as the ones Jimmie Hopper, Mary Austin, George Sterling, Ferdinand Burgdorf and others frequently organized, were regarded as Bacchanalian orgies. The women danced around the bonfires with bare feet, their long hair flying. A gallon jug of red wine was in evidence and anyone who stumbled upon these seemingly mad, wild gatherings was deeply shocked and went away thinking Carmel was getting to be as wicked as Paris.

Robinson Jeffers was only one of many writers who made their homes in Carmel, but while many of them lived here for just a short time, or came to visit, Jeffers stayed and through his writing helped make the region what it is today. If you're visiting on a weekend, plan to take a tour of Robinson Jeffers's **Tor House** and tower, which the poet built from stone with his own hands. *26304 Ocean View Avenue between Scenic Drive and Stewart Way; 831-624-1813 (weekdays), 831-624-1840 (weekends); by reservation only.*

■ ■ ■

Carmel Mission, as Mission San Carlos Borromeo de Carmelo at the southern end of town is popularly known, was founded by Father Junipero Serra in June of 1770. It has undergone extensive restoration and is, with its beautiful gardens, one of the prettiest and most restful places on the coast. Today, looking at the irregular, gold-brown contours of the old mission, it's hard to put it all together: the glorious site, the idealistic Franciscans who came north from Mexico, and the lives of the local Indians—whose culture was destroyed, and who, themselves, died in great numbers from diseases brought by Europeans.

The Carmel River, bordered by artichoke fields and sandy beaches, enters the ocean just south of the mission. Some of the beautiful land visible along the river belongs to a ranch donated to the state in 1997 by actor Clint Eastwood.

A sunset worth applauding at Carmel-by-the-Sea.
(following spread) Horse wranglers at Holman Ranch in the Carmel Valley.

■ **CARMEL VALLEY WINERIES**

Up Carmel Valley much of the landscape is as pristine as it was 200 years ago. Although some unfortunate malls have been built in the past few years, there are still signs by the side of the road alerting you to "Newts Crossing." In the acorn season, wild turkeys gobble up the tasty nuts underneath spreading oak trees; at all times of the year, deer, hawks, woodpeckers, and songbirds are plentiful. The Carmel Valley has several excellent wineries, which are well worth a short detour.

■ ■ ■

Chateau Julien
Because this winery occupies a French-style chateau (just off the highway), it looks the way many people think a winery should look. But it's more than just show. The wines, made from Monterey grapes, are excellent. *8940 Carmel Valley Rd.; 831-624-2600.*

Bernardus Winery
This state-of-the-art winery, tucked into the rolling hills southeast of the village of Carmel Valley, makes superb estate wines from its Jamesburg vineyards. If there's one winery that will add the Carmel Valley to the international oenophile's itinerary, this is the one. Try the cabernet franc and cabernet sauvignon, merlot, a lovely blend of reds called Marinus, sauvignon blanc, and chardonnay. Tours and tastings by appointment only. *5 W. Carmel Valley Rd.; 831-659-1900.*

Georis Winery
This tiny, up-valley winery makes only merlot—but what merlot. Production is minuscule—only some 500 cases per vintage. If you can't find the wine at local wine shops, look for it at the Casanova restaurant in Carmel (which is owned by winemaker Walter Georis) on Fifth Avenue between Mission and San Carlos streets. *4 Pilot Rd.; 831-659-1050.*

(There are more wineries in the valley: to learn more about them, consult the Compass Guide to the *California Wine Country*.)

■ **POINT LOBOS** *map pages 177 and 195*

This jagged, surf-swept headland, carved into sandy coves and rocky promontories by the constant pounding of waves, is one of the coast's most spectacularly scenic places. Wind-sculpted Monterey cypresses make their last stand on these cliffs; their ragged foliage and gnarled, salt-bleached trunks add an intensely dramatic accent to the barren cliffs, which rise straight from the white surf. Forests of dark Monterey pine and wildflower meadows cover the back slopes.

This landscape is not as virginal as it looks. It was once part of a cattle ranch and supported, at different times, a whaling station, a granite quarry, an abalone cannery, and a loading chute for a coal mine. One previous owner even tried to subdivide the point—laying out a town site with a harsh grid of streets.

Today, Point Lobos looks as pristine as any landscape trod by man can ever be. If you see some small (about 3-foot-high) people standing in the shadow of rocks or trees, watching you, ignore them. These "watchers" are said to pop up throughout the Big Sur area. Supposedly they leave you alone if you stick to the trails, but dire things are said to happen if you don't. Some of the folk who have seen the watchers have also seen elves at Point Lobos.

If you take the trail to the top of Whaler's Knoll, watch out for poison oak. The cypress loop is an easy hike with splendid views from the Sea Lion Point parking lot, even if you're out of shape.

■ BIG SUR COAST *map page 177*

While the term "Big Sur" was originally only applied to the valley of the river, it later came to connote the entire coast from Point Lobos to Lucia.

The 90-mile stretch of road from Carmel south along the Big Sur coast has some 30 turnouts with beach or cliff access and spectacular views; the road dips as low as 20 feet and rises to 1,200-foot cliff tops as it winds its way around precipitous headlands and into narrow canyons. In winter, be prepared for washouts, fallen rocks on the road, mudslides, and water over the roadway. In summer, there's usually a fair amount of traffic.

South of the Carmel River, the coast turns rocky, its steepness mitigated only occasionally by the gentler slopes of marine terraces. Here mountains edge up to the sea, and the pines and cypresses of Monterey give way to grassy slopes—brilliantly green during the winter rainy season, dotted with patches of golden poppies in spring, and clothed in a drab tan coat in summer, during the dry part of the year. Lofty bridges span creek chasms where redwoods grow. All along the Big Sur coast—wherever you can get close enough to the water—you should be able to watch sea otters. The stretch of shoreline from Monterey Bay south to Point San Luis has the largest concentration of these playful mammals in California.

Only one road (G 14) runs east across the Santa Lucia Mountains, and in places it is a mere track.

■ NORTHERN BIG SUR BEACHES AND WOODS *map page 177*

■ GARRAPATA STATE PARK

Located on the northern Big Sur coast, this beach stretches along 4 miles of coast. It is still undeveloped but has roadside turnouts for parking and rough trails leading to the water.

Jutting out into the ocean north of Palo Colorado Canyon (where the old coast road turned inland before the modern highway was built), **Rocky Point** offers some of the finest views of the Big Sur coast. Because I always seemed to pass it at odd times in my traveling day—too early or too late for lunch or dinner—I missed out on a visit to Rocky Point Restaurant until I scheduled a special visit. With its great view, it is worth a snack and a glass of wine even if you don't have the time for a full meal. Sit here and watch the fog caress the cliffs and sea stacks, listen to the surf, and check out the sea lions and, with luck, the dolphins and the resident sea otter while relaxing in the comfort of a warm room on a foggy morning or a hazy afternoon. *Hwy 1, 10 miles south of Carmel; 831-624-2933.*

The stands of eucalyptus trees and clumps of pampas grass that dominate the Central California Coast vegetation—especially along the Big Sur slopes—are not native but introduced species gone feral. (Many of the pines and cypresses growing here are not native either; while they may be native to the California coast; they are not native to this part of the coast.

■ ANDREW MOLERA STATE PARK

A trail here leads to the mouth of the Big Sur River, which may be impassable during winter high water. Trails lead to meadows and bluffs; the lagoon has some great bird-watching. The highway runs inland along the Big Sur River and into the redwoods before switching back to the coast. Walk-in campground.

■ PFEIFFER BIG SUR STATE PARK

There's no beach here, but redwoods and some great trails into the backcountry. More than 200 campsites, plus access to Big Sur River. Check out Pfeiffer Falls and the Gorge.

■ PFEIFFER BEACH

A truly magic place at the end of Sycamore Canyon Road (1 mile south of Pfeiffer Big Sur State Park; not well marked). Crashing waves, sea caves, and arches.

■ JULIA PFEIFFER BURNS STATE PARK

Wooded, tucked into a canyon above the ocean; a trail leads to an overlook where McWay waterfall plunges 80 feet into the sea. As the surf splashes against the rock, the water falls back in an arc, creating the illusion of a second, smaller, waterfall. When the sun breaks through the clouds and paints a rainbow onto the sea spray, it's fantastical.

During my last visit, I followed the waterfall overlook path to its end around the bend for the first time. To my surprise, I discovered palm trees, exotic shrubs, and the foundations of what must have been a substantial house. I learned that Lathrop Brown, a former New York congressman, and his wife, Helen Hooper Brown, moved to California in the 1920s, bought McWay's Saddle Rock Ranch, and built a home here called Waterfall House. In 1961 Helen Hooper Brown donated the entire property—about 1,800 acres—to the state for a park, stipulating that it be named for Julia Pfeiffer Burns, "a true pioneer." She also stipulated that the building was to be razed if it was not turned into a museum within five years. The state could not come up with the money, so the house was torn down in 1965.

From here south, much of the beach access is for experienced mountain climbers only; other parts of the beach have steep trails even energetic amateurs can scramble up and down on.

■ LIMEKILN STATE PARK

Limekiln State Beach takes its name from abandoned limekilns nearby, and is one of the few good camping spots on the Big Sur coast. Jade Cove has pebbles and boulders of nephrite. The state began getting a bit nervous about having jade removed from the beach after divers took a 9,000-pound jade boulder, worth $180,000, in 1971.

■ NEPENTHE

Nepenthe restaurant (just south of Big Sur on Highway 1) is the sort of place everybody loves, and not because it happens to be one of the few restaurants on the coast, and the only one with a spectacular view. I stopped here last on one of those rare winter days with pale sun and weak fog, the spindrift of the surf draping the coast in ethereal light. As I sat by the window, enjoying a superb Ahi tuna sandwich, I looked south for a long way, past gnarled live oaks, past redwood-filled creek canyons, and past Partington Ridge, where novelist Henry Miller lived during the 1940s and 1950s. He wrote:

> Big Sur has a climate of its own and a character all its own. It is a
> region where extremes meet, a region where one is always conscious
> of weather, of space, of grandeur, and of eloquent silence. . . . In
> summer, when the fogs roll in, one can look down upon a sea of
> clouds floating listlessly above the ocean; they have the appearance,
> at times, of huge, iridescent soap bubbles, over which, now and then,
> may be seen a double rainbow.

Miller's memory is kept alive by the **Henry Miller Memorial Library,** founded in
the 1960s by Miller's friend, the poet Emil White, in his home. It's about a mile
south of Nepenthe, in a sharp curve of the highway, half-hidden under tall redwoods. This shrine for Miller fans is open in the afternoon, but hours may vary,
especially in the off-season.

■ ■ ■

The stretch of coast south of here is among California's most rugged and beautiful.
The mountains drop into the surf at an even steeper angle than they do north of
the Big Sur River. There are hidden waterfalls and beaches, and splendid cliffs and
mountainsides (though a few are messed up by big, ragged clumps of pampas
grass, planted to combat erosion). The cliffs and steep mountainsides are covered
mostly with chaparral and scrub and a few trees (redwoods in the canyons), and
even a few succulents precariously clinging to steep cliff faces. But mainly it's
naked rock. Robinson Jeffers wrote in his poem "November Surf:"

> Like the steep necks of a herd of horses
> Lined on a river margin, athirst in summer, the mountain ridges
> Pitch to the sea, the lean granite-boned heads
> Plunge nostril-under . . . .

■ ROAD TO SAN SIMEON

If you've missed out on the elephant seals at Año Nuevo, you get a second chance
on this stretch of the San Luis Obispo coast, between San Carpoforo Creek to the
north (where the mountains begin to squeeze the coast highway) and San Simeon
in the south. According to an Año Nuevo park ranger, these elephant seals don't

Julia Pfeiffer Burns State Park.

"play fair," perhaps because they don't play hard to see. You'll spot them on beaches just off the highway (beware of rubber-necking motorists), and they're mostly unafraid of humans (some folks have even been known to place their infants on top of a sleeping seal to take family photos). But be careful—after all, elephant seals are wild animals, and they are BIG.

An elevated boardwalk at the cliff's edge winds south from the main parking area (marked Vista Point); it's a good overlook for the elephant-seal beaches. (Harbor seals haul out on a rocky point to the south; they're much smaller than the elephant seals.) Volunteers are often on duty to answer questions about the elephant seals and to make sure you don't molest the sea mammals.

William R. Hearst Memorial State Beach is a eucalyptus-shaded cove and wooden pier in San Simeon Cove, inviting to kayakers and fishermen. Seals dive for food among the rocks and kelp here and are then harassed by gulls; the seals in turn bother the pier fisherman by trying to steal their bait or catch. The pelicans try to get into the act but aren't quick or aggressive enough.

The shore north and south of the park, and the hills to the east, are owned by the Hearst Corporation (of newspaper fame). Until recently, public access has been tenuous at best. In 2004, the state came to an agreement with the Hearst Ranch to allow more public beach access. In return, Hearst gained some development rights but gave up plans to build a major coastal city on its property (which basically means most of the ranch will remain pristine).

■ HEARST CASTLES *map pages 177 and 223*

Hearst Castle rises from the rounded top of a hill southeast of the highway. The castle, officially known as Hearst San Simeon State Historical Monument, is the sort of place art snobs hate and the general public loves. There are good reasons for both opinions. Constructed between 1920 and 1950, as newspaper magnate William R. Hearst's private estate, the monument still contains pieces of Hearst's extensive art collection and herds of exotic animals. Herein lies the clue to understanding this place: Hearst was an eclectic collector (for background information, watch the Orson Welles movie, *Citizen Kane*, based on the newspaper magnate's life), and it is precisely this eclecticism that makes the castle so popular and qualifies it for folk-art status.

Hearst "found" his objects all over the world and paid big money for them. Instead of designing his pleasure dome bit by bit, he hired a famous architect (Julia

Morgan) to arrange the objects for him. It's fair to say that San Simeon is more than the sum of its parts. It remains a classic American nouveau-riche exuberance, beautiful in its own way, and was considered a fabulous getaway by the Hollywood stars Hearst entertained there—among them his mistress, Marion Davies, whose career he shamelessly promoted in his newspapers. *750 Hearst Castle Road. For tour reservations, call 800-444-4445.*

■ ■ ■

For a less famous sample of the same enthusiasm, see **Nitwit Ridge** in nearby Cambria Pines, an unusual residence built by local contractor Al Beal, also known as "Captain Nitwit." This several-story house, which covers a hillside plot, was built of concrete embedded with bits of seashell, glass, beer cans, auto parts, and other found objects. The home is a California Historical Landmark. *On Hillcrest Drive, off Main Street.*

■ SAN SIMEON STATE BEACH *map page 177*

Sandy San Simeon State Beach runs from Santa Rosa Creek north to San Simeon Creek. William R. Hearst Memorial State Beach has a swimming area that's protected from the worst excesses of the ocean by San Simeon Point and a picnic area in a eucalyptus grove.

At the south end of San Simeon State Beach, just north of Cambria, **Moonstone Beach** consists of low bluffs and pocket beaches bordered by the ocean to the west and Moonstone Beach Drive to the east. A wooden boardwalk (with observation platforms) winds through the low coastal scrub on the bluffs. Take a walk here and watch the passing whales, dolphins, and sea lions. Also look for harbor seals and sea otters on the rocks, rabbits and ground squirrels in the brush, and cormorants and brown pelicans offshore.

NOTE FOR DRIVERS CONTINUING SOUTH

The following chapter begins at Point Mugu near Malibu and ends just south of San Simeon on page 266. We hope drivers continuing south won't find it too onerous to switch directions as they read that chapter. Our reason for having done this? The majority of travelers come into the area south of San Simeon by driving north from Los Angeles.

■ TRAVEL BASICS

Driving

You may wish to begin a drive south to the Monterey Peninsula and Big Sur by traveling the faster inland roads, then cutting west over to the coast. If you choose to follow the Coast Highway out of San Francisco, you'll begin at Ocean Beach, described in "SAN FRANCISCO BAY" on page 61. Roads along the coast from San Francisco south to San Simeon—with the exception of two stretches of freeway near Santa Cruz and Monterey—are for the most part beautiful and rural but two-lane, making for slow driving on weekends and during the height of the summer travel season.

Climate

Expect some wind and fog in the summer, although many days will be clear and warm by noon. Spring and fall are brisk and clear. Winter can be rainy and damp with daytime temperatures in the 50s. Remember that if you travel inland a few miles, it's usually warmer. A mild climate is the rule along the entire coastline. Monterey is the driest coastal location north of Los Angeles, with only 15 inches of rain per season; just across Monterey Bay, Santa Cruz is the wettest with 28 inches. Summer (June through August) temperatures along the shore rarely rise above 70 degrees but are commonly in the 90s a short distance inland. Heavy winter (November to March) storms often cause mudslides along the Coast Highway, CA 1. Fall is magnificent, with warm temperatures and clear skies. **Water temperature** is cool year-round (50 to 60 degrees).

Food and Lodging

Santa Cruz and Monterey are in the heart of a culinary wonderland. The sea provides fresh seafood year-round. The Salinas Valley is the salad bowl of America. Regional wines, made from grapes grown in the neighboring valleys and mountains, enhance the local dishes.

A number of unusual and very comfortable inns are tucked away in coastal towns and sunny valleys. **Lodging and restaurant listings** by town in alphabetical order begin on page 362.

The trail above the beach at Julia Pfeiffer Burns State Park is just one of many wonderful places to hike along the Big Sur coast.

CENTRAL COAST RIVIERA

From Point Mugu north to Ventura, the Coast Highway runs away from the sea, through the fertile plain of the Santa Clara River. Offshore lie the wild and undeveloped Channel Islands, which can be visited by National Park Service concessionaire (see page 226). North of Ventura the coastal corridor narrows as the mountains push closer to the sea, leaving barely enough room between the steep, unstable bluffs and the surf for the highway to pass through. The pristine landscape of the coast is interrupted only occasionally by a few clusters of homes, oil derricks, and oil pumps.

The town of Santa Barbara is the urban highlight of this trip. Even if you only have time to get a glimpse of the town as it rises in tiers from the sea toward the mountains, topped by the two-towered facade of the mission, you'll be impressed by its picture-perfect aspects. Inland from Santa Barbara are several vineyard-laden valleys whose wineries are discussed in this chapter.

Highway 1 and U.S. 101 leave the coast at Gaviota Pass and separate. They do not return to the coast until they merge again in Pismo Beach and once again run together inland to San Luis Obispo. To the east is open ranch country; on the coast are towns of charm and interest.

■ POINT MUGU NORTH

This stretch of coast is at its prettiest on a misty morning, when the hillside houses float above the fog like the temples of a Japanese landscape painting, and when the blue ocean sparkles brightly beneath swirling bands of ocean vapors. Flowers and trees and bluffs look unreal at such times; only sand, the surf, and the water look real, making a visit to the beach seem like you're submerging yourself in a sea of liquid gold.

Point Mugu State Park, bordering the highway, has many sandy pocket beaches, including **Point Mugu Beach.** The last time I visited I saw brown pelicans catching their breakfast, and sea lions and common dolphins offshore. **Mugu Lagoon,** one of Southern California's largest remaining wetlands, lies entirely within the

A priest talks to visiting children at Mission Santa Ines, a historic (1804) mission.

U.S. Navy's Pacific Missile Test Center. A fine view of the lagoon can be enjoyed from the roadside turnout on CA 1, a half-mile north of Point Mugu Rock. Mugu Submarine Canyon, half a mile deep and more than 9 miles long, lies offshore. *Group tours during the winter birding season may be arranged by calling the U.S. Navy's public affairs office at 805-989-8094.*

At the mouth of La Jolla Canyon is the 10.8-mile **Ray Miller hiking trail**, a well-graded loop that leads into the coastal foothills and provides stunning views of the coastline below—and, on clear days, of the Channel Islands in the distance. There's overnight (permit-only) camping at La Jolla Valley Camp. *For more information, maps, and permits call Point Mugu State Park; 805-488-5223.*

CA 1 curves inland around the missile range, then becomes a freeway cutting through one of the most fertile agricultural areas in the world. To the left of the freeway is a different collection of birds—a display of all sorts of spiky rockets and things designed to kill and maim, but looking surprisingly like an assemblage of oversized spears protruding from the ground.

Due to shore erosion in the Point Mugu area, the coastal highway has been moved inland.

■ CHANNEL ISLANDS

Seen through the ocean haze of a clear day
on the beach, these offshore islands seem
to float above the sea like rocky wraiths.
They do indeed appear as elusive as
ghosts, for on most days you cannot
see them at all, even though they lie
just a dozen or so miles off one of
the most populated stretches of
the Southern California coast.

They're known as the
Channel Islands because
they are strung out like a
natural breakwater and
form the Santa Barbara
Channel, which stretches
from the northwestern
Santa Barbara coast southeast to Ventura County.

Because these islands lie
between the cold California
Current, which rushes south
from Point Conception, and the
warm Southern California Current,
which flows north along the shore
from Mexico, their shores are the battle-
ground of these two clashing ocean streams,
and they are often swathed in fog or buffeted
by wind. The climatic extremes created by the
mingling of cold and warm waters and chilly and
hot air, as well as the scarcity of fresh water, drove
away most of the early white settlers and may be the
reason why these islands have remained virtually
unsettled since the last of the native Chumash were carried off to mainland missions 200 years ago.

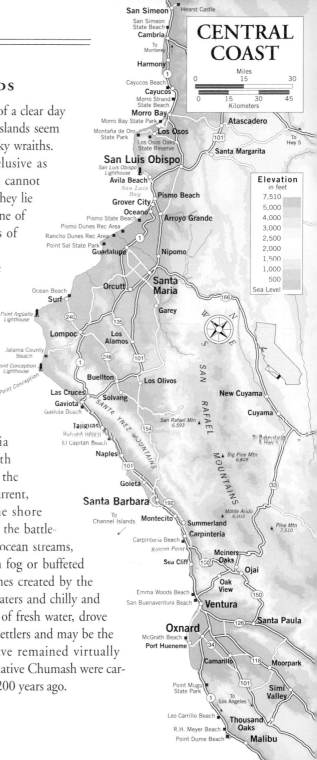

CENTRAL COAST

Miles
0   15   30

0   15   30   45
Kilometers

Elevation
in feet

| 7,510 |
| 5,000 |
| 4,000 |
| 3,000 |
| 2,500 |
| 2,000 |
| 1,500 |
| 1,000 |
| 500 |
| Sea Level |

San Simeon — Hearst Castle
San Simeon State Beach
Cambria
To Monterey
Harmony
Cayucos Beach
Cayucos
Morro Strand State Beach
Morro Bay
Morro Bay State Park
Montaña de Oro State Park — Los Osos
Los Osos Oaks State Reserve
Atascadero
Santa Margarita
San Luis Obispo
San Luis Obispo Lighthouse
Avila Beach
San Luis Bay
Grover City — Pismo Beach
Oceano
Pismo State Beach — Arroyo Grande
Pismo Dunes Rec Area
Rancho Dunes Rec Area
Point Sal State Park
Guadalupe — Nipomo
Ocean Beach — Orcutt — Santa Maria
Surf
Point Arguello Lighthouse
Garey
Lompoc — Los Alamos
Jalama County Beach
Point Conception Lighthouse
Buellton — Los Olivos
Point Conception
Las Cruces — Solvang
Gaviota
Gaviola Beach
Tajiguas
Refugio Beach
El Capitan Beach
Naples
Goleta
Santa Barbara
To Channel Islands — Montecito — Summerland
Carpinteria Beach — Carpinteria
Rincon Point
Sea Cliff — Meiners Oaks
Emma Woods Beach — Oak View
San Buenaventura Beach — Ventura
Oxnard
McGrath Beach
Port Hueneme
Camarillo — Moorpark
Point Mugu State Park
Leo Carrillo Beach
R.H. Meyer Beach
Point Dume Beach
New Cuyama
Cuyama
San Rafael Mtn 6,593
Big Pine Mtn 6,828
Monte Arido 6,003 — Pine Mtn 7,510
Ojai
Santa Paula
Simi Valley
Thousand Oaks
Malibu
To Los Angeles
To Hwy 5
SAN RAFAEL MOUNTAINS
SANTA YNEZ MOUNTAINS

Though cliffs and mountains dominate the insular landscapes, these islands may look surprisingly intangible—even when you approach them on a clear, sunny day by boat and run right under their surf-swept rocky shores. Rising sheer and straight-sided from the waves, they look like giant ships breasting the ocean. On windy days, when surf breaks high on the sharply pointed cliffs, the islands appear like a flotilla of aircraft carriers running out to sea.

But even that is part of the island illusion: these islands are much more than just barren sea rocks. They have sea caves, sandy coves, grassy glens, wildflower meadows, shady forests of oak and pine, and hillsides covered with chaparral and fragrant sage. Dry and golden under the summer sun, like most of Southern California, the islands turn lushly green after the winter rains.

■ ■ ■

When Spanish navigator Juan Cabrillo anchored off Santa Cruz Island in 1542, he found about 2,000 Chumash Indians living here. In the 18th and 19th centuries Spanish and American settlement followed a curious pattern. Because the islands were granted in toto as ranchos, they tended to stay consolidated under single ownership even after the Americans took over. (The one great exception is Santa Catalina Island to the south; see page 298.) They also continued to be used as cattle and sheep ranches. Santa Cruz Island, which was acquired in the 1860s by Justinian Caire, a French settler, became a private fief, self-sufficient in meat, vegetables, grains, and even wine.

Island diversions were few. Cowboys fought their boredom by roping sea lions and selling them to the San Diego Zoo, where they would be trained as circus performers. Other *vaqueros* used their roping skills to procure sea lions for the pet food, seal oil, and hide market.

In 1980, five of the islands were designated as part of a national park. (The Nature Conservancy owns 90 percent of Santa Cruz Island as a private holding within the park.) People come here to observe wildlife and experience natural beauty in a truly wild setting. Rangers lead guided walks along the island trails. Kayakers explore coves and sea caves, watching from the water the sea lions and elephant seals that haul up on the rocky coves, and the gray whales following their migration route to Baja in winter and to Alaska in early spring. San Miguel Island, especially the Cuyler Harbor area, is a favorite rookery site for pinniped sea mammals. Depending on the time of year, as many as 50,000 California sea lions,

CHUMASH MARINERS

The canoe, tomol or tomolo, was one of the glories of the Chumash. . . . The Chumash . . . were mariners; they took to their boats not only when necessity demanded, but daily, so far as weather permitted.

—Anthropologist A. L. Kroeber

If you travel to the Channel Islands today, you can't help but think about the Chumash Indians who came here by canoe, or tomol, in the 1800s. European explorers described tomols as holding from two to 12 people—one account even says 20. The boats were made of separate planks lashed together and calked with the tar that abounds on the beach.

Robert O. Gibson writes in *The Chumash* that tomols were usually about 30 feet long and could carry about 4,000 pounds. Using double-sided paddles, rowers could propel a tomol as fast as a person could run.

Possession of a tomol was a sign of high position in Chumash society, and only the members of the upper classes were allowed to own them. But according to Fernando Librado Kitsepawit, a Chumash interviewed by John P. Harrington, there seems to have been a bit of a Catch-22 proposition in Chumash society. Canoes brought wealth, but you could only own a canoe if you were wealthy. To make matters even more exclusive, you could become neither a canoe builder nor owner as an adult unless your parents had enough money to buy you a spot in a canoe society when you were young.

Canoes were essential for travel between the mainland and the Channel Islands, and it comes as no surprise that the islanders, who were the most dependent on these watercraft, were also considered the best canoe builders. Canoes were also used for fishing and for sea lion hunting.

Steller sea lions, elephant seals, harbor seals, northern fur seals, and Guadalupe fur seals can be seen at Point Bennet, which is a 15-mile round-trip hike from Cuyler Harbor. Divers and snorkelers find an extraordinary diversity of marine life in the kelp forests surrounding the islands.

Access to the islands is carefully controlled by park rangers. Camping permits must be obtained two weeks in advance; food and water must be brought in by campers.

OPÉRA BOUFFE BATTLE

An important battle was fought at Rincon Point in 1838—one of the many opéra bouffe civil wars that plagued Mexico. Juan Bautista Alvarado had appointed himself governor. When Don Carlos Carrillo, the governor appointed by the Mexican government, arrived, Alvarado suggested that Carrillo should challenge him by force, adding "I want to go speak with him, to see if he will wait for me or flee to hide with the deer amid the thickets of Baja California." He sent troops under Don Jose Castro down the coast, to head off Carrillo. Castro, by arranging for fresh horses for the soldiers at every stop, reached Santa Barbara in only two-and-a-half days.

Even though it was night, he immediately ordered an advance party to go to the point called El Rincon, a narrow pass between the ocean and the hill, to prevent anyone from crossing. Shortly afterward he left, accompanied by the garrison stationed there and enough artillerymen to handle a well-mounted eight-pound [shot] cannon. Castro succeeded in taking the high point of the ridge that dominates Mission San Buenaventura, where Don Carlos Carrillo had stationed his soldiers. Undetected, Castro had time to position his troops within firing range, and then waited for dawn to break.

Early the next morning, Castro's cannon sounded reveille for the *carlistas*. They were so surprised to be jolted out of their sleep that some of the officers wrestled with the sleeves of their jackets, believing them to be the legs of their pants. Some of them thought that the situation was similar to what happened at Troy, and soon a few began to speak of surrender.

The defenders held out until night. Historian Antonio Maria Osio sets the scene: "Since the nights in that area are typically foggy, they hoped to be able to escape and hide in the mustard fields." But Castro rooted them out: "They searched everywhere, even under the cloak of the great holy teacher and Doctor [San Buenaventura]."

After the men's unconditional surrender, Castro, in typical California fashion, "set the men free and offered apologies." Carrillo eventually left California. Little wonder the then-president of Mexico, Anastasio Bustamante, said that he did not really care who the governor of California was, and suggested that maybe the Californios should pick one of their own.

■ RINCON POINT *map page 223*

Every time I visit Rincon Point I pull over to look out at the view: big combers racing in from the vast reaches of the Pacific Ocean are refracted by a rocky offshore reef at the point, which is sandy below the bluffs on the Santa Barbara County side, and piled high with cobbles on the Ventura County shore. The cobbles were washed down from the mountains during rainstorms. They are also surprisingly stable, because their sides interlock and resist even the biggest waves. On both sides of the point, the mountains come close to the sea. The sun, reflected and muted by the spindrift of the surf, paints the shore with ethereal, otherworldly hues. No wonder this place is so popular with surfers and beachcombers alike, none of whom seem to mind the offshore oil drilling platforms. Because of the unique way in which the waves break on the reef, Rincon Point is considered to be one of the great surfing spots in the West. Depending on the light and weather, the water alternates between shades of green and blue, celadon to aquamarine, and is often clear even when other beaches become muddy after storms.

■ ■ ■

Long ago, dome-shaped houses of Chumash Indian villages clustered densely along this shore. Don't be surprised if you see a natural oil or tar seep on the shore or in the water; this is not man-made pollution but the hand of mother nature. The Chumash used tar they found on the beach in their technology of daily living. Tar served as glue to hold arrow- and spearheads to shafts, to glue beads onto bowls, and to hold together the pipes of reed flutes. It was applied as a waterproof coating to baskets, to the thatch of houses, and to the large Chumash canoes, unique artifacts among the native peoples of California.

During Spanish days, the point was a road hazard, since El Camino Real, the "royal" road that ran north from Baja California to the presidios, pueblos, and missions of Alta California, followed the beach. Many of the mudflats were covered at high water, and riders and *carreta* drivers had to carefully coordinate their schedules with the tides. They also had to keep watch for the tar that oozed from natural seeps and springs along the strand and was carried ashore by the surf in big sticky lumps.

Rincon Point is right off U.S. 101. Take Bates Road to its end on the Santa Barbara County side of the point (county park). Wooden stairs lead down the steep bluff to the beach. Harbor seals and sea lions haul out along this shore from December through May; if you're on the beach you may spot an occasional gray whale cruising past just outside the surf zone.

Santa Barbara's waterfront.

delight. Because the city is protected from cold north wind by the Santa Ynez Range (which rises right in its backyard to some 7,000 feet), the climate is so mild that pygmy date palms, bamboo palms, and tropical trees grown in greenhouses elsewhere in the United States flourish in roadside plantings. Flowers bloom year-round. Most of the city's attractions (with the exception of the Mission District) are within easy walking distance of hotels and motels.

Deposit your car in a parking garage (which might look more like a Moorish palace than like the concrete-slab, layer-cake garages of less enlightened cities) and walk. If you get tired, recover your stamina while sipping coffee or a glass of wine on the patio of a cafe or bistro. Or have a picnic. Fishmongers near the waterfront and on Stearns Wharf sell freshly cooked spiny lobsters and local crab (which they'll crack for you) and crusty bread.

You'd think that a place as thoroughly urbanized and overrun with visitors as Santa Barbara would have no wildlife. But nothing could be further from the truth. One warm summer day I spotted an acorn woodpecker setting up house in a palm tree near the courthouse, and a green heron fishing on the banks of Mission Creek, near the very busy intersection of State and Cabrillo. A flock of black-crowned night herons had established themselves in the evergreen fig trees, on the picnic tables, and on the pool fence at the west end of Cabrillo Boulevard, next to Los Baños del Mar, the public swimming pool. Gulls and herons were using the pool for bathing. Sparrows and rock doves brazenly search for crumbs under the patio tables of restaurants, and local pelicans are notorious for boldly walking up to fishermen and begging for handouts.

■ WHAT TO DO AND SEE IN SANTA BARBARA

Stearns Wharf and the Waterfront

Santa Barbara's waterfront is one long, sandy beach, lined with palms. The lagoon at the east end of the beach encompasses the Andrée Clark Bird Refuge. Walk down to the tip of the wharf (at the end of State Street) to watch the sun set over the Pacific, and then return early in the morning to watch the sun *rise* over the Pacific. This is possible, because the coast runs east to west, and the pier runs far out into the water.

One of the most pleasant walks in Santa Barbara, especially in summer when you can take full advantage of the sea breeze, is to walk to the end of the breakwater, which ends near Stearns Wharf, just south of the harbor entrance (where a large sandbank does duty as a sun-tanning and picnic beach). Watch for whales—in winter gray whales migrate past, but in summer you may see humpbacks and an occasional sperm or blue whale.

Getting around town is easy, even if you're not in the mood for walking. You can buy an all-day trolley pass (which will set you back less than a few hours of parking fees) at www.sbtrolley.com. Or you can rent an odd-looking "pedal mobile" (www.wheelfunrentals.com) that seats four pedalers.

State Street

Closed off from the through road in recent years, State Street is finally flourishing. Car dealerships and repair shops have given way to boutiques, restaurants, and studios; old hotels are being refurbished; and it is now possible to walk between the oceanfront and downtown (or take a waterfront shuttle bus). Earthling Bookshop is a good place to lose track of time. *Take the Garden Laguna Exit off Hwy. 101 and follow signs to downtown.*

laid-back Santa Barbara lifestyle, a Roman triumphal arch leads nowhere, but provides great views of Santa Barbara and the foothills of the Santa Ynez Mountains. The courthouse tower is about as tall as buildings in Santa Barbara can get, since zoning ordinances adopted in 1924 and 1930 restricted the height of buildings. Take time to linger in the garden and to enjoy the aromas of its exotic flowers.

The Fig Tree

You may notice the huge Moreton Bay fig tree just west of the U.S. 101 freeway at Chapala and Montecito streets. With huge root buttresses and a spread of some 160 feet, this tree, planted in 1877 by a local girl, is the largest tree of its kind in the nation. In some countries a tree of this magnificence would be considered sacred.

Santa Barbara Museum of Natural History

This museum has excellent exhibits of regional plants and animal life, geology, and Chumash culture. *2559 Puesta del Sol Rd. (via Mission Street and Mission Canyon Road); 805-682-4711.*

Santa Barbara Botanic Gardens

The canyon surrounding the former reservoir of the mission now serves as the Santa Barbara Botanic Gardens. Winding Mission Canyon Road leads through the canyon to the garden, an excellent showcase for indigenous California plants growing in a natural setting. Miles of foot trails wind through desert, arroyo, canyon, Channel Island, and redwood plantings above Mission Creek. There's a rock dam and aqueduct, once part of the mission's water supply system. The ruin of the mission's stone gristmill stands near the mouth of Mission Canyon. *1212 Mission Canyon Rd; 805-682-4726.*

Santa Barbara Mission

Founded in 1786 on a knoll at the upper edge of the coastal plain, the buildings of the Santa Barbara Mission date from 1815 to 1820 and later, but have undergone much reconstruction—most recently in 1950, when cracks appeared in the church and the entire sandstone facade had to be rebuilt. It is considered one of California's most beautiful missions, and it certainly has the most amazing view of any of the missions—all the way to the Channel Islands. It also had an almost curiously uneventful history. When Santa Ynez and La Purisima missions to the north were captured by insurgent Chumash, Santa Barbara Mission basked peacefully in the sunshine (due to the presence of the presidio down the hill); when other missions were secularized, Santa Barbara remained in Church control—which has helped to preserve its gardens and cloisters in perfect shape. An adjacent complex has served as a seminary for the training of priests since the late 19th century. Because this mission never abandoned the faith, it's a great place for soaking up the spirit of Old California. You'll need a car to get there. *Los Olivos and Laguna streets; 805-682-4713.*

■ UC SANTA BARBARA

The modern campus of the University of California at Santa Barbara, 10 miles north of Santa Barbara, is one of the most spectacular centers of higher learning in the country—not because of its ivy-festooned architecture, but because of the setting. It's truly stunning, laid out with the Pacific on one side and the Santa Ynez Mountains on the other. When you approach the campus from the beach, it looks more like a condo development in a tropical paradise than a college campus.

There are the usual lawns and tree-shaded campus walks, and all that, but what makes the place is the view. As is true for all UC campuses, parking is a mess (which is why the majority of students ride bikes). Ask for help. Access is via Highway 217 from U.S. 101.

The university town of **Goleta** offers affordable, though not particularly interesting, lodging, some of which has been lapped by the surf in recent years and is in the process of falling into the ocean. Some of these unstable buildings were rented to university students who wanted an ocean view and did not mind the risk. In 2004, however, the city declared several of these buildings unsafe and forced tenants to move. Despite this, UCSB students have been throwing wild parties at the "doomed" apartments above the beach. These parties, which have become nationally notorious, attract as many as 10,000 locals and visitors. (One had 62 kegs, according to a story in the local newspaper.) The **Isla Vista** neighborhood has a slightly trampled but lively look to it, thanks to the thousands of students who make up the majority of the town's population. The main streets are Embarcadero, lined with pizza joints, surf shops, bookstores, and thrift stores, and Del Playa, which runs along the beach and acts as a promenade for the parade of joggers, bicyclists, and in-line skaters.

(following spread) The Spanish Colonial Revival courthouse, built around a central courtyard and gardens.

Mission La Purisima, some 4 miles northeast of town, was built after the 1812 earthquake damaged the first mission, and a flood, triggered by the quake, destroyed the buildings. The new mission, which had crumbled almost as badly as its predecessor by the early 1900s, was fully and authentically restored by CCC workers during the 1930s. It is now the most complete of all the missions (and the largest historical restoration in the West), but administration by the California State Park System has led to neglect, and many of the buildings are suffering from premature deterioration. La Purisima Mission's sad claim to historic fame dates to the 1824 Chumash rebellion, when disenchanted Chumash converts held the mission for a month before being overpowered by superior Mexican forces. Seven rebels were shot, but the four ringleaders were merely sentenced to hard labor. *The mission is located just off Highway 246 (you can't miss the signs), 3 miles northeast of Lompoc.*

On September 8, 1923, a squadron of 11 U.S. destroyers steamed southward down the California coast. At Point Argüello (right) the lead ship ran aground in a thick fog. Before the captain could warn the others, six more destroyers followed the lead ship onto the rocks. The U.S. Navy lost more combat ships that day at Point Argüello than they did during the entire course of World War I.

■ JALAMA BEACH

A few miles east of Lompoc, winding, twisting Jalama Road curves southwest over hills, through draws, and down Jalama Creek to Jalama Beach, just 1.5 miles north of Point Conception and south of Point Argüello. The sandy beach and 28-acre county park at the end of the road are very popular with surfers and fishermen. The park borders Vandenberg Air Force Base (which allows beach access for the first mile north of Jalama). Intrepid hikers head south from here along the beach or trespass on the railroad tracks to Point Conception.

■ OCEAN BEACH

Ocean Beach, west of Lompoc, is among the wildest on the coast, and it has some of the best shorebird watching. To reach it, drive west on CA 246 from Lompoc to a small parking area at the mouth of the Santa Ynez River, where an extensive marsh inside the river mouth—with nearly 400 acres of fresh and salt water—and a hard-packed sandy beach are backed by sand dunes and low hills.

The beach, a county park, is on the Vandenberg base, but open to the public for 1.5 miles north and 3.5 miles south of the beachhead. A trail along the river shore leads to the dunes and the long beach of hard-packed sand. Many consider Ocean Beach more of a Northern California–style beach because of its pristine sand, wind-blown dunes, and powerful surf. The water, outside the foamy waves, is often steely gray or cold green. Long, straight rows of breakers have a hypnotic effect as they crash onto the beach at regularly spaced intervals.

■ GUADALUPE–NIPOMO DUNES

North of the Santa Maria River, in southern San Luis Obispo County, you'll encounter vast and mysterious dunes. The 6,000 acres of these ancient dunes (some of them began to pile up 18,000 years ago), plus the vast expanse of the Nipomo Dunes adjoining them to the north, offer more sandy waste than you may care to explore in a lifetime, but they are also eminently fascinating. Despite their Saharan appearance, the dunes have lakes, marshes, and wetlands supporting a great number of birds and other animals. The lakes are younger than the dunes— they only date back some 16,000 years. Rare plants grow here, and the giant coreopsis, a shrub with golden sunflower blooms, grows huge—the shrubs may be as much as 8 feet tall. The yellow pond lily reaches the southern limit of its range in local ponds. The dunes may look white, golden, or blue to you in late winter and spring. The wildflowers are in bloom. Grizzly bears once lived at the edge of the dunes; today the wildlife runs to smaller species, like kangaroo rats, which lead secret lives in the sands.

The dunes hold other secrets, as well: Hollywood used them for years as a stand-in for the Sahara Desert. Cecil B. DeMille shot *The Ten Commandments* in the dunes near Arroyo Grande and left the sets behind. The drifting sands soon hid them from view. Now and then someone launches an "archaeological" expedition to try and find them.

During the Great Depression, a gaggle of artists, writers, and camp followers lived in a village of driftwood huts in the Callender Dunes west of Oceano. They called themselves the "Dunites" and published a literary journal called *Dune Forum*. All traces of the driftwood village have been swallowed by the sands.

Some 4,000 acres of the Pismo Dunes and a section of the beach are open to motor vehicles. Here the dunes are considered healthy enough to take that sort of abuse. All other sections are closed to cars and off-road vehicles.

Nipomo Dunes is one of the few undeveloped coastal dune ecosystems in California. More than 180 species of birds inhabit this area and its surrounding wetlands.

The road leading to the southern part of the Nipomo Dunes at the mouth of the Santa Maria River was unmarked the last time I drove up CA 1, but it's easy to find. As you approach the small farming community of Guadalupe, head west on Main Street (which is the extension of Santa Maria's Main Street). The mouth of the river was once a county park but is now administered by the Nature Conservancy. There's a gate and a friendly guard, but no entrance fee. Watch for sand on the roadway and in the parking lot. This may be hard to navigate for rental cars, but the local beachcombers will happily pull or push you out of soft places.

■ ■ ■

CA 1 passes through vegetable fields on its way north, bypassing the dunes. It touches the beach near the motor-home parking lots (which pass locally for campgrounds) of south Pismo Beach before rejoining U.S. 101.

■ PISMO BEACH *map page 223*

This small, comfortable, down-to-earth beach town is a delight and still thoroughly unspoiled. The 1,250-foot-long fishing pier is an old-fashioned, laid-back place, where local kids cheer on surfer friends. It is nearly unchanged from when it was built back in 1881 to ship out local produce. Pomeroy and Hinds avenues, leading from CA 1 to the pier, have fish 'n' chips shops, cafés, surfboard and curio shops, and other seaside diversions. This is where farmers from the Central Valley come to vacation. The region's newspaper boxes carry Bakersfield and Fresno dailies. The pier is also a great place for watching surfers in action. It's lit at night.

Pismo State Beach, north of here, is flat and sandy until cut off by the cliffs of Shell Beach (which mainly consists of pocket beaches between rocky headlands). A stairway at the end of Wadsworth Avenue (a few blocks north) leads to volleyball courts.

Pismo Beach was once famous for its succulent clams, which were overharvested so badly by farmers plowing the beach and feeding the clams to their hogs that the shellfish almost became extinct. Of course, the locals don't blame the farmers for the clams' demise. A newspaper article prominently displayed on the pier places the blame right on the usual suspect: the sea otter.

North of Pismo Beach, the bay curves west. Shell Beach, the northern quarter of town, is an odd combination of tiny (formerly low-rent) cottages and new luxury lodgings.

U.S. 101 heads north from Pismo Beach across a low divide and then follows San Luis Obispo Creek into San Luis Obispo. Just after the divide, Avila Road runs west to the San Luis Obispo Riviera.

■ SAN LUIS BAY *map page 223*

You can tell that this warm bay, sheltered from chilly north winds by the San Luis Range (locally known as the "Irish Hills"), has a special climate, because castor beans grow wild by the roadsides—something you will encounter again in this region south of Gaviota Pass. A little more than a decade ago, San Luis Bay was marred by huge oil tanks, pipe lines, pump stations, and an occasional oil spill. But the oil company, Unocal, has pulled out of the area and cleaned up the marks of its activity. It has also given its former oil pier, where tankers tied up to load the black stuff, to Cal Poly in San Luis Obispo, to be used as a research platform for marine studies (with an endowment to keep it maintained). And increasingly, the natural beauty of the bay is reasserting itself. The bay has long sandy beaches, chaparral and tree-clad hills, hot springs and mineral springs in the Avila Valley (and two hot springs resorts: **Avila Hot Springs** and **Sycamore Mineral Springs**), three piers, and miles of hiking trails, including one trail, the Bob Jones City to Sea Trail, that will eventually connect San Luis Obispo to the beach at Avila. The **Avila Beach Barn**, a fruit stand, has the freshest, ripest fruit around.

■ ■ ■

Cave Landing, a rocky headland, juts some 150 feet into the bay and forms a natural pier, where in the early 19th century Yankee skippers once loaded hides and tallow from Mission San Luis Obispo. The Chumash buried their dead in the shallow seaside caves; today the caves are popular with fishermen and trysting students from Cal Poly in nearby San Luis Obispo. One cave is open on both sides, forming a large arch that goes clear through the cliff. A natural terrace on its western side offers great views of Avila Beach, Point San Luis, and spectacular sunsets. Giant clumps of artichokes grow wild at the edge of the chaparral. Steep trails lead down to beaches on either side of the headland.

Some locals call Cave Landing **Pirate Cove** because of the clothing-optional county beach below the cliffs to the east. (You can reach that by rough trail.) The access road is still called Cave Landing Road—you can't get lost. Just drive it to the end.

■ ■ ■

Avila Beach, about 6 miles north of Pismo Beach, is a small, cozy fishing village popular with college students from Cal Poly in San Luis Obispo.

During first years of the new millennium Avila has emerged from its cocoon as an oil city and become a beautiful beach town. When Unocal, the dominant oil production company, pulled out in 1999, it worked together with Avila residents to create a new town with the feel of an old, serene fishing village. Avila is now a funky little beach town with the most pleasant—and warmest—beach in San Luis Obispo County. The cleanup was not easy: it involved tearing down houses, digging up and replacing the soil, and rebuilding. The main drag along the shore is now partly a boardwalk and no longer a through street, which makes it much easier to enjoy the beach. There's a Friday-night seafood market on the waterfront, where fishermen sell their catch and local chefs show you how to cook it.

Port San Luis, in the lee of Point San Luis to the west of Avila Beach, has a 1,320-foot-long fishing pier that is lit at night. If you catch a really big one you can reel it in by feeding quarters to a coin-operated crane. I've enjoyed a lunch of fresh fish and local microbrew at the Olde Port Inn at the end of the pier. The restaurant also has an excellent wine list of local bottlings and glass-top tables that sit on wooden, boxlike bases above an opening in the floor—so you can look down into the water below the dock as you dine. A fish market on the pier sells fish fresh off the boats. The view from the pier is spectacular. Port San Luis is a scenic place, with scores of fishing boats anchored offshore beneath dark cliffs.

The hills above Cave Landing and the beaches are still wild, with black bears and cougars, deer, rabbits, raccoons, skunks, hawks, and eagles. Locals claim to have seen bobcats as well. RV parking is permitted on the bluff-top strip above the beach east of the pier (no hookups; sign up for spots at the port office).

■ PECHO COAST TRAIL

The shores north of Point San Luis are still remarkably unspoiled (except for the nuclear power plant in Diablo Canyon, decommissioned because it was built right smack on top of an earthquake fault). More than 7 miles of the planned 10-mile Pecho Coast Trail, which was supposed to go all the way to Montaña del Oro State Park, are now open (805-541-8735). It passes Port San Luis Lighthouse—a pre-fab 1894 wooden structure that's a clone of the Point Fermin lighthouse at San Pedro in Southern California—and continues on to Rattlesnake Canyon.

A peregrine falcon and a 2-week-old chick nesting on Avila Beach, just north of Pismo Beach.

■ What to Do and See in Morro Bay

El Morro

The city of Morro Bay is overshadowed by the monolithic 576-foot-high rock named Morro Rock, or El Morro, a Spanish nautical term meaning "bluff, rock, or hill serving as a landmark"—an apt description. The rock has indeed served as a landmark since the days when the Manila-Acapulco galleons sailed south to Mexico along the California shore. El Morro was even taller until rock quarrying operations, which lasted from 1891 to 1969, removed more than a million tons of rock for breakwaters and a causeway. The rock was not connected to the mainland until 1938. Today it is an ecological reserve protecting rare peregrine falcons. Climbing on the cliffs is prohibited, to protect the nesting resident falcon. And watch out for rattlesnakes. According to locals in the know, the rock has more than its share of these venomous, long-fanged, and easily riled critters. There is, by the way, only one peregrine falcon nest on the rock: this predatory bird rules a territory 10 miles in diameter.

Fishing

The docks here bustle with fishing boats. Morro Bay and Avila Beach to the south account for more than half of all the commercial fish caught in the southern half of California. The **"clam taxi"** takes day trippers from Virg's Fish'n at 1215 Embarcadero on the waterfront across the bay to the 3 mile-long sand spit protecting Morro Bay from the fury of the ocean. **Charter vessels** leave for full-day and half-day fishing trips; 805-772-1222. These are particularly popular when the albacore are biting. Morro Bay was once a major abalone processing center until overfishing led to the decline of the tasty snails. Of course, the blame is put on the sea otters.

Embarcadero

The Embarcadero runs all the way from Morro Rock past the town's waterfront to Morro Bay State Park, south of town. The state park stretches across the marshes at the mouths of Chorro and Los Osos creeks inland to the slopes of Black Hill and Hollister Peak. The **Morro Bay Natural History Museum** (805-772-2694) has exhibits focusing on the bay's ecology.

Morro Bay is dominated by Morro Rock, a 576-foot rock easily visible for miles around.

■ CAYUCOS TOWN AND BEACH *map page 223*

North of Morro Bay the Coast Highway passes sandy **Morro Strand State Beach South** (until recently known as Atascadero State Beach) and **Morro Strand Beach.** You might want to pull off the highway at **Cayucos Beach** for some bird-watching. Willets, black and ruddy turnstones, semipalmated plovers, and others hang out here even in summer, when their more enterprising brethren are north in the Arctic, raising broods. Access is from parking lots (follow signs) and from trails and steps at street ends.

Cayucos itself is a delightful small town, so popular with vacationers that its rooms are booked all summer long. You'll understand why, if you stroll along Ocean Avenue and walk out onto the narrow, rustic wooden pier. This town has grown considerably in the last few years, mostly on the hillsides to the south. The old part of town, near the pier, is still charming. Look for storm petrels fluttering around the pier (they're the size of blackbirds).

Point Estero, west of Cayucos, marks the northern end of Chumash territory and the beginning of the Salinan territories. When the Portola Expedition passed through here in 1769, Chumash canoes lined the beach at Cayucos. Cayucos got its pier in 1875. It was a regular stop for the Pacific Steamship Company ships and was used to ship out local dairy products. Later abalones were dried here, for export to San Francisco and Japan. At Estero Bay, Chinese gathered sea lettuce and dried it for export until China closed its ports following World War II.

Estero Bay, a new (and, as yet, mostly undeveloped) state park, has wetlands, low bluffs, stream canyons, a cove and pocket beach at Vila Creek, tide pools, sea stacks, and 4 miles of trails along bluffs and through meadows. Estero Bay marked the northern border of Chumash territory and several of their village sites are protected in the park. *San Luis Obispo Coast District; 805-549-3312.*

In 2003, with the help of conservation organizations, the state acquired the Sea West Ranch north of the estero. This ranch, about halfway between Cayucos and Cambria, has 3 miles of shoreline and bluffs, plus tidelands, wetlands, and costal terraces. It's not yet open to the public. For updates, go to www.parks.ca.gov.

Beyond Cayucos, CA 1 runs inland, past **Harmony,** a hamlet with a couple of restaurants, galleries, a pottery, and a winery.

■ **CAMBRIA** *map page 223*

One of the friendliest towns on the central coast is tucked off the highway in a pretty valley. Cambria had its beginnings in 1862, when cinnabar ore, from which quicksilver (mercury) is extracted, was found in the Santa Lucia Mountains to the east. Copper, quicksilver, dairy products, and cattle hides produced in the area were loaded onto schooners at San Simeon Bay, until Cambria got a pier in 1874. The coastal shipping trade ended in 1894, when a rail line from San Luis Obispo reached Cambria. Yet the village remained relatively isolated until 1937, when the Coast Highway opened between Carmel and Cambria. The pines on the knolls to the west are one of only four native stands of Monterey pines in the world (the others are in Monterey, Santa Cruz, and San Mateo counties, near Point Año Nuevo; and in Baja California).

Downtown Cambria, inland and east of CA 1, continues to better itself, but life near the shore seems to be almost immutable, thanks in part to the tough regulations

The idyllic town of Cambria.
(following spread) Watching the tide at Cambria's beach.

of the California Coastal Commission, which frowns on too much new construction within sight of the ocean.

West Village, on the seaward side of CA 1, is the newer, residential part. In the 19th century few people lived here because this was the port district—and because there was a rather smelly whaling station here as well.

Shamel County Park, west of CA 1 on Windsor Road, has trails leading to tide pools and surf fishing spots, plus a picnic area and swimming pool.

Moonstone Beach, at the northern end of Cambria, is named for the milky white agates that can be found in the sand. It marks the southern boundary of the California Sea Otter Game Refuge, which extends from here north to the Carmel River in Monterey County. At Motel Row, along Moonstone Beach Drive (which is part of San Simeon State Beach to the north), motels and a couple of restaurants line the eastern curb of the highway, but they are tastefully done and have great views of the ocean. From Moonstone Beach the Coast Highway winds north above the shore to San Simeon.

NOTE FOR DRIVERS CONTINUING NORTH

The preceding chapter, Golden Gate to San Simeon, describes sites along the coast from San Francisco, traveling north to south, because most travelers to that area begin their trip from the north. Thus its description of Hearst Castle begins at the end of that chapter on page 216. We hope drivers continuing north won't find it too onerous a task to switch directions when they read that chapter.

■ TRAVEL BASICS

Climate

The coast from Point Mugu to Santa Barbara and Point Conception has an ideal climate—sunny virtually year-round, with an occasional winter storm between December and March. Summer temperatures average near 80 degrees; winter, 65 degrees. A hot offshore wind, the Santa Ana, occasionally blasts the coastal communities between September and November, raising temperatures to extreme levels (115 degrees once in Santa Barbara) and creating danger of wildfires. From Point Conception north to San Simeon the climate is a little cooler and wetter (15 to 25 inches of rain). **Water temperature:** From Malibu to Santa Barbara water temperatures average 65 to 70 degrees in late summer and in the low 60s the rest of the year. From Point Conception—which marks the dividing line between a cold northern current and a warmer current coming up from the south—the water is 55 to 65 degrees and unsuitable for swimming.

Food and Lodging

This stretch of coast has some of the most delicious foods found in all of California—fresh fish and shellfish, including tuna, rockfish, squid, red rock crabs, spiny lobsters, and mussels; avocados and other subtropical fruits, including locally raised bananas; and from the Santa Maria Valley, strawberries and winter vegetables. Both Santa Barbara and San Luis Obispo counties have world-class wineries (see pages 242-244 and 254-255).

Lodging ranges from the comfortable to the sublime. While Santa Barbara seems to foster the utterly sybaritic away from the immediate shore, some of the most comfortable lodgings with a view can be found along San Luis Bay, from Pismo Beach northwest to Avila Beach. In Santa Barbara hotel rooms fill up quickly, especially in summer. **Lodging and restaurant listings** by town and in alphabetical order begin on page 362.

L.A. METRO
& ORANGE COUNTY

The Santa Monica Mountains drop sharply into the ocean at Malibu in northwestern Los Angeles. Because they run east-west (instead of north-south), the ocean shore also runs laterally—so the beaches face south, protecting the waters from cold northerly currents and allowing them to soak up a maximum of sunshine.

Where the mountains meet the sea, the coastline is broken by rocky headlands and sandy pocket beaches. A wide crescent of sand sweeps around the shores of Santa Monica Bay to the Palos Verdes Peninsula. These beaches are backed by a wide coastal plain packed with houses, industrial parks, and shopping malls. South of Venice, power plants and refineries tower over the shore in several places.

The 15-mile-long shoreline of the Palos Verdes Peninsula has spectacular views of the ocean, small coves, and tide pools. South of the Los Angeles–Long Beach superport lies Orange County, the "SoCal" of the popular imagination. Filled with fashionably casual people in excellent physical condition and wearing Italian sunglasses, the beaches are awash with surfers and sunbathers exuding a golden immortality.

■ EARLY MORNING LIGHT

Early in the morning, as the sun cleared the eastern horizon, I was ready. Brush poised, watercolor paper moistened, paints squeezed from their tubes, I waited for the light. I tried to capture the pastel colors the morning sun sheds on the coastal ridges of the Santa Monica Mountains, dissolving the outlines of land and sea, sky and earth, and merging everything into one other for a few evanescent moments.

I had tried to catch the images on film, with no success. And high on a dry ridge above Latigo Canyon, I struggled with paint and reality. My eye could see, but not grasp the fleeting changes: ridges and mountains became translucent and bled into each other, and the bulk of a distant peak shone through a nearby range. Hills rose to float away. Then, in an instant, it all changed. The land resumed its solid shapes and earth-drab colors; the ridges once again rose sharply against the pale morning sky.

I suspect this optical illusion of transcendental light is the interplay of the sun's rays, filtered through the dry land air and moist ocean air (and perhaps the smog from the San Fernando Valley to the east). This illusion of light does not happen

A surfer races out, at Huntington Beach.

when fierce Santa Ana winds sear the slopes with desiccating desert air, or when fog drifts inland, up the canyons from the beach.

Fog sustains life on this coast of little rain. Its minute water particles cling to the clumps of grass, to sage and wild lilac, and to the leathery leaves of oaks. The film of water flows downward, forming drops that fall to the ground and moisten the soil, much like rain, but slower, more patiently.

As the sun warms rocks and bluffs, hawks rise on the updrafts to scan the chaparral for prey. Kangaroo rats and mice live here, as do rabbits, deer, sparrows, jays, and quail. The hawks share the top of the food pyramid with coyotes, bobcats, and cougars. You're not so likely to see these but you may see vultures, which, like hawks, are easy to spot as they glide on the wind, patiently drawing circles in the air, waiting for a meal.

When the fog drifts in from the sea and thickens over the land, the vultures and hawks float inland, toward the sun, as do the human sun worshippers; only a few visitors stay to enjoy the long, empty strand with the gulls, terns, sanderlings, and snowy plovers.

■ SANTA MONICA MOUNTAINS

In the heart of the Santa Monica Mountains and along their ocean front are pre-served some 150,000 largely undeveloped acres of mountains, seashore, grassy glens, and rocky hillsides—home to the southernmost stands of valley oak, as well as mountain lions and golden eagles. What these mountains lack in altitude—the highest point, Sandstone Peak, is only 3,111 feet above sea level—they make up for in ruggedness. The hills are deeply folded and cut. Malibu Canyon, a spectacu-lar gorge 1,400 to 1,800 feet deep, bisects the mountain range. There are a variety of parks within the system, many offering horse, bicycle, and hiking trails.

Sycamore Canyon and Cove

Lying on either side of the Pacific Coast Highway (PCH), both Sycamore Cove and Canyon are part of the much larger Point Mugu State Park. The cove provides access to a pocket beach where campers and day visitors swim, fish, and bird-watch. Sycamore Canyon is a riparian woodland with a trail that leads into Point Mugu. *The cove is west of the highway; Sycamore Canyon is across the highway in Ventura County; 805-488-5223.*

Malibu Creek State Park

The park's 5,000 acres support portions of Malibu Creek, streams, Century Lake, and miles of hiking and horse trails. There's also a campground and picnic area. Twentieth Century Fox Studios once owned part of the park and used the area to film the scenes for *Butch Cassidy and the Sundance Kid,* "Dukes of Hazzard," and "M*A*S*H," among others. *Take Malibu Canyon Road, 6 miles north from PCH; 818-880-0367.*

Topanga State Park

Thirty-five miles of trails (hiking, bicycling, and horseback riding) wind through canyons and along ridges in this 9,000-acre park. The popular Eagle Rock/Eagle Spring trail from Eagle Junction affords panoramic views of the ocean and the San Fernando Valley. There are both hike-in and equestrian campsites. *20825 Entrada Rd., off Topanga Canyon Blvd; 310-455-2465.*

Will Rogers State Historic Park

Former home to humorist, silver-screen star, and "Cowboy Philosopher" Will Rogers; polo matches are played every Sunday in his honor. Facilities include an interpretive nature center and exhibits on local flora and fauna; house tours are also available, and the lawn is a good picnic spot. Hiking, horseback riding. *16000 block of PCH, Pacific Palisades; 310-454-8212.*

Temescal Gateway Park
The most popular hike here is the waterfall, but as with all the waterfalls in these mountains, don't expect a violent gush of water. Most times of the year, you'll be lucky to find any water at all. The park, spread out across both sides of Temescal Canyon Road, has a playground, picnic tables, and hiking trails with ocean views, plus free roadside parking. *Temescal Canyon Rd. and Sunset Blvd., Pacific Palisades; 310-454-1395.*

■ ALONG THE SHORE

If the mountains provide a welcome respite from the hurried life of the city, the beaches are the centers of action. One reason the beaches along the Malibu shore west of Santa Monica Bay are so popular is because they face south, and are thus exposed to less fog and more sun than nearby urban beaches. That's also why they are crammed with houses and flower gardens—and why the public strand is often jammed even in midweek. Malibu has long been the place for stars and starlets, the well-to-do and the ostentatious. Practically the entire entertainment industry owns real estate on Broad Beach (6 miles north of Paradise Cove), including Goldie Hawn, Neil Simon, Robert Redford, Michael Ovitz,

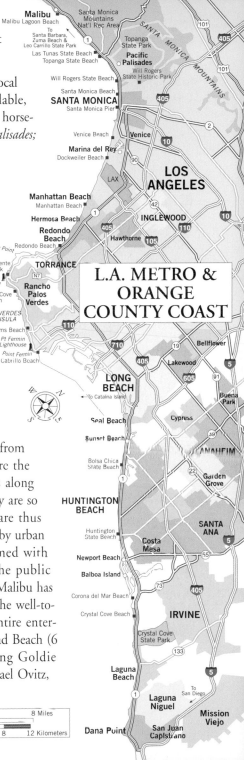

Sylvester Stallone, Eddie Van Halen and Valerie Bertinelli, Mel Gibson, Emilio Estevez, and Ted Danson. Steven Spielberg owns a couple of houses on the beach.

The shore has many public beaches —a few of them between the sea and exclusive, gated housing compounds. Anyone listening to the surf will have to agree that Malibu is aptly named: the Chumash Indians called this place *humaliwo,* "the surf sounds loudly."

■ LEO CARRILLO STATE PARK

Just south of the Los Angeles County line, this park has one of the best campgrounds on the coast. It's a collection of sandy beaches, rocky shores, meadows, and streamside woods—one of the most magic places on this coast. It's large enough (2,190 acres) to allow urban refugees to escape from the crowds, yet compact enough to make a hike from campsite to beach a pleasing walk. The rocky promontory of Sequit Point has shallow sea caves and tide pools, the creek is lined with shade-giving trees, and the hillsides are covered with fragrant chaparral. Coveys of California quail visit campsites at dusk, before they fly into nearby shrubs to roost. At night, the canyon is filled with the chirping of frogs and the refreshing aromas of coastal sage and yerba santa.

The tide pools at Leo Carrillo are arguably the best in Southern California— look for sea hares, starfish, and fronded sea palms. The rangers are quite helpful.

DRIVING AROUND THE AREA

From Leo Carrillo State Park east to Point Dume, the view of the ocean from the road is relatively clear, but houses crowd the shores and block the view entirely from Point Dume to Topanga. Yet the beaches are still there in their expansive glory and more accessible to the public than ever. For points of access, look for signs by the side of the road.

■ MALIBU *map page 271*

What *is* Malibu? There is no downtown and no obvious center of town here. Rather, Malibu is that most typical of Southern California towns, an incorporated city that takes in various housing developments in the Santa Monica Mountains and along the 27-mile stretch of shore from the southern end of the Ventura County line south to Pacific Palisades. This means the City of Malibu has a continuous 27-mile shoreline that stretches from Leo Carrillo State Park to Topanga Beach. There are

LEO, "PANCHO," AND THE NONPLUSSED ANGELENOS

Few people seem to know that Leo Carrillo, after whom the park is named, was not only the actor who played Pancho in the *Cisco Kid*, but also a member of one of California's most prominent pioneer families who traced his lineage back to Raymundo Carrillo, a sergeant who helped found the Presidio of Santa Barbara in 1782. I heard much of the family history in the mid-1960s from Theo, a brother of Leo's who owned orange orchards in the Santa Ana Canyon and oil wells in the hills. With old-fashioned California generosity, Theo once made me a special-occasion gift of an electric orange squeezer (one of the first ones made), saying that the juicer came with as many oranges from his orchards as I needed. The orange groves were replaced long ago by shopping malls and tract homes, but the juicer still works.

It seemed like a fitting tribute to Leo's memory that a movie crew was shooting at the beach. It was a low-key affair, with the surfers and swimmers hardly taking any notice of the actors and technicians. Angelenos take everyone, even their stars, in stride. One week earlier, Kevin Costner had been shooting some movie scenes in Washington State, and the state parks department shut down and blocked off one entire section of Deception Pass State Park (the most popular park in the state). In Southern California, it would be decidedly uncool to stare at a star or ask for an autograph.

I mentioned this a few days later, over lunch, to beach resident Bill Burden, who agreed with my observation but said that some shows are more popular than others. The shooting of a "Baywatch" segment at Will Rogers State Beach used to attract so many spectators, he said, that vendors would put up bleachers and sell refreshments

few commercial ventures along the Coast Highway—a few small shopping centers, fronting on the non-ocean side of the highway, but no large malls (that's what Malibu keeps Santa Monica for) and seemingly no industry.

There is a Malibu shopping area of course, but I only learned this recently, after I stopped by the market at the intersection of the Coast Highway and Trancas Canyon looking for picnic supplies. After squeezing my nondescript car between a BMW and a Porsche, I went inside and found the selection of foods not at all what I had expected to see in affluent Malibu. I began complaining about this to a woman who was waiting in the check-out line with me. My fellow shopper explained that this market is a neighborhood market, one of the few remnants of the "old Malibu," where ranchers and ranch-hands outnumbered the movie moguls and personal assistants.

If I wanted fresh breads and good produce, she suggested, I should try the Hughes Family Market (at Webb Way and PCH), where she had once stood in line with Olivia Newton John. Hughes Market, apparently, has a turbo cooler that can chill a liter of 7-Up in 30 seconds, with settings for four temperatures. Or, if I wanted to check out the local scene, she thought I might want to try the Malibu Country Mart, east of PCH on Cross Creek Road, with its boutiques, cafes, and restaurants, including Bambu—a sushi, chili fries, and "movie-star hot spot."

■ MALIBU BEACHES *map page 271*

Public access points to Malibu beaches can be difficult to spot, especially in the residential areas; look for the brown signs.

El Pescador, Las Piedras, and El Matador

These narrow, sandy beaches are often quite deserted when other beaches are packed to capacity. These are ideal places for an oceanside picnic. El Matador, with its natural rock arches, is the prettiest. Bodysurfing tends to be poor here because of rip tide. Each has 20 to 40 parking spots and rough trails or stairways down to the ocean. *32000 PCH and north.*

Zuma Beach

If the surf is up, even if it's a Monday, the parking lots at wide, sandy Zuma will most likely be full. More than 2 miles long, Zuma is one of the finest white-sand beaches in California. The crowd largely consists of teenagers and bodybuilders. Teens commune especially between towers 6 and 7 at Zuma. Immortalized in "Some Girls" by the Rolling Stones, this broad, flat beach has volleyball, a fast-food stand, and waves strong enough for bodysurfing. *30000 PCH.*

Point Dume State Beach

A steep set of stairs leads down sandstone cliffs to Point Dume's sandy beach. Rocky tide pools have giant green sea anemones and other intertidal animals.

Point Dume is fairly difficult to reach, but it's worth the effort. You have to hike to the point up from the beach, over a stairway from Westward Beach Road, and then take a trail to the Point Dume Whale Watch. Take up surveillance from one of the benches here, and keep an eye out for the California gray whales during their migration from November to May. Offshore kelp beds teem with fish and support many seabirds, like the brown pelicans roosting on offshore rocks.

The beach community of Malibu embraces one of the most famous stretches of coastline in California.

Madonna and Sean Penn's wedding took place at a friend's estate on Point Dume, beneath helicopters filled with photographers. Barbra Streisand owns a compound of three houses on Point Dume.

There's free parking on the road (Westward Avenue) between Zuma and Point Dume. Fees for beach access. *South end of Westward Ave.*

Westward Beach

Technically part of Zuma and part of Point Dume County Beach, this pleasant beach is a good place for surfing, boogie boarding, and swimming, and is often less crowded than its better-known neighbors. (It's also referred to by locals as "Free Zuma" because there's street parking on Windward Beach Road off PCH.) One of the best coastal hikes in Malibu (especially during low tide) begins here. The 2-mile trail leads past Point Dume's whale-watching spot, a number of tide pools teeming with marine life, and finally to Paradise Cove. Near the parking lot is the spot where Charlton Heston fled from the apes in *Planet of the Apes*. *West of Point Dume off Westward Ave.*

WELCOME TO
BEAUTIFUL PARADISE COVE
SEA THE VIEW
BRING THE KIDS
HAVE A SEAT
ENJOY MALIBU

Malibu Lagoon State Beach

This beach is known for serious surfers, who come here for the perfectly shaped waves. Longboarding is popular and some surfers use antique wood boards. The park has a 700-foot-long wooden pier originally built in 1903 and rebuilt in 1946.

Surfrider Beach was popularized by surfing movies in the 1950s and 1960s (think *Gidget*) and has needed no advertising since. I do sometimes wonder if surfing would have become as popular a sport as it is, if it had not attracted the attention of film directors and song writers. Once it was glorified in the movies, it just had to catch on—especially since it was practiced on warm, scenic beaches. *Pacific Coast Highway and Cross Creek Rd.*

Malibu Lagoon

This lagoon was the site of the southernmost village of the Chumash, who fished here and gathered mollusks. More than 200 species of birds have been observed on or near the lagoon, including elegant terns, belted kingfishers, and American goldfinches.

Paradise Cove

Except for the days when movie crews take over, this is a quiet cove, ideal for swimming and sunbathing. But ever since 1963, when movie audiences went to Frankie Avalon and Annette Funicello's first *Beach Party*, Paradise Cove has appeared as the quintessential Southern California beach in countless movies (including three more of Frankie and Annette's beach parties), rock videos, and television shows. There's ample but expensive parking at this privately owned beach. The approach by foot is down a big hill. Paradise Cove has a beach and fishing pier, a restaurant, and a snack bar (the latter is open only in summer). *28128 PCH; 310-457-2511.*

Crowded Surfing Beaches

From Malibu Canyon east to Santa Monica, the beaches are crowded even on weekdays. The parking strips at **Las Tunas State Beach** and **Topanga State Beach** are usually full, and the waves are crowded with surfers floating just outside the surf line like sea lions waiting for a run of smelt. Surfers are the most amphibious of Americans. In their wet suits, water-permeable like the skin of

Friendly signage tells you to enjoy the beach.

■ SANTA MONICA *map pages 271 and 280*

Santa Monica's oceanfront is one vast beach, backed by low bluffs and tall palm trees, condominiums, and hotels. Santa Monica is more than surf and sand and sun, more than palm trees swaying in the ocean breeze. It has wide boulevards, sidewalk cafes, great restaurants and shops, and beautiful homes with large gardens and red-tiled roofs. It also has a large population of drifters and homeless people, and busloads of tourists crowding the Promenade, Boardwalk, and Pier.

It was named by Father Juan Crespi of the Gaspar de Portola Expedition of 1769, which camped at a spring hereabouts. For some unfathomable reason, the spring reminded Crespi of St. Monica's tears shed for her heretic son, St. Augustine. In 1828, the extensive local grasslands were granted to Francisco Sepulveda, a former alcalde of the Pueblo de los Angeles.

In the 1880s, railroads linked Los Angeles to the east coast and the city's population skyrocketed. Beach resorts and private clubs began to spring up all over Santa Monica. William Randolph Hearst threw extravagant Hollywood bashes at his seaside mansion, and Santa Monica Pier's grand ballroom, once the largest in the world, welcomed 5,000 nightly. In the 1920s and 1930s, illegal gambling ships were anchored offshore, and Raymond Chandler portrayed it as sleazy "Bay City" in *Farewell, My Lovely*. After Cary Grant and Mary Pickford bought land here, it became known as "The Gold Coast."

Santa Monica's beach is still one of the most popular in Southern California, not only with people, but with movie and television producers. David Hasselhoff's lifeguard station on "Baywatch" was at 16000 Pacific Coast Highway and the beach club on "Beverly Hills 90210" was at 415 Palisades Beach Road (PCH). A short list of contemporary movies using Santa Monica backdrops include

A Santa Monica beach scene in the early 1900s.

Speed, The Truth about Cats and Dogs, White Men Can't Jump, Heat, and *Forget Paris.* Movie stars even own some of the restaurants here and in adjacent Venice, including 72 Market Street (Liza Minnelli) and Schatzi on Main (Arnold Schwarzenegger).

■ ■ ■

Today, the price of Santa Monica real estate is among the highest in L.A. County. Along Ocean Boulevard there are a number of large hotels and upscale apartment buildings overlooking the ocean, but the streets are so wide it doesn't seem as crammed as most popular beachfronts. (At the same time, many of the town's apartments are surprisingly down at the heels.) The quality of the food in the area is quite high, and there is some interesting architecture, including a few buildings by Frank Gehry—the most outrageous being the much-magnified pair of binoculars that houses the Chiat-Day advertising agency.

Nuns have tea on Santa Monica Pier.
The Santa Monica Farmer's Market is a treasure trove of agricultural diversity.

■ WHAT TO DO AND SEE IN SANTA MONICA

Santa Monica Pier

Santa Monica's original Pleasure Pier, the brainchild of Coney Island showman Charles Looff, opened in 1917. It has a hand-carved carousel; a variety of amusement park rides, including a giant Ferris wheel with a dizzying view of the Pacific; game booths; and arcades. Free summer concerts (the Twilight Series) are held on the pier every Thursday evening. UCLA's Ocean Discovery Museum is located *under* the pier. Walking the pier at night is still one of the more romantic ways to enjoy the city, especially now that the Jetsons-style police station guards the pier's entrance. At any time of day you'll be sharing the pier with families, fishermen, and street musicians. The Mexican restaurant Mariasol, at the end of the pier, has the best outdoor deck in the city, and if you're lucky you might find a good chili dog at one of the food stands, such as **Mariasol Cocina Mexicana** (401 Santa Monica Pier; 310-917-5050). Near the pier, on the beach, is **Big Dean's Cafe** (1615 Ocean Front Walk; 310-393-2666), a typical, and popular, no-fuss beach bar dishing up beer, wine, chili, grilled chicken, fish, and meat—plus music, steps from the sand. The tacos are a local favorite. Almost above the surf, at the foot of the pier near the carousel, **Rusty's Surf Ranch** (256 Santa Monica Pier; 310-393-7437; www.rustyssurfranch.com) has an upbeat beach-bar style, complete with surfboard décor. The menu is SoCal–eclectic, with dishes running from fried clams and calamari to chicken wings, crab cakes (and crab cake sandwiches), and quesadillas.

Santa Monica State Beach

A 3-mile beach that extends south from Will Rogers State Beach is not only one of the most popular beaches in the L.A. area, but also one of the few where the melting pot truly works: members of all races mingle here splendidly.

Shopping

The European-style, pedestrians-only **Third Street Promenade,** mobbed on weekends, is the liveliest shopping district in Santa Monica. You'll find upscale restaurants side by side with ethnic fast-food outlets, the best of which is Benita's Fries, whose menu contains only Belgian-style French fries (and dozens of dipping sauces). Also here: three multiplex movie theaters; unusual shops like Dom, with its seemingly infinite assortment of kitschy housewares; and three exceptional bookstores (Midnight Special, Arcana, and Hennesey and Ingalls). At the southern end of the Promenade is the enormous, pastel, and angular Santa Monica Place shopping mall,

Mr. Hearst's Beach House

Newspaper magnate William Randolph Hearst is known for his castle, San Simeon, but he also built himself a beach house in Santa Monica—it had 100 bedrooms and 55 bathrooms. The 37 fireplace mantels were from English estates, and the paintings on the walls were by Rembrandt, Hals, Reynolds, and Rubens.

The beach house did not have the pretense of a museum or a castle, but was a sunny, light, informal place devoted to endless fun . . . and it quickly became the epicenter of the movie colony's social activities. On weekends there were always at least fifty or sixty visitors about. . . . Guests who liked to swim had their choice of the ocean a few feet away or a beautiful hundred-foot pool with a Venetian marble bridge spanning the center of it.

■ ■ ■

[Mr. Hearst] devised some of the most ingenious events the town had ever seen.

There was the kid party, where the handsome Clark Gable came dressed as a Boy Scout and Norma Shearer and Joan Crawford were frilly little Shirley Temples. Another was the sumptuous Early American party with Mr. Hearst appearing as James Madison, another firm believer in the Constitution and gracious living, and his five sons all outfitted as sailors of our young Republic. In keeping with the theme, Norma Shearer came as Marie Antoinette, representing our French ally during the Revolution. But the *pièce de résistance* was the five-tiered cake fashioned like a replica of Independence Hall.

—Ken Murray,
*The Golden Days of
San Simeon,* 1971

*Mr. and Mrs. William
Randolph Hearst*

Santa Monica Pier

designed by architect Frank Gehry. (The Promenade is on Third Street, between Wilshire Blvd. and Broadway.) Toney **Montana Avenue** and eclectic **Main Street** are both lined with trendy restaurants, furniture stores, sidewalk cafes, and boutiques.

Farmers Market

There are farmers markets every day of the week in Los Angeles, but the largest is in Santa Monica, two mornings a week at the Third Street Promenade and Arizona Avenue. Flowers, fruits, vegetables, and herbs are sold every Wednesday from 9:30 A.M. to 3:30 P.M. and on Saturday from 8:30 A.M. to 1:00 P.M. Don't miss the fantastic tamale stand; its gourmet varieties include spinach and leek, sun-dried tomato, and barbecued chicken with habañero salsa.

Palisades Park

Set on a cliff overlooking Santa Monica Beach, this palm-lined park is a good place for running, walking, and watching the sunset. Pedestrian bridges and stairways lead from the park down to the beach. The park runs parallel to Ocean Avenue, between Colorado Avenue and Adelaide Drive.

Biker dude cruises Venice Beach.

■ **VENICE** *map pages 271 and 280*

If Southern California is the epicenter of the nation's wackiness, Venice is the very heart of that epicenter. When I last approached **Venice Boardwalk,** I was greeted by a "pink man," dressed in pink Spandex and fluttering his pink cape at me. He was friendly without trying to sell me anything. He pointed to the top of some palm trees where, high above the beach, a tightrope walker in formal dress casually strutted, waving a black parasol.

Scantily clad skaters, some wearing little more than a G-string, scooted by, zigzagging around the bicycle riders, who in turn cruised past the palm readers, the crystal sellers, and T-shirt vendors at a slightly slower pace. All about swirled the aromas of tacos, chiles, and cilantro. It's not surprising to me that Venice is very popular with tourists from Europe and Asia who come here to learn what Americans are really like. *The Boardwalk runs parallel to Venice Beach, between Navy Street and Washington Boulevard.*

Muscle Beach, actually part of the boardwalk, is a local institution where both men and women show off their bodies. It was originally named for the mussels attached to the pilings of the Santa Monica Pier. During the Great Depression, mussel became muscle, when WPA workers started an exercise program for local kids. Today, the name has traveled south to Venice Beach. You can't miss Muscle Beach, due to the unique architecture of the workout center: huge dumbbells are incorporated into the design. *20th Street and Ocean Front Walk.*

Lined with palm trees, **Venice Beach** is a wide, sandy, and surprisingly uncrowded beach set between the Venice Boardwalk and the ocean. Many of the folks coming to experience the Boardwalk never actually walk out onto the beach. *Extends from Marine Street to Spinnaker Street.*

Venice eccentricity goes back all the way to 1904, when a tobacco magnate named Abbot Kinney bought 160 acres of coastal salt marsh south of Santa Monica and set out to create a new cultural center for the nation by carving canals and a central lagoon from the briny fens and naming the place "Venice." He built an arcaded hotel, the St. Mark; spanned the canals with Venetian-style bridges; and began to attract crowds with appearances by such notables as author Helen Hunt Jackson, actress Sarah Bernhardt, and the Chicago Symphony. As it turned out, the

Youth enjoying themselves at Venice Beach.

Miller Beer Bikini Contest, Hermosa Beach

■ ORANGE COUNTY OVERVIEW

Orange County is an enigma. It can be both beautiful and unattractive. Thirty years ago there were still more orange groves here than housing tracts or freeways. On winter nights the orange blossoms would open and their dense, tropical scent would permeate the air. Today, one of those orange groves is part of a freeway—named the "Orange" Freeway.

Northern Orange County is part of the flat Los Angeles basin; southern Orange County is hilly or mountainous. In the north, the shores are primarily sandy beaches or coastal lagoons and marshes; to the south they are dominated by rocky cliffs with sandy pocket beaches.

Much of northern Orange County (including its coastal plains and terraces) has been swallowed by urban sprawl, but there are still open, wild spaces, mostly in the San Joaquin Hills and Santa Ana Mountains. The dense chaparral and big-cone Douglas-fir forest surrounding Santiago Park (Old Saddleback) are as wild as any western mountain landscape. The reason so much wilderness has survived is because much of the mountainous back country is U.S. Forest Service land.

Orange County has all of the amenities you would expect from a 20th-century American suburban community, and several of the beaches are spectacular. To find parking on a sunny summer weekend, try to arrive early—by 9:30 or 10 at the latest.

■ TRAVELING AND ACCESS TO ORANGE COUNTY BEACHES

Orange County can be reached via I-5 from Los Angeles and San Diego; via CA 1 (PCH) along the coast; and via the Riverside Freeway (Highway 91) and CA 55 from I-15 and Riverside. Many north-south and several east-west roads end at the beach, but the easiest way to reach the coast is by Beach Boulevard/Highway 39; the Costa Mesa Freeway/Highway 55; and Laguna Canyon Road/Highway 133.

■ ■ ■

Because so many Orange County beaches hide behind fences, and because too many people live here on too little land, trips to the Orange Coast should be planned with care. Driving trips here can be disappointing and frustrating. Try to avoid driving during the morning or evening rush hours, and be prepared for delays on any warm weekend day.

Commercial orange groves have long since disappeared from this Southern California county. Workers pick oranges in the town of Orange, in 1911.

Surfers near the pier at
Huntington State Beach.

hood of his Lincoln convertible with its surfer hood ornament. The exhibit also includes the groovy tunes of surf music. *411 Olive Ave., two blocks up from the Huntington Beach pier; 714-960-3483.*

The paved, multi-use **Santa Ana River Bike Trail** runs along the Santa Ana River from the mouth inland to Gypsum Canyon Bridge in Yorba Linda.

■ NEWPORT BEACH *map page 271*

The unique topography of this beach city is determined by the way the city spreads along the shores of Newport Bay (the old Santa Ana River estuary), a wide inlet that's the drowned mouth of the river. Part of the city covers the Balboa Peninsula, a several-miles-long sandy spit formed in 1825 by a huge Santa Ana River flood. The river has since been diverted and enters the ocean to the north of town. Several artificial islands in the bay serve as exclusive and very expensive residential neighborhoods (where you can rent houses in the summer months).

Newport Beach has been a fashionable resort since before 1908, when this photo was taken.

The town of Newport Beach is famous for its wealth and for its vast yacht harbor, with more than 10,000 boats. The annual Christmas Boat Parade of Lights is the town's most important event—kind of like a Christmas-themed Rose Parade at night.

Newport Beach—the beach—is a delight. There are no fences in sight—you can walk onto the beach from the ends of peninsular streets, and I have found free all-day parking only two blocks from the pier. My old rule has long proved its value: if you're looking for free parking, follow a surfer.

Newport Aquatic Center on Newport Bay offers lessons in canoeing, kayaking, and Olympic rowing. *1 Whitecliffs Dr. From PCH head north on Dover Dr. and turn right on Whitecliffs Dr.; 949-646-7725.*

The popular **Newport Dunes Resort** has a 15-acre lagoon with swimming, boating, a picnic area, camping facilities, and a restaurant. *714-729-3863.*

Once scheduled for housing and commercial developments, **Upper Newport Bay,** an important 752-acre estuary, was saved in the nick of time. It has an intertidal mudflat and a salt-marsh wildlife reserve, which together serve as wintering areas for migratory shorebirds and waterfowl. Trails wind through and around the reserve. North Star Beach has a small-craft launch and kayak rentals. *714-973-6820.*

The adjacent **San Joaquin Freshwater Marsh Reserve** protects 202 acres of marsh above Newport Bay. It's part of the University of California Natural Reserve System. *For information on visiting or fishing permits, call 949 824-6031.*

■ ■ ■

You reach the **Balboa Peninsula** by taking the well-marked Balboa turnoff from the Coast Highway. Main Street runs between Balboa Pier on the ocean and the bay. The beach (as opposed to the town) of Newport Beach faces the ocean at the west end of the peninsula.

Along the road to the pier you'll notice the Victorian **Balboa Pavilion** at 400 Main Street. Facing Newport Bay, it is a California classic: it served as a dance hall well into 1940s, was restored in 1962, and is now the terminus for the *Catalina Flyer,* a fast catamaran that leaves from here daily for Catalina Island (see page 298).

The "Wedge" at the end of the peninsula is a famous place for bodysurfing. The break can be punishing and the currents swift, making it unsafe for all but the strongest swimmers. When the waves are up, they often reach over 15 feet. Watching experienced bodysurfers skip along the waves makes for a great morning of free entertainment.

■ NEWPORT BEACH PIER

You have to arrive early at the foot of the Newport Beach Pier, where the dory fleet lands, if you want to have the pick of the freshest fish and shellfish. On my last visit, I was slowed down by one of those ubiquitous Orange County traffic jams, and by the time I made it there several dories had already returned, and the sales counters were covered with fish. Because I'd heard rumors that some of the dorymen might be buying their fish from larger boats instead of catching them themselves, I took a close look at these fish. The rumors were malicious. These fish were *fresh*, and in no time at all, the catch was sold.

Soon, more dories came in, racing through the surf to run the boats up on the beach as high as possible. I watched as one dory went out again. The doryman nonchalantly edged it up to the surf, began to push harder as the boat began to float, waited for a lull between the breakers then, after a final shove, he jumped in and started the outboard motor. By the time the next breaker hit the beach he was ready. The dory almost stood straight up on its tail as it hit a large breaker. Then, with a big splash, it was safely outside the surf.

Since the mid-1990s, dory-fleet catches have included some of the odder seafood searched out by Orange County's ethnic communities, like sculpin, small rockfish (to be cooked whole), whitebait, and sea snails.

■ BALBOA ISLAND

A tiny car ferry runs from the pavilion to Balboa Island, a small, quaint wonder of a place in Newport Bay. The island is encircled by a boardwalk and tiny waterfront houses, boat slips, and small sandy beaches. Marine Avenue, which crosses the island, has small shops, food stores, and cafes. You can return to the mainland via Marine Avenue, which connects directly to Highway 1.

■ CORONA DEL MAR *map page 271*

Corona del Mar is a southern extension of the city of Newport Beach. Along the highway it looks like a miles-long strip mall, but its back streets are filled with small, attractive houses, and the coves below have smooth, sandy beaches.

China Cove Beach

A pair of sandy coves on the east side of the harbor, near the channel, forms this beach. *Pedestrian access is by stairs from Ocean Blvd.*

Rocky Point

A small sandy cove at the east side of the harbor channel, with many small caves, this beach was formerly called "Pirates Cove." Access is from Ocean Boulevard, by path from China Cove Beach, or over the rocks from Corona del Mar Beach to the east.

Corona del Mar Beach

This very popular sandy beach just east of the Newport Harbor entrance has picnic tables, volleyball nets, and other amenities. The harbor jetty breaks are popular with surfers. There's a pay parking lot at the beach, and metered parking on the bluff above.

Little Corona City Beach

This gem of a beach is tucked away in a sandy cove with rocky reefs and tide pools. To reach it follow the walkway from Poppy Avenue.

■ CRYSTAL COVE STATE PARK *map page 271*

If you're driving the Coast Highway, you'll breathe a sigh of relief when you leave the coastal housing and shopping developments behind and drive through the wide open spaces of Crystal Cove. Marvelous tide pools are here; there's nothing like poking among them at sunset when the water is bright with color.

This half-wild area, with its sandy and rocky coastline, beaches, coves, and wild hills, has developed into the most exciting park on the Orange County coast. The park's El Moro Canyon in the San Joaquin Hills has campsites and 18 miles of hiking, bicycling, and equestrian trails. *949-494-3539.*

The adjacent, undeveloped Laguna Coast Wilderness Park stretches over the hills west of Laguna Canyon Road between Crystal Cove and Aliso and Wood canyons. This park can be entered only on special public-access days. *949-494-9352.*

■ LAGUNA BEACH AREA *map page 271*

Laguna Beach has preserved the timeless charm of its cliffs, trees, buildings, and cascades of flowers. The town is as delightful as ever, especially at those magic spots where a gap in the cliffs reveals a sandy beach. (Prepare for traffic jams on your way into town; parking can be a problem.)

The junction of Broadway and PCH, known as the "village," is the heart of Laguna Beach. It is here, at **Main Beach,** where Laguna Canyon meets the ocean.

The broad sweep of Laguna Beach.

At times it seems that all of the town's life takes place on the boardwalk along the strand. You'll find the usual volleyballers here, plus kids on skateboards, surfers, divers, young boys strutting like Adonis and girls who look as fresh as if they had stepped newly formed from the sea foam.

But this is also a beach where families stroll on the boardwalk or spread blankets beneath the bluff for *al fresco* meals, and where old folks come to soak up both the sun and the youthful energy of this village beach. Laguna has long been the home to one of the biggest volleyball competitions on the coast. Main Beach has three courts with nets, one with a net strung between two palm trees. It's also home to one of the most competitive (and definitely the most scenic) pick-up basketball courts anywhere. Top-notch athletes, including college players from UCLA and ex-professionals, do battle against a backdrop of the blue Pacific and swaying palm trees.

Because artists have always lived here—especially when Laguna Beach was considered to be way out in the boonies and rents were more affordable—there have always been crafts shops and galleries bordering the Pacific Coast Highway and lining Forest Avenue. Exhibits often include plenty of pastel seascapes and unhappy clowns, but there's serious art as well. The summer-long Pageant of the Masters and Sawdust Festival offer a diverse and in-depth look at the art scene.

■ LAGUNA BEACHES

Crescent Bay Point Park

A lawn and paved walkway off the Coast Highway has views of Laguna Beach and of the Seal Rocks, where sea lions haul out. *Turn off CA 1 onto Crescent Bay Drive toward the ocean.*

Pocket Beaches

A good number of beaches are hidden in small coves accessible by well-marked walkways or stairs. Look for them off Cliff Drive and on street ends south of Main Beach. The beaches at the end of Oak, Brooks, and Thalia streets are particularly appealing.

Heisler Park

This pretty, grassy park, on the bluff above Picnic Beach and Rock Pile Beach, is connected by paved walkway south to Main Beach.

Junior lifeguards are put through their paces prior to a tough day on Laguna Beach.

Aliso Creek

Dominated by a short, uniquely designed pier, this beach has an appealing stretch of fine white sand and invitingly blue water. The currents can be powerful, and the shore break makes it a popular place for skimboarding. The parking lot is almost right on the sand, making for easy access. This is one of the southern California beaches where, because of the configuration of the shore, swimmers should avoid "body whomping" (bodysurfing in shallow water, at the shore break) because the surf can toss them into the sand and cause spinal injuries or broken necks.

Salt Creek Beach Park

Just south of Laguna, this long, sandy, beautiful beach is popular with surfers, swimmers, and sun hounds. Head north along the sand toward Monarch Bay to escape the crowds. Easy access off the highway. Large metered parking lot, grassy area, basketball courts.

Cliffside homes are perched precariously over the ocean along this stretch of the coast.

■ DANA POINT *map page 271*

The natural beauty of this cove has been destroyed by its breakwater and marina, and the last piece of natural beach on the west end of the cove is now hidden beneath the sprawling buildings of the Orange County Marine Institute.

Exhibits inside the building celebrate what used to be here. Big placards sport renderings of an even bigger institute planned for the cove, and solicit donations. Fragile cliff tops are crowned by oversized edifices that look as though they had been assembled from a mail-order catalog of generic California beach houses.

On the waterfront sea wall, you'll find a replica of the brig **Pilgrim,** in which author Richard Henry Dana sailed to these shores in the 1830s. Dana, who called this cove "the only romantic place on the California coast," would be appalled if he could come back and see the change. The *Pilgrim* is not a true replica but a modified Portuguese schooner. There's another ship moored there, too; the *Spirit of Dana Point.* Both ships were wrapped in fumigation tarps in the summer of 2004, presumably for termite control.

A paved walkway runs along the shore of the boat basins. Most of the restaurants overlooking the boat basin are so generic they might as well be in a mall. But one place, **Jon's Fishmarket**, has character, and excellent fish 'n' chips and seafood chowders. The outdoor dining area is always packed with happy diners.

■ ■ ■

At **Ken Sampson Overlook,** you can see the ocean and harbor from a gazebo built on the very spot where author Richard Henry Dana and his fellow sailors threw "California bank notes" (dried cattle skins) off the bluff to be loaded onto the brig *Pilgrim* anchored in the cove below. *South end of Amber Lantern and Violet Lantern streets.*

Heritage Park (at the foot of Golden Lantern Street and El Camino Capistrano) has a grassy bluff-top overlook with benches and wheelchair-accessible paths overlooking Dana Point Harbor. A stairway leads down to the harbor.

Doheny State Beach, just south of the harbor, has something for everyone. There is a campground with 120 sites, a great beginners surf spot, a bike path, visitors center, divers park, and more. Before the harbor jetty went in, Doheny was a famous surf spot known as "Killer Dana" to the locals; it was mentioned in the Beach Boys' ode, "Surfin' USA."

■ MISSION SAN JUAN CAPISTRANO *map page 271*

The cove at Dana Point was once part of the vast landholdings of Mission San Juan Capistrano, whose partially reconstructed ruins stand several miles inland, in the small town of San Juan Capistrano.

This town—which 19th-century visitors referred to as "San Juan," not "Capistrano"—once had the largest stone church of any of the missions, but it collapsed during an early-19th-century earthquake, killing several worshippers, and was never rebuilt. The original mission chapel is still intact, and it is the only church still standing at any of the missions where Father Junipero Serra celebrated mass.

The mission grounds are beautifully landscaped and offset by fawn-colored arches and a low, multi-bell campanile, considered to be the most romantic of any California mission. The reconstructed sections of the mission's work areas will give you a good idea of how the missionaries and Indians prepared food, made wine, and performed their daily tasks of maintenance. The mission's old stone church ruin has been stabilized and made earthquake-proof, and several of the original church bells have been restored.

The mission chapel in San Juan Capistrano.

One reason this mission is so popular with visitors is because flowers—bougainvillea, roses, birds-of-paradise—bloom here profusely, even in midwinter. This mission is quite definitely worth a short detour from the coast (follow I-5 and look for signs directing you to San Juan Capistrano and its mission). The Ortega Highway, CA 74, runs east from San Juan Capistrano through the very rugged Ortega Mountains. It eventually drops down the sharp escarpment of the Coast Range to Lake Elsinore in a series of hairpin turns. There's a great view of the lake and the interior valleys from the top of the cliff. Far in the distance to the southeast, you can just make out the hills of the Temecula wine district. The Capistrano Creek Bike Trail runs from the beach along Capistrano Creek to the mission.

■ SAN CLEMENTE *map page 323*

Much of this town sits on top of cliffs, but at the main beach and municipal pier the cliffs open like the tiers of an amphitheater, allowing for easy access to the shore. With the sun lighting up the flowers and the sea, and with throngs of smiling people walking to the beach, San Clemente can lay claim to being one of the

Women shop on Avenue Del Mar.

most delightful places on the Orange County coast. It's also a funky seaside village—a cultural hodgepodge where Marines in fatigues, barefoot and shirtless surfers, Latin American immigrants, and *nouveau riche* meld together among one-room bungalows and multimillion-dollar mansions.

Casa Romantica, the opulent cliff-top Spanish Colonial Revival mansion built in 1928 by Ole Hanson (one of the founders of San Clemente), has been restored and reopened as a cultural center. While most of the events at the center run to classical music concerts and poetry readings, it seems fitting for the hometown of the Surfriders Foundation that the first event after opening was a surf lecture. *415 Avenida Granada (P.O. Box 191); 949-498-2139; http://casaromantica.org.*

The last time I walked the streets of this town, passing surf shops, thrift stores, sushi bars, authentic Mexican markets/restaurants, and throngs of healthy, laid-back locals, I ended up at the Fisherman's Restaurant and Bar. Situated at the foot of the San Clemente pier, it's a longtime favorite for tourists and locals alike. Over a wonderfully fresh cut of yellowtail, I stared out at the sea and tried to envision President Richard Nixon sneaking out of his nearby "Western White House" back in the late 1970s, to sit at the bar with the tanned crowd dressed in flip-flops and tank tops, enjoying an afternoon beer or two. (Nixon owned this place, tucked into the bluffs at the southern end of town, from 1968 to 1979.) But my mind could not conjure up the image. Instead, I took a long, leisurely stroll on the sandy beach that runs from San Clemente south to San Onofre and listened to the sea wind soughing in the grasses, and the gulls shriek at the surf while gray whales splashed offshore on their southward migration.

■ TRAVEL BASICS

Driving

Los Angeles is known as a chaotic place, an anti-city, where even a network of freeways fails to create order. Many of L.A. and Orange County's major attractions—museums, celebrity cemeteries, temples, theaters, movie studios, shopping malls, Rodeo Drive, Universal City, and Disneyland—are strewn all over the place, like meatballs on a plate of freeway spaghetti. Even worse, they are separated by miles of congested roads. The area's coastal attractions, on the other hand, are lined up like beads on a string.

Practically speaking, no one wants to drive along the coast between Malibu and San Clemente. It's too slow, too crowded, and in a sense too depressing, with urban sprawl and ubiquitous oil derricks. Better to pick a few of the places described here and go enjoy them—but don't try to do too much.

Coast Road Names: CA 1 starts out as the Pacific Coast Highway in Malibu, changes its name to Palisades Beach Road in Santa Monica, then heads away from the coast at Colorado Avenue (whose end is the Santa Monica Pier) and merges with I-10, the Santa Monica Freeway, for a few blocks. When CA 1 leaves the freeway to head south, it becomes Lincoln Boulevard, a name it keeps until it takes a turn around LAX airport and becomes Sepulveda Boulevard. It keeps that name through El Segundo and Manhattan Beach until it crosses Artesia Boulevard (CA 91) and resumes its proper name: the Pacific Coast Highway, popularly referred to as PCH.

Climate

Dry and warm year-round. The rare winter rainfall only amounts to a total of 12 inches per season, usually falling in January or February. Fog is common along the beaches between Santa Monica and Palos Verdes during the summer, but usually burns off by midday. Summer temperatures average between 75 and 85 degrees. **Water temperature** averages 65 to 75 degrees year-round.

Food and Lodging

Excellent restaurants can be found in the L.A. area, and all major hotel and motel chains are well represented. **Lodging and restaurant listings** by town in alphabetical order begin on page 362.

SAN DIEGO COAST

North of the city of San Diego, small seaside towns are strung all along the coast, interrupted now and then by a lagoon. You'll understand why people flock to these beaches when you step into the water and feel how warm it is. There's also a special quality to the light that makes you want to linger on the sand, looking across the blue swath of the Pacific.

The city of San Diego, which is central to this area, spreads from the northern, hilly shores of San Diego Bay west to the ocean and east up the valley carved by the San Diego River.

San Diego manages to be both a generic U.S. city and one with a distinct personality. If its downtown architecture is much like that in the rest of the U.S.—high rises, malls, and all that—the scene is heavily leavened by the restored Victorians in the Gaslamp Quarter and, more commonly, by the neo-Mediterranean architecture: arched entrances, white walls, and red tile roofs. This feels appropriate, not only because it's set in a Mediterranean climate, but also because the area was a Spanish colonial outpost between 1769 and 1820, and later, for another 28 years, part of an independent Mexico. Late-20th-century Mexican influences, brought north by immigrants, have turned quarters like Old Town into vibrant centers of Mexican culture. Drive just a few miles south of San Diego and you'll be in Mexico.

■ About North County

San Diego's North County offers broad, wide-open, sandy beaches pummeled by roaring surf, along with quiet, protected coves, flocks of shorebirds, and friendly people. The beaches here are wider and less crowded than those of San Diego to the south and Orange County to the north. The water is temperate enough for swimming, the waves shaped right for surfing, and the sand is soft and warm underfoot.

Shorebirds are plentiful because many of the best beaches form sand barriers across the mouths of creek or river lagoons. Since this gives sanderlings, willets, dunlins, dowitchers, and other sandpipers a chance to double dip, they hang out in great flocks. The local folk are friendly because their beaches have not yet been taken over by city crowds. Even the local surfers are friendlier than they are

Children pet a hedgehog at the San Diego Zoo.

the Marines have also introduced (non-native) bison. Stop at **Las Flores Vista Point** for a great view of the mountains to the east and the bluffs and beaches to the west. You have to be a VIP, however, to watch marines in action from the viewing stand bleachers at nearby Practice Landing Beach.

You can tour the former ranch house (now the Commanding General's Residence) by appointment. Tours are on Tuesdays and Thursdays at 10 A.M. from the last week in September to the end of May. You can request an appointment by email (jonasonfa@pendleton.usmc.mil). There's a landing craft museum in Building 21561 in the base's boat basin. Self-guided tours of the base are not available. *To schedule a visit to the museum, call 760-725-2195; www.pendleton.usmc.mil.*

■ **OCEANSIDE AND SAN LUIS REY** *map page 323*

The San Luis Rey River, which rises near Mount Palomar, debouches into the ocean just south of **Oceanside Harbor,** a rather drab and dull small-boat port with the usual facilities. **Harbor Beach** is the port's only highlight. **Oceanside City Beach** runs along the town's oceanfront and is partially accessible by the Strand, a paved road that dead-ends at pay parking lots. (There's plenty of on-street parking as well and it's free a few blocks from the beach.) Steps lead down to the Strand from **Linear Park,** a landscaped concrete walkway along the bluff with benches and view platforms.

This uncrowded beach, shadowed by tall palm trees swaying in the wind, is about as close to the ultimate Southern California beach as you'll get. At Oceanside, the color of the water changes, taking on a turquoise sub-tropical hue, and you see more swimmers in the water than you do to the north. Palm trees look healthier than they do up the coast, and tender tropical and sub-tropical shrubs and flowers—which hide their pretty heads behind tall garden walls from Santa Barbara to San Clemente—proudly expose their bright faces to the sea breeze.

People thrive here too, as you can tell by all the cheerful faces that greet you on a walk to the end of the 1,900-foot Oceanside Pier. And if the hike along the pier makes you hungry, satisfy your appetite with turkey pot pie, hearty chili, or a fresh-baked apple pie at Ruby's Diner, a retro-50s restaurant at the tip of the pier.

Oceanside is a tad more grungy and has a blue-collar feel to it, unlike Carlsbad and the other spiffed-up beach towns to the south. The beach is popular with marines and families from nearby Camp Pendleton.

■ CARLSBAD *map page 323*

Interestingly, the town of **Carlsbad** originally got its name from a mineral spring whose waters were supposed to have the same qualities as the famed Carlsbad spring in the Czech Republic. Luckily Carlsbad has managed to keep its village character intact, even while attracting plenty of visitors with its beaches, restaurants, and excellent lodging.

Carlsbad Oceanfront

The Carlsbad oceanfront is divided between **Carlsbad State Beach,** a sandy and rocky beach with overlooks on the blufftops, and **Carlsbad City Beach** to the north. (This beach is accessible by stairs at the north end of Ocean Street, and at several cul-de-sacs.)

Carlsbad has 5 miles of easily accessible beach bordered on the land side by a bluff, a retaining wall, and a pedestrian walk. Picnic areas and restrooms have been upgraded in recent years (and are plentiful). The beach is very popular with families, teenagers, and surfers.

South Carlsbad State Beach

This beach extends north for 4 miles from Batiquitos Lagoon, an important resting place for migratory fowl. Bird-watchers may watch the birds from trails along the eastern and western shorelines. The state beach has campsites along the bluffs, hot showers, a laundromat, and a grocery and bait store. The Encina Fishing Area on the Coast Highway is popular with fishermen because the fish of Agua Hedionda Lagoon are known to bite eagerly. Much of the small town of Carlsbad sits on bluffs between Agua Hedionda Lagoon and Buena Vista Lagoon.

Buena Vista Lagoon

The lagoon, which separates Carlsbad from Oceanside, is one of the best bird-watching places on the south coast. At **Maxton Brown Park** on the Carlsbad shore, a paved path leads to an overlook with benches and picnic tables. To the east, a duck feeding area on Jefferson Street, south of CA 78, has a paved parking lot and benches. The **Buena Vista Audubon Nature Center** in Oceanside has nature exhibits and a short trail along the shoreline; *2202 Coast Highway; 760-439-2473.*

■ ENCINITAS AND CARDIFF-BY-THE-SEA *map page 323*

Encinitas is a sleepy seaside town with small but quaint main streets, flowering gardens, and some good vegetarian restaurants. **Quail Botanical Gardens,** just off Encinitas Boulevard (one block east of Interstate 5), is worth a visit to see its ancient cycads, palms, flowering trees, and the largest collection of bamboo in the United States. You might not want to visit the garden at the height of the summer drought, when it's dry and dusty, and the tempers of the volunteers are as frayed as the leaves of the banana plants. But even in summer you can admire the majesty of some of the garden's bamboos—some are as thick as small trees. *760-436-3036.*

The town of **Leucadia,** which is actually a part of the city of Encinitas, grows and sells more flowers (especially poinsettias) than any other town in the United States. In the early spring the hills north of Palomar Airport Road are a blanket of brightly colored blossoms. It appears that houses on the bluffs overlooking the beaches are quite literally teetering at the edge of disaster as the ocean gnaws at the soft, unstable escarpments.

A Mexican-American woman sells poinsettia flowers in Leucadia.

Nearby **Cardiff-by-the-Sea** is a small, laid-back coastal community. If you're looking for a place to stock up on picnic provisions before heading to one of the area's fine beaches, try the Seaside Market or pick up a smoothie and veggie burger at Ki's, both on Highway 1. Or you can hang out at Miracles Cafe at 1453 San Elijo Avenue (until the place closes, at least: it lost its lease in 2004, but may be able to hang on for a year or two), a coffeehouse that gives you a good sense of what North County is all about. For instance, a local recently told me that Rob Machado (one of the most famous surfers competing today) lives nearby and if he's at Miracles, or simply walking by, on the same day you're there, good luck getting any of the normally friendly staff to pay attention to you. There's also a famous bar right on the beach: the **Kraken** at 2531 S. Highway 101.

Beacon's Beach (formerly known as Leucadia State Beach) is at the end of Leucadia Boulevard. It has more cobblestones than sand and is often strewn with kelp, but once you make it to the water, the fishing, swimming, and surfing are great. South from Beacon's Beach is narrow, sandy **Encinitas Beach**. To reach narrow, cobbled **Stone Steps Beach,** just south of Encinitas Beach, take Portal Street west from Highway 101 (South Coast Highway). This short street becomes El Portal, splits north and south, and dead-ends quickly west of Neptune Avenue—a narrow, northbound, one-way street that runs along the bluffs, parallel to the beaches. Stone steps lead to the beach. There's only on street parking here.

Moonlight Beach

Especially popular with the pre-teen boogie-board set and families, Moonlight Beach, in Encinitas, has volleyball and tennis courts, a snack bar, and picnic tables. This picture-perfect beach got its name from the moonlit picnics locals held on the beach in the late 19th century. The restrooms, outdoor showers, and other facilities received a major upgrade in the spring of 2004. Note that this beach is popular with families, and parking can be tricky on warm summer days. Moonlight Beach is at the western end of B Street, which is the continuation of Encinitas Boulevard (it changes its name when it crosses the Coast Highway (old U.S. 101) about half a mile from the beach. There are no steps leading down to Moonlight Beach, because access is through a gap made in the bluffs by a creek, although there are steps leading from the Moonlight Beach parking lot (on the bluff) down to the beach.

Boneyard Beach—south of Moonlight Beach, between E and J streets in Encinitas—is the local nude beach. You reach it via stairs from D Street. There are no facilities.

Swami's

The golden cupolas, lush gardens, and meditation area of the mosque-like **Self-Realization Fellowship Hermitage** sprawl conspicuously on the ocean side of the highway. The grounds are open to the public, however, and don't worry—no one will try to convert you. The "exotic" property (the towers are topped with golden onion domes) inspired locals to name the beach below Swami's—it's a narrow strip popular with both surfers and surf fishermen. *Stairs at 216 K St.*

Swami's is one of the beaches immortalized by the Beach Boys in "Surfin' USA." The cobblestone beach makes sunbathing a tad difficult, so the crowd is mostly restricted to serious surfers—and they're not always kind to outsiders. The foot of the stairway is often washed by surf, complicating the transition from land to water.

San Elijo State Beach

San Elijo is the southernmost state beach that has full camping facilities. Park headquarters have a tide-pool display and a native plant garden. Even though the beach is mostly cobble rather than sand, it is popular with swimmers, surfers, divers, and fishermen.

Even though the campground on the bluff has been renovated and is usually full, this is a quiet beach, great for taking long walks (at low tide). At high tide, the surf may wash the base of the cliffs. In the water, surfers have the right of way (or think they do).

Cardiff State Beach

A stretch of warm sand between the ocean and San Elijo Lagoon segregates surfers (southern half) and swimmers (northern half). The southern part of the park also has tide pools. If the surf isn't cooperating, you can always look at marine critters or watch the birds in the lagoon do their thing.

This cobblestone beach, which is popular with surfers, kayakers, and fishermen, used to be sandy until erosion carried off the sand (this also happened at other north county beaches). The south end has tide pools. The *San Diego Union-Tribune* reports that this beach can be unsafe during storms, when heavy surf may close Highway 101 and its restaurants (and toss cobblestones onto the road).

Garden cactus at the Self-Realization Fellowship Hermitage.

■ SOLANA BEACH *map page 323*

The town of Solana Beach seems modest compared to its glamorous neighbor Del Mar, but it has a rather funky, post-modernist city hall that looks like a colorful, overblown clock radio, and a couple of good beaches: **Fletcher Cove Beach**, with basketball and shuffleboard courts for those not limber enough to surf or play volleyball; **Seascape Shores**, with volleyball courts in the sand and good surfing offshore (reached via stairways near the 500 and 700 blocks of Sierra Avenue); and **Tide Beach**, another good surfing and swimming spot, with some great tide pools where you can spend hours observing the marine life. Most of the local beaches have been heavily eroded by surf in recent years; in fact, the town has been sued by the Surfriders and other conservationist organizations for putting up illegal seawalls to shore up unstable bluffs. On the positive side, the lack of sand has created great tide pools. But Solana Beach's greatest local fame stems from a seemingly humble quonset hut converted into a music club: the Belly Up Tavern (143 S. Cedros Avenue), which draws big-name blues and rock stars.

■ DEL MAR *map page 323*

You haven't experienced true relaxation until you get to Del Mar. Even though the town is best known for its famous racetrack, and the horse racing season is in full swing by mid-July, you wouldn't know it if you hadn't read about it. The beach marches to a different drummer. There isn't even a traffic crush, because the track is easily accessible from I-5 to the east. But the beach parking lots are full, and bobbing out in the water beyond the breaking surf, surfers are lined up waiting for the next perfect set.

Del Mar has two excellent beaches: wide and sandy City Beach, where surfers and grunions run in season; and Del Mar Bluffs City Park, at the mouth of the San Dieguito River. City Beach is wide and sandy, and popular with surfers, swimmers, beach walkers, and grunion hunters.

Grunions are 4- to 8-inch smelt-sized fish that spawn in summer on some southern and central California beaches during full moon. The females leave the water and wiggle themselves into the wet sand, then the males wrap themselves around them to fertilize them. You need a fishing license and may catch the tiny—and very wriggly—fish, and may only use your bare hands—you are not allowed to dig holes in the sand to entrap them. That's why so few people ever catch any and others consider it to be an urban legend. It is not. One source claims that

Del Mar City Beach.

"Observing grunion can be much more interesting than catching them." Another states that "they appear to exert a powerful and magic effect on the human psyche. More than one student has related to me their success in love following a grunion run." Grunion hunters usually built bonfires on the beaches during the nights of the runs and throw some darn good parties.

Well-heeled Del Mar Plaza has a number of ritzy shops, galleries, and best of all a glorious sundeck. Colorful wooden chairs invite you to relax with a Pellegrino and look out over Camino del Mar, the picturesque train station, grassy Del Mar Park, and, of course, the sparkling ocean.

■ TORREY PINES *map page 323*

Torrey Pines is a place *and* a type of pine tree—a unique yellow pine with five long needles (8 to 13 inches) instead of the more common two or three. In coastal gullies, they slowly grow from 20 to 60 feet tall, and take on spectacular shapes, because branches broken off by the wind die back to the main trunk. Living branches stretch away from the ocean, as though they were trying to flee the sea wind. Oddly enough, even though this pine has such a limited natural habitat, it

geophysics, climatology, oceanography, and biology, and has a fleet of four ships in seas around the world.

There are surfboards in most, if not all, of the cliffside labs at Scripps. Dave Fields, a Ph.D. candidate from Scripps, admits that many of the students and teachers surf between classes. (Sandbars on either side of Scripps Pier turn out reliable peaks year-round.)

The beach and tide pools are part of a series of underwater reserves stretching from the southern city limits of Del Mar south to Goldfish Point in La Jolla. If you want to learn more about the shore and the ocean, be sure to visit the associated **Stephen Birch Aquarium,** perched on a cliff above La Jolla Sands. This dazzling place has a number of interactive, hands-on exhibits and is a wonderful place to take children. There's even a "Dive after Five" event where for $20 guests stand outside near the kelp tank, munching on tacos, drinking cocktails, watching the sunset, and, via microphones, chatting with divers feeding fish in the tank. The aquarium also arranges two- and three-hour whale-watching cruises. *2300 Expedition Way (from I-5, exit on La Jolla Village Drive; turn west on Expedition Way); 619-534-3474.*

The thousand-foot Scripps Pier, built by one of the world's foremost institutions of oceanography, is just south of Scripps Beach and tide pools. The institution's research ships, which study the ocean floor, moor here and are occasionally open to the public.

SALUBRIOUS AIR, *THERE*

The charm of Southern California is largely to be found in its air and light. These are really one element: indivisible, mutually interacting, interpenetrated. Without the ocean breezes, the sunlight would be intolerable; without the sunlight and imported water, virtually nothing would grow in the region.

■ ■ ■

The geographers say that the quality of Southern California's climate is pure Mediterranean—the only specimen of Mediterranean climate in the United States. But such words as "Mediterranean" and "subtropical" are most misleading when applied to Southern California. Unlike the Mediterranean coast, Southern California has no sultry summer air, no mosquito-ridden malarial marshes, no mistral winds. A freak of nature—a cool and semimoist desert—Southern California is climatically insulated, shut off from the rest of the continent. As Helen Hunt Jackson once said, and it is the best description of the region yet coined, "It is a sort of an island on the land."

—Carey McWilliams, *Southern California Country,* 1946

. . . UNTIL THE SANTA ANA WINDS STRIKE

About 1 o'clock P.M. [on June 17, 1850] . . . a blast of hot air from the northeast swept suddenly over the town, and struck the inhabitants with terror. It was quickly followed by others. At two o'clock the thermometer exposed to the air rose to 113°, and continued at or near that point for nearly three hours, while the burning wind raised dense clouds of impalpable dust. No human being could withstand the heat All betook themselves to their dwellings. . . . Calves, rabbits, birds, etc., were killed, trees were blighted, fruit was blasted and fell to the ground, burned only on one side; the gardens were ruined. At five o'clock the thermometer fell to 122° [sic], and at seven it stood at 77°.

—*As recalled by Walter Lindley, M.D., and Joseph Widney, M. D. in 1888*

■ LA JOLLA *map page 323*

San Diego's coastal communities were described by historian Kevin Starr as "a seaside celebration of sun and sky, an urban area for the Mediterranean encounter of line, color, warmth, and spaciousness." Nowhere is this more true than in La Jolla, with its very Mediterranean coast and narrow winding streets. Houses crowd right up to edge of cliffs; fragrant flowers are everywhere; sandy beaches and sea caves sit below rocky precipices; and ocean waters are pleasantly warm for swimming. Here, more than anywhere else, beach neighborhoods are part of the shore; the houses and gardens are fully integrated with the sea, sand, surf, and rock. No one seems quite sure how La Jolla got its name or who named the place. "Jolla" is supposedly a corruption of either Spanish *joya* ("jewel") or *hoya* ("hollow,") depending on which writer you believe. Both explanations are plausible.

La Jolla has been a popular wintering place since long before the first Anglo settlers arrived. Beaches and other attractions are usually crowded; it may be hard to find parking after 10 A.M. Streets can get very congested and traffic often slows to a crawl, if it moves at all. Relax and give yourself plenty of time.

From a visitor's viewpoint, La Jolla is an embarrassment of riches. After a couple of days, you feel like you'll need at least a year or two to begin exploring, and much more time to experience it all. The beaches are delightful sandy pockets tucked into rocky coves. Some are sandy year-round; on others, winter storms wash away and expose the underlying boulders, until the gentle currents of summer restore the sand.

Downtown La Jolla is a very compact place; consider parking your car and walking. Locals say the true test of positive thinking is finding a parking place at the cove in summer. But it's really much easier to discover all the special little beaches if you walk rather than drive.

La Jolla is bliss for shoppers, and La Jolla folks have distinct style: even a mail carrier looks like her short skirt and airy blouse are tailor-made. The **main shopping areas** are Prospect Street and Girard Avenue. Shopping in La Jolla is not as intimidating as it used to be. A few resale designer stores have crept in next to the snooty Armani and Ralph Lauren boutiques. The dress code in La Jolla is decidedly different than in all other parts of San Diego. "Expensive-casual" is the style here—Cole-Haan sandals rather than drugstore flip-flops, for one. If you don't already own this type of wardrobe there are plenty of shops to suit you up in style.

Local cookies from Girard Gourmet.

If all the shopping wears you out, stop at the **Whaling Bar** in the beautiful La Valencia Hotel on Prospect for a cooling martini, and reflect on the fact that such movie greats as Greta Garbo, Mary Pickford, and Douglas Fairbanks were here before you. You'll get spectacular views from the patio. There are also several pleasant cafes nearby, including **Girard Gourmet** at 7837 Girard Avenue.

The **San Diego Museum of Contemporary Art** (700 Prospect Street; 619-454-3541) on Prospect Avenue is starkly elegant, with enormous windows that face the ocean. Modern and contemporary art is on display, including the very cutting edge of what's in right now—painting, sculptures, prints, drawings, videos, installations, and design. A few miles away on the on the UCSD campus is the highly regarded **La Jolla Playhouse** (2910 La Jolla Village Drive; 619-550-1010), founded in 1947 by Gregory Peck and Dorothy McGuire.

■ La Jolla Beaches and Beach Walks

La Jolla Shores Beach–Kellogg Park
A mile-and-a-half north of downtown La Jolla is La Jolla Shores, where grassy lawns, palm trees, and picnic tables front a wide, sandy beach. Launch a kayak, swim, or dive. Native American artifacts have been uncovered by divers at the north end of the park, but remember: if you find anything interesting, be sure to call a ranger's attention to it. This is La Jolla's prime family beach, so it's usually very crowded in summer. If you want a sandwich to take to the beach, try the marvelous **Cheese Shop** on nearby Avenida de la Playa.

La Jolla Cliffs
Gulls, cormorants, brown pelicans, and other seabirds roost on shelves and ledges carved into seaside cliffs, which extend along the shore for several miles south of downtown. A grassy cliff-top picnic area at **Ellen Scripps Park** is very popular on summer weekends. A path and stairs lead down to **Boomer Beach,** a world-famous spot for bodysurfing (experienced surfers only!)

Pelicans watch over La Jolla Cove.

La Jolla Cove

The small beach at the cove has been popular with locals and visitors since 1960. It looks more pristine now than ever. At one time, there was a heated saltwater pool here; at another, the main attraction was a diver who doused himself with oil and set himself aflame before plunging into the sea.

The cove's clear waters and abundant sea life (protected as an underwater reserve) attract divers, snorkelers, and—some feel—way too many numbers of harbor seals. Considered by some to be the crown jewel of La Jolla beaches, it's great for sunbathing, swimming, and diving.

La Jolla Caves

The sea has carved the rocks into caves beginning east of the cove, near Goldfish Point. Once accessible only by boat, one of the seven caves can now be entered through an artificial tunnel, via the La Jolla Cave and Shell Shop; 1325 Coast Blvd. You don't have to go all the way to Acapulco to watch cliff divers brave death. If you pick the right time you can watch them in action as they fly off the cliffs above La Jolla Cove. The jumping has been going on for more than a century and it continues even though the city of San Diego banned it back in 1996, when several jumpers died. (There's a $290 fine if you get caught "flying.") The lowest of the jumps is only about 7 feet above the water of the bay, the highest is some 107 feet.

The cliff-diving area is colloquially known as **the Clam**, taking its name from the most popular jumping-off place, which is shaped roughly like a clamshell. Other jumps in the 30-foot-plus range include the Point, at 35 feet; the Washing Machine (which puts you into a turbulent pool of water); and the Bear Paw, at 37 feet. The Thread the Needle jump is also only about 35 feet high, but you have to jump through a 3 foot-wide gap to reach the water. (The Clam website says about one of those gaps: "Sections of the wall have barnacles on them. Bad, bad, bad to hit them.") The most dangerous of these jumps is called Dead Man's Cliff—for a very good reason. Not only is it 107 feet high, but you have to get a running start and jump out to avoid hitting the cliff wall itself. The water at the bottom is only 8 to 15 feet deep, depending on the tide. Despite the ban, it's questionable if the cliff-diving will stop. Several decades ago, San Diego banned nude bathing, without much success. There will probably still be jumpers on these cliffs a hundred years from now. You just have to be there at the right time to see them. For details about the jumps (and short videos), go to *www.theclam.com*.

The Coast Walk

This dirt path along the bluffs provides a panoramic view of ocean, beach, and caves. Unfortunately, the trail has been severely damaged by storms and erosion, making portions of it decidedly unsafe. *Found on Torrey Pines Rd. just east of Prospect St. or on a path adjacent to 1325 Coast Blvd.*

Children's Pool Beach was taken over by a harbor seal colony in the 1990s. The city of San Diego blocked off the beach with ropes to leave the seals undisturbed, and to make sure that human swimmers did not become ill because of the high E. coli bacteria count (seals poop onto the beach and into the water). In late summer of 2004, under pressure from residents wanting to use the beach, the city removed the ropes and declared the beach open for both seals and humans.

■ WINDANSEA BEACH *map page 323*

It's easy to see why surfers love this beach below Neptune Place. A large rock 500 feet offshore helps kick up the large surf, which dramatically adds to the already spectacular scenery. The beach supposedly was the setting for the surfer subculture mocked by Tom Wolfe in his "non-fiction" book *The Pump House Gang*. In the 1950s, beat poets like Allen Ginsberg and Lawrence Ferlinghetti read their poems at the Pour House, a popular but now defunct restaurant a few blocks up the hill on La Jolla Boulevard. Windansea surfers have a reputation for being extremely territorial and rude to newcomers. But photographers (and their subjects) love Windansea. Commonly seen here are large families having a group portrait taken, fashion shoots, and high school volleyball teams posing for the yearbook. And just as vacationing Arizonans are always found at Mission Beach, Brazilian tourists are a fixture at Windansea during the summer, and are easy to spot—just look for thong bathing suits.

Don't bodysurf unless you know how, and don't underestimate the power of the surf if you are a stranger to the ways of waves. Waders who misjudge the depth of the water and dive in head-first often suffer spinal injuries or even broken necks when they're tossed onto the beach or onto rocks, as do inexperienced bodysurfers thrown by a wave head-first into the sand. Body whomping, a crude form of bodysurfing in which a wader standing in shallow water leaps forward to catch a shore break (a wave that breaks at the water's edge), can also cause serious injuries. There

Windansea Beach is one of the most popular surfing beaches in Southern California.

are usually a lot of experienced surfers in the water who make swimming and surfing look easy, but it's not—especially in areas with complex shore breaks.

Walking north across the sea-carved boulders of Windansea will lead you to **Marine Street Beach,** a pleasant swimming and sunbathing beach with fine white sand and warm water. **Horseshoe Reef,** a bit farther north of Marine Street, is popular with surfers.

■ BIRD ROCK

One of La Jolla's southernmost beaches, Bird Rock supposedly got its name not from the large guano-covered offshore rock where cormorants and pelicans like to hang out, but from a Mr. Bird, who first developed this area in 1907. The Bird Rock Inn, built from local beach stone, once stood at the foot of Bird Rock Avenue. Charles Lindbergh enjoyed dinner here before he flew the *Spirit of St. Louis* from North Island to New York and Paris. A stairway at Bird Rock Avenue provides access to the beach below with its fascinating tide pools. This is a great place for watching the birds, the surf, and the tide pools; it's not for swimming and picnicking.

■ ARRIVING IN SAN DIEGO

San Diego has always brought out the superlatives in visiting writers. Henry James was bowled over by a surfeit of "nature and climate, fruit and flowers," and warbled that "The days have been mostly here of heavenly beauty, and the flowers, the wild flowers just now in particular, which fairly rage, with radiance, over the land, are worthy of some purer planet than this. I live on oranges and olives, fresh from the tree and I lie awake at night to listen, on purpose, to the languid list of the Pacific which my windows overhang." (A tough man, that Henry James, eating olives fresh from the tree and not puckering up.)

Kevin Starr, in *Americans and the California Dream, 1850-1915,* called San Diego the "fulfillment of the dream of California as a Mediterranean littoral."

While the Spanish-style buildings of Balboa Park, San Diego's palm-lined boulevards, and its mission-style homes have been described as representing "nostalgia for an imagined past," it is a nostalgia that works, making San Diego uncommonly attractive. Since the city borders a protected bay, it also has a long and interesting waterfront. There's enough to see here to take up an entire vacation. Highlights include the Commercial Basin, with its fleet of tuna clippers; Shelter Island, created from dredge material; La Playa, the beach where Yankee ship captains cleaned and dried the hides they acquired from California missions and ranchos; Spanish Landing Park, where the galleons supplying the presidio and mission moored; the Embarcadero, with its walking trail; the Maritime Museum, home to the old windjammer *Star of India*; and a former San Francisco Bay ferry, the *Berkeley*.

Across the bay lies the U.S. Naval Station on North Island, at the tip of the Coronado Peninsula, where naval aviation was invented in 1911 and where Charles Lindbergh took off in 1927 on the first leg of his flight to fame. Just below the base, the resort town of Coronado hugs the shore.

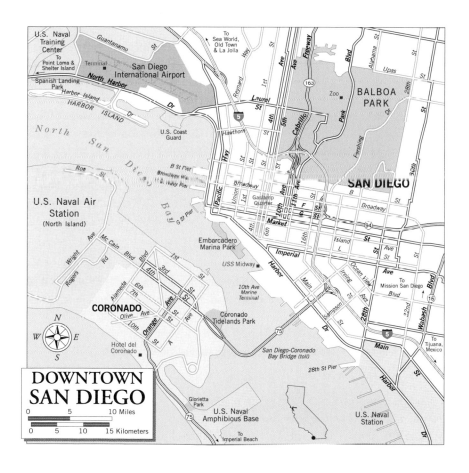

DOWNTOWN
SAN DIEGO

The Mexican border is half an hour south of San Diego, and its presence makes itself felt everywhere. Just turn on your car radio and you'll be surprised how many stations play Mexican music for a Spanish-speaking audience. Flip through the channels in your San Diego hotel room, and you'll discover several Spanish-language TV stations. As you drive through San Diego's neighborhoods, look around, and you'll find many restaurants serving Mexican food—as well as, primarily in the suburbs, shop signs entirely in Spanish. South of the border it's the other way around—you'll find many shop signs in English.

■ WHAT TO DO AND SEE IN SAN DIEGO

Balboa Park
This 1,400-acre park is one of the great urban parks of the West. It contains the San Diego Zoo and has more attractions than you can possibly enjoy in just one visit. **El Prado** has beautiful gardens and 10 museums, including the **Natural History Museum** (619-232-3821), the **San Diego Model Railroad Museum** (619-696-0199), the **Museum of Photographic Arts** (619-238-7559), the **Museum of San Diego History** (619-232-6203), and the **San Diego Museum of Art** (619-232-7931). There's also a Moreton Bay fig tree (rubber tree), 40 feet tall, with a limb spread of more than 100 feet. A replica of Shakespeare's **Old Globe Theatre** is part of a three-theater complex (619-239-2255). Many of the park's Spanish-Mediterranean–style buildings were erected for the 1915 Panama-California Exposition. *Off I-5 at Park Blvd., or by Hwy. 163, which cuts through the park.*

Balboa Park [San Diego] Zoo
This world-famous zoo, with a beautiful setting amongst hills, shrubs, and trees, has more than 4,000 exotic animals (926 species) living in as natural a habitat as possible. Note the absence of wire cages. *Balboa Park, east of downtown, off Hwy. 163; 619-234-3153.*

The affiliated 2,200-acre **Wild Animal Park** has even more wild animals living in a wild habitat. *15500 San Pasqual Rd., Escondido; 760-747-8702.*

Flamingos duck down for food at the San Diego Zoo.

One of the best shows (and jobs) at Sea World.

Old Town

San Diego was founded here in 1769, on a slope above its bay, by a Spanish expeditionary force. Buildings dating from 1821 to 1872 survive and have been beautifully preserved in a state historic park that looks and feels authentic, down to the unpaved dusty streets and plaza. Highlights include the 1820s **Casa Estudillo** and **Casa de Bandini** (a restaurant with a courtyard, and a local favorite for Mexican food); the **Casa Carrillo,** the first house built outside the presidio, which once occupied this site; the **Casa de Machado y Steward;** the 1865 **Mason Street School,** the original home of the *San Diego Union* newspaper (1868); and the **Light-Greeman House,** which dates from the 1840s (it was originally a saloon operated by a liberated slave and his friend, who were among San Diego's first black settlers).

There's ample free parking off Pacific Highway west of the railroad tracks (reached by a pedestrian underpass). *Old Town State Park headquarters, Old Town Plaza; 619-220-5422.*

Sea World

On 150 acres on the southern shores of Mission Bay, this aquarium-cum-amusement park packs in a lot of sea life, ranging in size from sea stars to orcas. There are daily shows, plus nighttime shows in summer, followed by fireworks. *On Mission Dr., off I-5 or I-8; 619-226-3901.*

Bay and Waterfront

San Diego's downtown borders an interesting waterfront, over which many of the city's better hotels look out. The West End has restaurants and galleries. Amtrak stops at the historic, Spanish-style Santa Fe Railroad Station. **The San Diego Museum of Contemporary Art** is in the American Plaza; 619-234-1001. There's also a Centre City stop of the **San Diego (Tijuana) Trolley**. Along the Embarcadero, the **B Street Pier** is an international cruise ship terminal.

On some weekends, **Navy ships** tying up at the Broadway Pier are open for visitors. If you've never clambered all over an aircraft carrier, here's your chance.

The highlight of the **Maritime Museum,** just north of the Broadway Pier, is the three-masted *Star of India*. Workshops teach visitors how to raise sails on an old-fashioned windjammer. *1306 North Harbor Dr.; 619-234-9153.*

The USS *Midway*, the nation's longest-serving aircraft carrier (1945–1997; Persian Gulf flagship in Operation Desert Storm), is now a museum—moored at the Navy Pier, North Embarcadero, on the San Diego waterfront. It has carried flight simulators, restored aircraft, a gift shop, and a cafe. *910 Harbor Drive; 619-544-9600; www.midway.org.*

Shelter Island

This man-made island holds yacht clubs, restaurants, the **Commercial Basin**, with its fleet of tuna clippers, and San Diego's oldest and most respected charter boat outfits. *H&M Landing, off Scott St.; 619-222-1144.*

Spanish Landing

Spanish ships *San Antonio* and *San Carlos* anchored here in May of 1769 and established a camp, where they greeted the overland party led by Portola (and including Father Junipero Serra). From here began the exploration of California. Later ships supplying San Diego's presidio and mission moored here. *Spanish Landing Park on N. Harbor Dr., west of Lindbergh Field.*

Mission San Diego

The first mission in California was founded on July 16, 1769, near the presidio in what is now Presidio Park in Old Town (San Diego Viejo). Five years later, the mission was moved upriver, away from the interference of presidio soldiers who preyed upon the Indians whom the padres were trying to convert. The mother mission of Alta California, San Diego's buildings were completed in 1813 only to fall into ruin as an independent Mexico withdrew its support from missions. They were rebuilt between 1915 and 1931. *Take I-8 east from I-5; go north on I-15 to Friars Rd. and take the exit going east. At the bottom of the hill turn left onto San Diego Mission Blvd. The mission is two blocks east, on the left side of the street; 619-281-8449.*

Gaslamp Quarter

This 16-block downtown district, centered at Fifth and Market, has so many old buildings that it's been designated a National Historic District. Beautifully reconstructed buildings now house restaurants, nightclubs, galleries, and shops. *Fifth and Market; pay parking lots.*

Hillcrest

This uptown neighborhood is San Diego's gay district (one local radio station called it the "Castro District of San Diego"—a nod to San Francisco's gay-culture hub). It is known for its tree-shaded streets, chic restaurants, bars, and shops. Many turn-of-the-19th-century homes have been beautifully restored. *Centered on University Avenue near Fifth and Sixth.*

■ GETTING TO SAN DIEGO'S BEACHES

It's the first hot Saturday of summer, and the San Diego beaches (and all of the roads leading to them) are packed with cars. Beach parking lots have been full since 9 A.M., and San Diegans eager to cool off in the surf circle the beach blocks, hoping for an elusive parking space. Mixed in with the locals are many cars with out-of-state license plates, mostly from Arizona (where the day's temperature is 104 degrees, with thunderstorms). Despite the 80-degree heat and the traffic, drivers don't loose their tempers. As car air conditioners overheat, drivers roll down the windows to let in the ocean breeze. It's part of the local lifestyle to be laid back—even for the Angelenos who have driven south to escape the frenzy of their megalopolis. A billboard along the Coast Highway, announcing the start of the horse-racing season at nearby Del Mar racetrack, happily proclaims: "May the horse with the coolest name win."

Mission San Diego was founded in 1769.

I had been forewarned about the gridlock by a friend: "At this time of year," he said, "you have to hit the road at 4 A.M. to avoid traffic jams."

It wasn't quite that bad. Traffic moved, albeit slowly. And who was in a hurry anyway? If you got tired of circling the same block over and over again, you could always drive south to the less crowded shores of Coronado, Silver Strand, and Imperial Beach.

■ PACIFIC BEACH *map page 323*

A boardwalk runs from Mission Beach north to **Pacific Beach** ("**PB**"), which is known, despite its somewhat sedate image, as the "party spot" of San Diego County. Most of these parties do not happen on the beach, but in beachside (or near-beach) apartments and condos, or in the bars and music clubs strung along Garnet Avenue. Crystal Pier, at the foot of Garnet Avenue, is a combination fishing and pedestrian pier and hotel; there's a good farmers market here on the weekends. Though it is known for being the only place on the coast with lodgings over the ocean (which were recently upgraded), the rooms are actually above the sandy beach (unless the tide is very high). You can't miss Crystal Pier—there's a huge arch at the entrance. Mission Boulevard is also one of the best places in Southern California to shop for bathing suits.

Enjoy a drink or a meal at a boardwalk restaurant (like the Green Flash) while observing skaters, bikers, joggers, surfers, tourists, and homeless people—they pass by on the boardwalk or sit on the concrete wall to chat with each other. The beach is wide and sandy. Keep in mind that alcohol is permitted on the beach only between noon and 8 P.M. Glass containers are not allowed.

Pacific Beach Park has a grassy picnic area, street-end access to the beach, as well as separate paved pedestrian and bicycle pathways. At Palisades Park to the north, paths lead from a grassy picnic area down to the wide sandy beach. The waves breaking onto the rocky shores of **Tourmaline Surfing Park,** below False Point, are popular with surfers (especially beginners and longboarders) and kayakers. To sign up for a surfing lesson contact the Mission Bay Aquatic Center (see page 351). There are many more splendid little beaches, most of them accessible via the dead ends of roads, between Pacific Beach and La Jolla. (See page 336 for more on La Jolla).

Tourmaline Surfing Park is a favorite beach for beginners.

■ MISSION BAY *map page 323*

Mission Bay, to the immediate east of Mission Beach, is the world's largest civic aquatic park, and borders the eastern shore of the Mission Beach peninsula. This bay is Southern California's most popular water playground. Mission Bay Park is one of those places that tries to have something for everybody: it encompasses the entire shoreline of the bay. People come here to sun on protected sandy beaches, and to water ski, snorkel, swim, sail, paddle, or dine. *(Call the Mission Bay Visitors Center for information; 619-276-8200).*

A few years ago, Mission Bay was the center of activities for the America's Cup races. But no one much wants to talk about the race anymore, perhaps because the American boat lost the cup to New Zealand.

The **Mission Bay Aquatic Center** rents Hobie cats, windsurfers, and sailboats, and offers classes in sailing, surfing, windsurfing, water skiing, and diving. *Santa Clara Point, east off Mission Boulevard in Pacific Beach; 619-488-1036.*

■ MISSION BEACH *map page 323*

Popular Mission Beach, west of Mission Bay (and Sea World), is divided into an eastern and western half by Mission Boulevard and into northern and southern sections by an amusement park called Belmont Park.

Mission (as it's locally called) is filled with an old-fashioned beach vibe: children chasing each other through the sand, sailors on leave eyeing the girls, roller-coaster riders screaming their heads off, junior high kids thronging arcades, and skate boarders weaving in and out of the crowd. **Belmont Park** has restaurants; a carousel; the Giant Dipper, a recently restored 65-year-old roller coaster; and the Plunge, a vast indoor saltwater swimming pool.

The crowds here are even livelier and more colorful than those at Pacific Beach to the north (into which Mission Beach smoothly blends). While the surf here is generally manageable; the big (and often dangerous) waves at the jetty are for experienced surfers only. Alcohol (no glass containers) is permitted on the beach from noon to 8 P.M., but is not allowed on the boardwalk, on the seawall, or in parks. As in Pacific Beach, parking near the sand can be hard to find. Come early.

Shops line the paved boardwalk running south along the beach. On a warm, sunny day this can be a very active place, with joggers, bikers, skaters, and attention seekers—a bit like Venice Beach, but imbued with that unique San Diego live-and-let-live mellowness. Watching the sometimes overt sexual antics of the local pleasure seekers makes you understand why San Diego is the adult video capital of the nation. (No, not rentals: they're *produced* in San Diego.)

■ OCEAN BEACH *map page 323*

Ocean Beach to the south is separated from Mission Beach by the mouth of the San Diego River. Just east of here is the crossing point of I-5, the major north-south highway, and I-8, a major east-west route. I-8 runs west from the interior valleys almost to the beach, funneling folks from Mission Valley and the San Diego State University campus (as well as from the Imperial Valley and Arizona).

Ocean Beach got its start in the early 1900s, as a cluster of weekend beach cabins. In the 1920s and 1930s, when San Diego began expanding toward the beach, many of these cottages were converted into year-round homes. Because they were small, they provided inexpensive housing near the beach and were popular with surfers and beach bums during the 1950s and 1960s.

This beach is surprisingly quiet and laid-back for an urban beach. It's popular with families, volleyball players, swimmers, boogie boarders, and fishermen. Even on a sunny, hot summer's day, not everyone is here to swim and sunbathe. Fishermen stand shoulder by shoulder on the **Ocean Beach fishing pier**, hoping to catch a mess of yellowtail, bonito, corbina, or surfperch for the backyard barbecue. At 2,100 feet long, this is the longest public pier on the West Coast. Other visitors just walk onto the pier to catch a whiff of the cooling ocean breeze; stroll along the palm-shaded boulevards; or browse in the eclectic antique shops of Newport Avenue, a block north of the pier (which has no parking meters!). Alternately, they while away the afternoon at the **O.B. Pier Cafe**, a funky coffeehouse on the pier, or the **Sunshine Company Saloon** (5028 Newport Avenue), or revitalize their systems with a burger from **Hodad's** (5010 Sunset Avenue). A sign reflects the local spirit: "No shirt, no shoes, no problem."

Some of the nearby beach towns have gone upscale only in recent years, as waterfront property anywhere in the West has skyrocketed in value. Ocean Beach is a good example, but it has kept its populist atmosphere and is still funky—and very popular. The Ocean Beach vibe—a mix of reggae, hippie style, and second-hand antique shops—is unique to this part of town. It looks and feels more like Eugene, Oregon, than Southern California (if you take away the palm trees). Locals hang out at a great bar called **Pacific Shores** on Newport Avenue.

Winston's Beach Club, just off Newport Avenue on Bacon Street, books reggae and local bands nightly.

There are more interesting restaurants in Ocean Beach than you can possibly sample in one visit. **Nati's,** the most popular breakfast place is, fittingly, on Bacon Street. In contrast to the shimmering newness of most San Diego neighborhoods, Newport Avenue is a throwback to the era of small towns and Main Streets, with an old-fashioned movie theater, diners, family-run businesses, and faded signs and storefronts.

Every Wednesday from 4–7 P.M. (till 8 in spring and summer) a farmers market is held in the 4900 block of Newport Avenue. This is a great place for checking out the tasty and uncommon produce of San Diego's backcountry, from apples and cherimoyas to macadamia nuts and piñon pine nuts.

Ocean Beach Park, north of the pier, has a sandy beach interspersed with rocky outcroppings and tide pools. It is a prime surfing beach where the famed Hawaiian surfer Duke Kahanamoku gave surfing exhibitions back in 1916. Expect the hardcore surfers to yell at the mere swimmers (or "speed bumps") to get out of the way, but it's all good-natured fun—even if surfing and volleyball seem at times more a vocation than a vacation.

If the surf looks right, rent a surfboard at the South Coast Surf Shop and give it a try. If the waves are low, surfing can be relatively easy—but beginners should not attempt waves that are more than knee high. Doug Werner, in his excellent book, *Surfer's Start-up: A Beginner's Guide To Surfing,* has some very good advice for novice surfers. It's a good book to read *before* you head for a surf shop.

Dog Beach, at the north end of the park, is the only beach in the city of San Diego where dogs are allowed to run free during the day. (Coronado and Del Mar also have designated dog beaches.)

Ocean Beach City Park, south of the pier, has a rocky shore with pocket beaches and tide pools; it's accessible by stairs from Santa Cruz, Bermuda, Orchard, and Narragansett avenues.

■ SUNSET CLIFFS PARK *map page 323*

Sunset Cliffs Park, along Sunset Cliffs Boulevard, is about as wild as a city park can get. Rough trails lead down rather unstable cliffs to secluded sand or cobble pocket beaches. Many of these trails start at a parking area at the end of Cornish Drive. Beware: both the cliffs and trails are heavily eroded and can be quite dangerous.

Chances are you'll decide the spectacular scenery is worth the risk, however. This cliff area with small pocket beaches area is more popular for surfing and for its scenic beauty than for its beaches, and it's a great spot for watching sunsets. Be careful when you take trails along the cliffs, however: the soft rocks are very unstable.

Sunset Cliffs is considered one of the three or four best surfing beaches in San Diego. Although the water is cooler here than in La Jolla and points north, the surf in winter is especially good. Large, flat rocks, strewn over a narrow strip of sand, extend far out into the water. The kelp beds offshore are responsible for the distinctive smell of seaweed onshore. There are fine tide pools here and great diving (for more experienced divers).

■ POINT LOMA *map page 323*

On a clear day, the view from Point Loma is spectacular. You can look all the way south to Tijuana, Mexico, and may even discern the Coronado Islands a few miles offshore, just south of the border. You can look east to San Diego, with its bayside waterfront, and see two airfields from Point Loma: the Naval Air Station on North Island, at the head of the Coronado Peninsula; and Lindbergh Field near the bay's shore.

From Sunset Cliffs Boulevard, a left (east) turn on Hill, and right (south) turn on Catalina will take you to Point Loma. Eighty-one acres of the Point Loma Peninsula are set aside as the **Cabrillo National Monument.** The 1854 lighthouse at the tip of Point Loma has an interpretive center with a great bookstore, views from lookout points above the cliffs, nature walks, and tide pools. Curiously, no direct arterial route leads to this monument, one of the most popular in the nation. Note that Point Loma Boulevard does not take you directly to Point Loma, but rather to Ocean Beach. However, a left on Nimitz and a right on Catalina will take you all the way to the Point Loma Lighthouse.

En route to the monument, you'll pass the somber grave markers of **Fort Rosecrans National Cemetery**. You can't miss the lighthouse and Cabrillo National Monument. They're at the very end of the road. The **whale overlook** is a great place to observe California gray whales as they pass by on their way from the Bering Sea to Baja. *At the southern end of Catalina Blvd., reached from downtown and I-5 via Rosecrans and Canon sts. and Catalina Blvd.; 619-557-5450.*

■ ■ ■

Lover's Leap at Point Loma, 1905.

The monument (where you must park and from which you walk to Point Loma) charges a parking and admission fee, and closes at sunset in summer and at 5:15 during the rest of the year. The **Old Point Loma Lighthouse** was built in 1854 with sandstone and bricks shipped south from Monterey. From its perch on the rocky spine of the peninsula, 462 feet above the ocean, you have a clear view, because the native vegetation of the point, coastal scrub, does not grow very tall. This lighthouse has been out of commission (and a major visitor attraction) since 1891, when the Point Loma Lighthouse farther down the slope replaced it; fog had often obscured the beam of the higher light.

Below the lighthouse is a **visitors center** with an excellent bookstore. The 1.5-mile **Bayside Trail,** which runs through the scrub along the eastern slope of the point, passes abandoned World War II gun emplacements and is a great place for watching local sea birds, hawks, herons, and pelicans. During a visit in the summer of 2004, I discovered for the first time that the point was heavily fortified during the last two World Wars. The slopes are still dotted with concrete bunkers, a few of which are open to the public. One showed videos of how disappearing guns—which recoiled from the enemy's view, thanks to the camouflaged steel-and-concrete parapets they were mounted on after being fired—were loaded and fired. More fascinating still is the fact that this former fortification has become obsolete in an era of high-tech coastal defense. I got a glimpse of the new-style defense at an overlook on the other side of the hill, where I identified several navy ships steaming into port with the help of a fleet identification chart I bought in the park gift shop. A destroyer turned out to be DD 992 *Fletcher*, but I could identify a big submarine only as a *Los Angeles*–class attack sub. As I looked at the chart, then at the ships, I noticed that I attracted some curious glances from folk with a military bearing. I'm glad, I now think, that my digital camera ran out of juice or I might have been tempted to take photos of the ships—at the risk of being detained by Homeland Security as a suspicious character.

Above me, black-chinned hummingbirds buzzed around the flowers on a tall agave flowering stalk, accompanying feedings with bell-like calls; an Abert's towhee scurried through the scrub, oblivious to the saber rattling at the foot of the hill. The **Point Loma Ecological Reserve,** on the southwest shore of the monument, has great tide pools with sea snails, sea stars, green sea anemones, giant keyhole limpets and, in deeper water, abalone and spiny lobsters. If you're lucky, you'll come across a sea hare, a shockingly large marine slug that may grow to a length of 15 inches.

Just offshore is one of the largest kelp beds in California. Vast as they are, these kelp beds were almost destroyed between 1947 and the 1960s by herds of voracious

Beach attire at the Hotel del Coronado today.

sea urchins. Urchin populations had once fallen and risen with the supply of kelp but the urchins, scientists learned, were subsisting on sewage effluents, giving the kelp no chance to regenerate between attacks. All sorts of measures were tried to cut back on the urchin population. But when divers learned that Asian gourmets paid high prices for sea urchins, the spiny creatures were in trouble. Within a few years their status went from oversupply to overharvested. The kelp took advantage of the respite, and vast kelp beds once again sway in offshore waters.

■ CORONADO PENINSULA

Geologically speaking, the Coronado Peninsula is part of Mexico, since it was formed by sand carried to sea by the Tijuana River and washed north by ocean currents. Originally, the tip of the peninsula consisted of two sandy islands connected by marshes, but they, like many of the San Diego Bay marshes, have long been filled in.

Even though Coronado is connected to San Diego Bay by a narrow sand spit that runs south to Imperial Beach, it is for all practical purposes an island, and it acts like one. The northern tip (technically known as "North Island") has a naval air station, while the southern part has fancy resorts, restaurants, and splendid beaches.

CA 75 crosses San Diego Bay from I-5 near downtown San Diego to Coronado, runs south over the spit to Imperial Beach, and turns back to I-5, allowing for a leisurely loop trip. You can reach the Coronado Peninsula via the 2.3-mile Coronado–San Diego Bay Bridge, or you can take the passenger-bicycle ferry, which departs from the foot of the Broadway Pier in San Diego every hour on the hour, and leaves Coronado on the half-hour; *619-234-4111; fee parking at the Broadway Pier.*

■ WHAT TO DO AND SEE IN CORONADO *map page 343*

Hotel del Coronado
A vast, turreted Victorian complex built of wood, Hotel del Coronado dominates the Coronado oceanfront. It looks like a big, white wedding cake. While the hotel has maintained its standards of excellence and is as popular now with visitors as it was back in 1888, when it first opened, friends who spend a lot of time in Coronado prefer to stay at the Meridien and visit the Coronado for drinks and atmosphere.

Town of Coronado
This is a pleasant, albeit pricey, beach town with the usual shops and restaurants, and several excellent beaches.

Coronado Beaches

The peninsula holds two very popular beaches: **City Beach,** which runs north from the hotel to the naval air station, and **Coronado Shores Beach** which runs south to Silver Strand State Beach. The water here may reach 70 degrees by late summer, and the sand holds pismo clams (which are eagerly sought after by local as well as visiting clam diggers).

North Beach can be a good place for summer surf, since it's the only south-facing beach. There's also great bodysurfing here and it's rarely crowded. Navy Seals train on Coronado, just north of Silver Strand State Beach. Head for RRR's Cafe to stock up on picnic supplies.

These sandy beaches are frequented by an upscale crowd of vacationers and local families, who spread their beach blankets out early in the morning and stay all day. In January and February, with luck, you may see migrating whales pass by (gray whales often root for crustaceans and mollusks in the surf).

Coronado Beach Historical Museum

The museum provides background information and sells an excellent self-guided tour booklet; *1126 Loma Ave., 619-435-7242.*

■ SILVER STRAND STATE BEACH *map page 323*

The long and narrow sandy spit that runs from Coronado south to Imperial Beach has access to both the ocean beach and the bay, and is as narrow as half a city block in places. The beach is popular for swimming, clamming, catching grunion, surf fishing, and combing the high-tide line for shells. (There are a multitude to be found here, including some unusual ones not found farther north.) The bay-side beaches are in the wind shadow of the dunes and the highway, making them warmer; they can be reached from the parking lots via pedestrian tunnels running beneath the road.

A bike path runs along the bay side of the peninsula for almost 10 miles. Bicyclists, hikers, and inline skaters use it. The surf is rarely high, which makes for great ocean swimming.

Silver Strand Beach is bordered on the north and south ends by Navy property and is patrolled by Navy military police. They appear to be more lax in enforcement than the state park rangers, since the far northern section of Silver Strand, near the Navy's Amphibious Base, is popular with nude sunbathers. *619-435-5184.*

A family on the way to San Diego on the ferry from Coronado.

■ IMPERIAL BEACH *map page 323*

Imperial Beach, which likes to call itself an all-American city, was founded by promoters who wanted to attract vacationing farmers from California's Imperial Valley. Today it's a very pleasant and relatively low-cost beach town with a splendid sandy strand (which was widened a few years back by dredge spoils from San Diego Bay). The beach is popular with surfers and swimmers but is not always safe, because of dangerous currents and riptides. Another danger is less visible: effluent from the Tijuana River to the south—"a green ribbon of sludge," as a writer for a San Diego newspaper described it, "which is carried north by ocean currents."

Imperial Beach can get quite crowded during hot summer days. Dunes Park, along Seacoast Avenue near the pier, has shaded picnic tables, a playground and restrooms. The annual U.S. Open Sand Castle Competition in July draws competitors from around the nation.

A sewage treatment plant is being planned for the U.S. side of the border. In the meantime, an odoriferous cloud continues to hang above the estuary. The Tijuana sewage doesn't deter birds and other wildlife, however, making the **Tijuana River National Estuarine Reserve,** south of Imperial Beach, uncommonly rich in species. Who knows for how long the treatment plants will remain one step behind the flush of the growing population? But for now, the birds (and the phytoplankton, algae, insects, crustaceans, fish) who live in the marsh are thriving. One-quarter of California's endangered lightfooted clapper rail population hangs out in the marsh's tules. Harriers are common. You'll occasionally encounter black skimmers, reddish egrets, and peregrine falcons. There's an excellent visitors center whose rangers give guided tours of the marsh. *301 Caspian Way; 619-575-3613.*

"America really begins at Imperial Beach," one writer stated. Border Field State Park to the south is a no-man's-land abutting the Mexican border fence, where *La Migra* (U.S. Border Patrol) rounds up illegal Mexican immigrants. Curiously, Border Field is the only beach south of San Luis Obispo County where horseback riding is legal. Go, by all means, if you feel an urge to visit the southwesternmost point in the continental United States.

Mexico: Sixteen miles south of San Diego, I-5 ends at the Mexican border, just north of Tijuana. The border crossing is open 24 hours a day. For a short visit, a passport is not necessary, but it's not a bad idea to bring one anyway. Highway 1, a toll road, will take you south to Ensenada's beaches and restaurants, hotels and condos, and eventually down the length of the Baja California peninsula, to the resort of Cabo San Lucas.

■ TRAVEL BASICS

Getting There

Between Oceanside and La Jolla, old U.S. 101 is a four-lane highway whose narrow lanes wind along bluffs. It opens to a boulevard between Pacific Beach and Point Loma. From Coronado, a four-lane highway runs south along Silver Strand Beach to Imperial Beach and the U.S. border with Mexico. **Rental car companies** warn about driving in San Diego because of the high rate of auto theft. Few such companies allow their cars across the Mexican border.

Climate

This stretch of coastline boasts the most equable climate in the United States. Temperatures hardly vary from the 70s in the summer and the 60s in the winter. Annual rainfall is less than 10 inches, usually falling in a handful of winter storms, or the odd summer monsoon thunderstorm, when moisture from the southwest makes its way as far west as San Diego—a rare event and unique to this part of the California coastline. **Water temperature** is in the upper 50s and 60s year-round, occasionally reaching the low 70s.

Food and Lodging

You'll find good, fresh food in San Diego County and a great deal of excellent Mexican cuisine. Strawberries ripen to perfection in the coastal valleys, and apples in the nearby mountains, as do avocados (which you can buy ripe from farmers markets), cherimoyas, lemons, limes (which taste better here than almost anywhere else), macadamia nuts (grown to perfection in the foothills east of San Luis Rey), tree-ripened oranges, and pine nuts collected from piñons growing on the desert side of the mountains. There's even a limited supply of local wine.

The ocean produces great variety of fish and shellfish, including some warm-water fish like yellowtail, bream, tuna, marlin, and swordfish. The spiny lobsters from near-shore water are particularly fine (especially if you can enjoy them grilled and swathed in olive oil, garlic, and chile sauce).

As for lodging, there are many fine hotels and resorts in this area as well as inexpensive beach motels. **Lodging and restaurant listings** by town in alphabetical order begin on page 362.

LODGING & RESTAURANTS

LODGING RATES
Per night, one room, double occupancy
$ = under $80 $$ = $80–130 $$$ = $130–200 $$$$ = over $200

RESTAURANT PRICES
Average dinner entree
$ = under $10 $$ = $10–17 $$$ = $17–25 $$$$ = over $25

ALBION *map page 107*

✕⊞ **Albion River Inn.** 3790 CA 1; 707-937-1919 or 800-479-7944 **$$$**
One of the finest inns on the Northern California coast. Ocean views from New England–style cliff-top cottages, with fireplaces and decks. Spa, gardens. Full breakfast and dinner; straightforward cuisine but nicely done.

APTOS *map page 187*

✕ **Cafe Sparrow.** 8042 Soquel Dr.; 831-688-6238 **$$**
French country cooking at its best, in comfortable, intimate quarters decorated with lots of flowers. Excellent wine list.

ARCATA *map page 141*

⊞ **Hotel Arcata.** 708 Ninth St.; 707-826-0217 **$**
This 1915 downtown hotel was once the town plaza's showcase, then fell on hard times, and has recently been restored. It feels comfortably old; were it not for the sushi restaurant in-house, you might feel you've stepped back in time.

✕ **Abruzzi.** 791 Eighth St. (Arcata Plaza); 707-826-2345 **$$**
Delectable, garlicky Italian food, prepared with gusto, arranged beautifully, and served with a smile.

AVILA BEACH *map page 223*

✕⊞ **Sycamore Mineral Springs Resort.** 1215 Avila Beach Dr., San Luis Obispo (Avila Beach); 805-595-7302 or 800-234-5831; www.sycamoresprings. com. **$$$-$$$$**

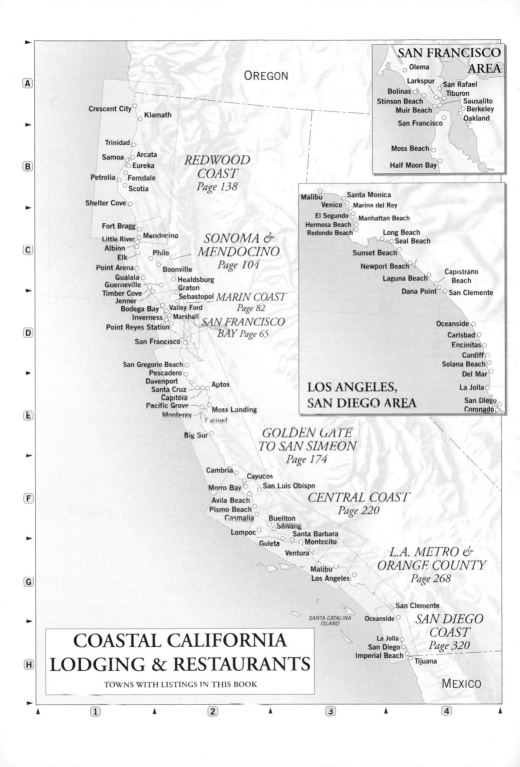

COASTAL CALIFORNIA
LODGING & RESTAURANTS

TOWNS WITH LISTINGS IN THIS BOOK

OREGON

SAN FRANCISCO AREA

Olema
Larkspurg
San Rafael
Bolinas
Tiburon
Stinson Beach
Sausalito
Muir Beach
Berkeley
Oakland
San Francisco

Moss Beach

Half Moon Bay

Crescent City
Klamath

Trinidad
Samoa
Arcata
Eureka
Petrolia
Ferndale
Scotia

Shelter Cove

REDWOOD COAST
Page 138

Malibu
Santa Monica
Venice
Marina del Rey
El Segundo
Manhattan Beach
Hermosa Beach
Redondo Beach
Long Beach
Seal Beach

Sunset Beach

Newport Beach
Capistrano Beach
Laguna Beach
Dana Point
San Clemente

Fort Bragg
Little River
Mendocino
Albion
Philo
Elk
Point Arena
Boonville
Gualala
Healdsburg
Guerneville
Graton
Timber Cove
Sebastopol
Jenner
MARIN COAST
Page 82
Bodega Bay
Valley Ford
Inverness
Marshall
SAN FRANCISCO
Point Reyes Station
BAY Page 65

San Francisco

SONOMA &
MENDOCINO
Page 104

Oceanside
Carlsbad
Encinitas
Cardiff
Solana Beach
Del Mar
La Jolla
San Diego
Coronado

**LOS ANGELES,
SAN DIEGO AREA**

San Gregorio Beach
Pescadero
Davenport
Santa Cruz
Aptos
Capitola
Pacific Grove
Monterey
Moss Landing
Carmel

Big Sur

*GOLDEN GATE
TO SAN SIMEON*
Page 174

Cambria
Cayucos
Morro Bay
San Luis Obispo
Avila Beach
Pismo Beach
Casmalia
Buellton
Solvang
Lompoc
Santa Barbara
Goleta
Montecito
Ventura

CENTRAL COAST
Page 220

Malibu
Los Angeles

L.A. METRO &
ORANGE COUNTY
Page 268

SANTA CATALINA ISLAND

San Clemente
Oceanside

*SAN DIEGO
COAST*
Page 320

La Jolla
San Diego
Imperial Beach
Tijuana

MEXICO

In the woods above a creek, this is truly one of the great resorts on the coast. Parts date to the 1800s, while other parts are new, but they blend seamlessly with the help of beautiful gardens. The resort has full spa treatments, massages, and hot tubs in the woods and in each room. Accommodations range from plain to very comfortable to luxurious. The Gardens of Avila restaurant, tucked into a wooded hillside, serves flavorful spa food.

✕ **Olde Port Inn.** Port San Luis Pier 3; 805-595-2515 **$$$**
The best fresh fish around, excellent local wine list. Fine views of fishing boats bobbing in the lee of the rocky headlands.

BERKELEY *map page 65*
✕ **Chez Panisse.** 1517 Shattuck Ave.; 510-548-5525 Downstairs: **$$$$** Cafe: **$$**
Chef Alice Waters and the kitchen staff at this renovated Craftsman-style home are California cuisine legends. Downstairs, they do a pre-set, prix fixe dinner; call ahead to find out what's being served on which night, and to reserve a space. Upstairs you get salads, risottos, pizzas, and other lighter fare.

BIG SUR *map page 177*
✕☷ **Ventana Country Inn Resort.** CA 1, 2.5 miles south of Pfeiffer–Big Sur State Park; 831-667-2331 **$$$$**
An upscale, modern, weathered-cedar resort with Swedish-style rooms—lots of glass to enable views of the ocean, 1,200 feet below. Cielo, the inn's restaurant, dishes up seafood and salads prepared with a Mediterranean touch.

✕ **Nepenthe.** CA 1, 4 miles south of Pfeiffer–Big Sur State Park; 831-667-2345 **$$**
A relaxing place with great food and super service. Henry Miller and Jack Kerouac ate here. The view down the coast alone is worth a visit. Downstairs, Cafe Kevah (831-667-2331), has less expensive food and an oceanview deck, but it's closed in the off-season.

BODEGA BAY *map page 107*
☷ **Inn at the Tides.** 800 CA 1; 707-875-2751 or 800-541-7788 **$$$**
Wood-shingled cottages on a hillside overlooking the Bodega Head bay and the ocean.

✕ **Lucas Wharf.** 595 CA 1, Bodega Bay; 707-875-3522 (restaurant); 707-875-3562 (deli) **$-$$**
Fresh seafood, a deli that sells great fish 'n' chips, and a fish market to let you buy the stuff raw and fresh.

BOLINAS *map page 85*
✕ **Smiley's Schooner Saloon.** 41 Wharf Rd.; 415-868-1311 **$**
Considered the oldest continually operating saloon in the country.

CAMBRIA *map page 223*
▥ **Cambria Sea Otter Inn.** 6656 Moonstone Beach Dr.; 805-927-5888 **$$**
A comfortable inn with gas fireplaces in all rooms.
✕ **Sow's Ear.** 2248 Main St.; 805-927-4865 **$-$$**
Regional American cuisine is given a Central Coast lift with fresh local shellfish, produce, and cheeses. Divine chicken-and-dumplings, plus upmarket dishes like salmon in parchment.

CAPISTRANO BEACH *map page 271*
✕ **Olamendi's Mexican Cuisine.** 34660 PCH; 949-661-1005 **$$**
Very popular place, with great burritos.

CAPITOLA *map page 177*
▥ **Capitola Venetian Hotel.** 1500 Wharf Rd.; 831-476-6471; www.capitolavenetian.com **$$$**
A funky 1920s hotel plus an adjacent condo complex—the first of its kind in the state (and brought fully up to date). Make reservations several months ahead of time in summer and for off-season weekends.
▥ **The Inn at Depot Hill.** 250 Monterey Ave.; 831-462-3376 **$$$**
A former railroad station that's now a lavish inn. All rooms have fireplaces; many have hot tubs. Excellent breakfasts.
✕ **Gayle's Bakery and Rosticceria.** 504 Bay Ave.; 831-462-1200 **$**
You'll have to wait in line for this extremely popular place's sandwiches, salads, pastas, and stews—but they are worth it.

CARDIFF-BY-THE-SEA *map page 323*
✕ **Beach House.** 2530 S. U.S. 101; 760-753-1321 **$$$**
Posh seafood restaurant close to the beach, with valet parking. The seafood is fresh and well-prepared; the views are great.

CARLSBAD *map page 323*
▥ **Carlsbad Beach Terrace Inn.** 2775 Ocean St.; 760-729-5951 **$$$**
A popular motel across the highway from the beach. Some rooms have a beach view.

⛝ **Carlsbad Inn Beach Resort.** 3075 Carlsbad Blvd.; 760-434-7020 **$$$**
Old World–style hotel set on a wide landscaped lawn in the center of town.
✕ **Harbor Fish South.** 3179 Carlsbad Ave.; 760-729-4161 **$**
An outdoor patio where you can eat fried fish and shellfish and hamburgers.
✕ **Neiman's.** 300 Carlsbad Village Dr.; 760-729-4131 **$$$**
In the oldest Victorian structure in town. This place is rather formal (proper attire required). **Niemans' Seagrill** is less formal.
✕ **Pelly's Fish Market.** 7110 Avenida Encinas; 760-431-8454 **$**
Great seafood chowder and grilled fish.

CARMEL *map page 177*
⛝ **Cypress Inn.** Lincoln and Seventh sts.; 831-624-3871 **$$$**
A local landmark for decades. At one time partly owned by Doris Day, this Moorish-style inn has a spacious lobby, large marble bathrooms, and 34 cozy guest rooms.
✕⛝ **Los Laureles Lodge and Restaurant.** 313 West Carmel Valley Rd.;
831-659-2233 or 800-533-4404 **$$-$$$**
This former horse ranch about 10 miles up the valley from CA 1 has been reincarnated as a comfortable country inn. The restaurant is in the 1890 ranch house; some of the guest rooms occupy former stables. Large swimming pool, terraced garden.
⛝ **Sandpiper Inn.** 2408 Bayview Ave.; 831-624-6433 **$$-$$$**
A block from the beach, this 1920s Prairie-style inn has large, airy rooms with skylights, fireplaces, and sea views. The gardens are filled with rhododendrons and azaleas.
✕ **Casanova.** Fifth Ave., bet. Mission and San Carlos sts.; 831-625-0501 **$$$**
This romantic, family-run restaurant serves Italian and Continental classics: rich pastas, grilled salmon, rack of lamb, and veal Provençal.
✕ **Rocky Point Restaurant.** (10 miles south of Carmel on CA 1); 831-624-2933;
www.rocky-point.com **$$-$$$**
A clifftop restaurant with large portions of straightforward but tasty American food. The view's gorgeous; you can watch sea lions, sea otters, and dolphins splash in the surf while you eat.

CASMALIA *map page 223*
✕ **The Hitching Post.** 3325 Point Sal Rd.; 805-937-6151 **$$-$$$**
Run by the same family for half a century. Think choice, aged beef cooked slowly over live-oak coals. Meats here are grilled on an indoor oak wood barbecue grill. There's also chicken, quail, and fish.

CATALINA *map page 271*

⊞ **Inn on Mount Ada.** Avalon; 398 Wrigley Terrace Rd.; 310-510-2030 **$$$$**
This intimate, lavish hotel occupies the old Wrigley mansion. The 6 guest rooms
have ocean views; all meals are included.

✕ **Avalon Seafood.** On the pier; 310-510-0197 **$**
Don't miss fish 'n' chips at this quaint spot. You can buy bait here, too.

✕ **Cafe Prego.** 603 Crescent Ave.; 310-510-1218 **$$**
Feast on sumptuous pastas and Italian seafood dishes by candlelight, or come for a
satisfying Sunday brunch.

CAYUCOS *map page 223*

⊞ **Beachwalker Inn.** 501 S. Ocean Ave.; 805-995-2133 **$$**
A plain motel within walking distance of the beach. Try to get in during the height
of the summer beach season. The beach, of course, is spectacular.

✕ **Sea Shanty.** 296 S. Ocean Ave.; 805-995-3272 **$**
A small restaurant serving fresh fish.

CORONADO *map page 323 or 343*

✕⊞ **Hotel Del Coronado.** 1500 Orange Ave., Coronado; 619-435-6611 **$$$$**
This ritzy old Victorian hotel is a relic that somehow works. There are two giant
outdoor pools, six tennis courts, a croquet green, fancy shops, and two formal dining rooms dishing up a variety of food, from the opulent to the dietetic.

✕ **Peohe's.** 1201 First St., Coronado; 619-437-4474 **$$-$$$**
Restaurants with tropical themes seem a bit odd in most places, but here the décor
fits (and works) quite well. The views of San Diego Harbor are spectacular—as
you'd expect from a restaurant located on the ferry plaza.

CRESCENT CITY *map page 141*

⊞ **Crescent Beach Motel.** 1455 U.S. 101, 2 miles south of town; 707-464-5436 **$**
Crescent City has no fancy hotels, B&Bs, or restaurants. This oceanview motel is
your best option, as is the Beachcomber restaurant next door (707-464-2205 **$$**)
Make reservations! In summer, Crescent City motels fill up fast.

✕ **Chart Room.** 130 Anchor Way, Crescent City; 707-464-5993 **$-$$**
Locals and visitors dine family-style at the long tables of this old-fashioned restau-
rant at the end of a busy wharf. The large dining room overlooks the boat basin;
it's a great place for watching fishing boats and sea gulls.

DANA POINT *map page 271*
✕ **Jon's Fish Market.** 34665 Golden Lantern St.; 949-496-2807 **$**
This moderately priced seafood market and eatery is the most popular place in the harbor. Outdoor dining near the boat slips.

DAVENPORT *map page 177*
✕ **Whale City Bakery & Grill.** 490 CA 1; 831-423-9803 **$**
Burgers, ice cream, and other plain fare in a pleasant setting.

DEL MAR *map page 323*
▤ **L'Auberge Del Mar.** 1540 Camino del Mar; 619-259-1515 **$$$$**
A posh, European-style hotel on beautifully landscaped grounds.
✕ **Fish Market.** 640 Via de la Valle; 619-755-2277 **$$**
Unpretentious place with well-prepared fresh seafood, very popular with locals.
✕ **Kirby's Cafe.** 215 15th St.; 619-481-1001 **$**
Eating popovers on the patio at Kirby's has to be one of the best ways to start the day in Del Mar. The food is surprisingly imaginative. Lunch only.

EL SEGUNDO *map page 271*
✕ **Panama's Bar and Grill.** 221 Richmond St.; 310-322-5829 **$**
A popular, low-key local hangout and blues bar (live music Thursdays through Sundays; no cover). They serve standard bar food.

ELK *map page 107*
✕▤ **Greenwood Pier Inn.** 5928 CA 1; 707-877-9997 **$$$**
On a lawn high above rocky, secluded beaches, this inn includes a main house and small cottages equipped with private baths, fireplaces, skylights, and water views. There are gardens, a country store, and a garden shop onsite (707-877-3440). Breads, desserts, and pastries are baked on the premises; most herbs used in cooking come from the garden. Open seasonally.
✕▤ **Harbor House.** 5600 CA 1; 707-877-3203 **$$$-$$$$**
This inn, beautifully and completely crafted from redwood, was built as a lumber executive's residence in 1916 and overlooks a private beach.

ENCINITAS *map page 323*
▤ **Moonlight Beach Motel.** 233 Second St.; 760-753-0623 **$**
A comfortably upgraded motel with balcony views of the beach.

✕ **Ki's Restaurant & Juice Bar.** 2591 U.S. 101; 760-436-5236 $
Catering mostly to a health-conscious crowd, Ki's has built a statewide reputation
for its smoothies.

✕ **Roxy Restaurant & Ice Cream.** 517 N. U.S. 101; 760-436-5001 $
A vegetarian favorite for decades. Hearty baked casseroles, interesting salads, pastas,
and pizzas, plus some fish and chicken and the celebrated Niederfrank's ice cream.

EUREKA *map page 141*

✕⊡ **Cafe Waterfront.** First and F sts.; 707-443-9190; www.cafewaterfront.com $$
This nicely appointed restaurant overlooking Humboldt Bay occupies a historic
building (once a waterfront saloon and brothel). Today this local hangout serves
pasta, fresh local fish and shellfish, and a standard assortment of (nicely prepared)
chicken and meat. Sunday brunch with live jazz.

Upstairs, you can rent a restored Victorian apartment (the former brothel). It
has a full kitchen, antique furniture, soaking tubs, and splendid views from every
window. It won the Governor's Award for Excellent Design back in 1993.

✕ **Lost Coast Brewery & Cafe.** 617 Fourth St.; 707-445-4480 $
A friendly local hangout with good beer and simple but tasty food.

✕ **Sea Grill.** 316 E St.; 707-443-7187 $$
An old-town eatery serving fresh fish prepared multiple ways. Lunch during week,
dinner every day but Sunday.

FERNDALE *map page 141*

⊡ **The Gingerbread Mansion.** 400 Berding St.; 707-786-4000 $$$-$$$$
About as fancy and elaborate as a Victorian can get. All rooms have private baths.
Splendid breakfast in formal dining room overlooking the gardens.

✕ **Curley's Grill.** 400 Ocean Ave.; 707-786-9696; www.humboldtdining.com/
curleys $-$$
Since its inception in the mid-1990s, this storefront restaurant has turned into one
of Ferndale's favorite dining spots. The food is basic—sandwiches, cheeseburgers,
pastas, fresh seafood, and New York steaks—but good.

FORT BRAGG *map page 107 (or 141)*

⊡ **Beachcomber Motel.** 1111 N. Main St.; 707-964-2402 *or* 800-400-SURF;
www.thebeachcombermotel.com $$-$$$
A very pleasant modern motel with views of the ocean from most rooms, and with
easy access to the Old Haul Road trails to McKerricher State Park and the coastal
bluffs and beaches. Within walking distance of downtown Fort Bragg.

⛫ **Cleone Garden Inn.** 24600 N. CA 1; 707-964-2788 **$$**
A beautifully maintained place that was originally a motel, but which has evolved into a comfortable inn.

⛫ **Noyo River Lodge.** 500 Casa del Noyo; 707-964-8045 **$$**
Think fireplaces, soaking tubs, private decks, sumptuous breakfasts, antique furnishings, landscaped gardens and paths. From here it's an easy walk to Noyo Harbor, the fishing docks, party boats, and restaurants.

✕ **North Coast Brewing Company.** 455 N. Main St.; 707-964-3400 **$$**
The twist here is the drink: servers match good food (seafood, fresh pasta, chili, regional specialties like beer-batter red snapper, fish 'n' chips) with brews.

✕ **The Restaurant.** 418 N. Main St.; 707-964-9800 **$$**
This storefront restaurant is one of Fort Bragg's culinary treasures: all the food (except the bread) is prepared from scratch on the premises. It's seasonal and delicious, in the best California style, and exceedingly popular with locals. Call ahead; hours are quirky.

✕ **The Wharf Restaurant.** On N. Harbor Dr. in Noyo Harbor; 707-964-4283 **$-$$**
This local hangout overlooking the harbor (with a glimpse of the ocean beyond the bluffs) serves very fresh fish cooked with just the right touch and sauced very lightly. The place has barely changed since it opened 40 years ago—except it's a lot less smoky.

GOLETA *map page 223*
✕ **Beachside Bar Cafe.** 5905 Sand Spit Rd.; 805-964-7881 **$$**
This Goleta Beach County Park restaurant is a good place to sip a beer while eating a simple sandwich or fresh, expertly prepared local fish.

GUALALA *map page 107*
✕⛫ **Gualala Hotel.** Center of town on CA 1; 707-884-3441 **$**
Nineteen recently renovated, smallish rooms. Dining room, bar, wine shop.

✕⛫ **St. Orres.** 36601 CA 1 (2 miles north of town); 707-884-3303 **$$-$$$**
A lodge inspired by the Russian architecture of the first European settlers on this coast. The lodge has shared baths; cabins are private. Close to a sheltered sandy cove. Great restaurant, regionally renowned, with outstanding Northern California wine list. No credit cards.

✕ **Pangaea.** 39165 S. Hwy. 1, Gualala; 707-884-9669; www.pangaeacafe.com **$$$**
Locally grown, organic ingredients are prepared with flair; on a recent visit,

offerings included house-cured duck prosciutto, wild Point Arena salmon, wood oven–roasted pork chop, and grilled lavender duck breast. The proprietors make their own charcuterie and bake bread in their wood-fired oven. Lunch in summer and dinner Wed.–Sun. only.

HALF MOON BAY *map page 177*

🏨 **Cypress Inn on Miramar Beach.** 407 Mirada Rd.; 650-726-6002 or 800-83-BEACH (23224) **$$$-$$$$**
A luxurious inn right on the beach.

🏨 **Mill Rose Inn.** 615 Mill St.; 650-726-8750 **$$$-$$$$**
This romantic inn is set among lovely gardens. Guest rooms are furnished with Eastlake and arts-and-crafts antiques and have private entrances, as well as balconies that face the courtyard.

✕🏨 **San Benito House.** 356 Main St.; 650-726-3425 **$-$$**
This restored country inn is a local favorite. A sauna, redwood deck, restaurant, and reasonable prices add to its charms. Come to the restaurant for a delicious Sunday brunch, or a weekend dinner of Northern Italian/French country cooking.

🏨 **Zaballa Inn.** 324 Main St.; 650-726-9123 **$$-$$$**
This 1859 building (Half Moon Bay's oldest) houses nine guest rooms, some with whirlpools and/or fireplaces.

✕ **Half Moon Bay Bakery.** 514 Main St.; 650-726-4841 **$**
This bakery offers sandwiches and salads, plus pastries fresh from the 19th-century oven.

HERMOSA BEACH *map page 271*

✕ **Good Stuff.** 1286 The Strand (just north of Pier Ave.); 310-374-2334 **$**
Denizens of the beach scene—body builders, strand skaters, volleyball players—and other folks come for healthy, tasty, inexpensive dishes (omelets, sandwiches, burritos, fresh fish). Outdoor seating. On the beach close to the pier.

IMPERIAL BEACH *map page 323*

✕ **Cafe Jalisco.** 1669 Palm Ave.; 619-575-4955 **$**
This small, unpretentious, storefront Mexican cafe has been around since the 1940s, thanks to its great food and the loyalty of local customers.

INVERNESS *map page 85*

🏨 **Ten Inverness Way.** 10 Inverness Way; 415-669-1648 **$$$**
The redwood living room of this homey B&B has a large stone hearth and lots of

bookshelves. The simple but pretty guest rooms have hand-sewn quilts. Delicious breakfast menu.

✗ **Vladimir's Czech Restaurant.** 12785 Sir Francis Drake Blvd.; 415-669-1021 **$$$**

Good Central European cooking—beef tongue, lamb shank, cabbage rolls, goulash, and other stick-to-your-ribs fare. No credit cards.

JENNER *map page 107*

✗ **River's End.** 11048 CA 1; 707-865-2484 **$$$**

Burgers, roasted baby pheasant, and fresh fish specials—this place has them all, plus great views of the mouth of the Russian River. Excellent Sonoma County wine list.

LA JOLLA *map page 323*

🛏 **La Jolla Cove Motel.** 1155 Coast Blvd.; 619-459-2621 **$$**

Comfortable motel near Ellen Scripps Park and overlooking La Jolla Cove.

✗🛏 **La Valencia Hotel.** 1132 Prospect St.; 619-454-0771 **$$$**

Beautiful old salmon-colored stucco hotel near the beach, with lovely views. The **Mediterranean Room ($$$)** serves a seafood-oriented brunch. La Valencia also has the **Sky Room,** a formal Continental-style restaurant with impressive views **($$$$)**, and the **Whaling Bar ($$$)**.

✗ **Bird Rock Cafe.** 5656 La Jolla Blvd.; 619-551-4090 **$$**

Reasonable prices help make this a La Jolla favorite. Mussels (harvested locally) are served in a savory Thai curry; other seafood dishes are also very good. A bustling, fun scene.

✗ **George's at the Cove.** 1250 Prospect St.; 619-454-4244 **$$$**

A local favorite, with semi-formal indoor dining and more casual dining on the deck overlooking La Jolla Cove. In both places, the cuisine is California eclectic with an emphasis on seafood (one recent example: applewood-smoked salmon with fennel, miso, and Hawaiian pesto). Upstairs, **George's Ocean Terrace ($$)** is a rooftop aerie with stunning views and palate-tempting meals at a reasonable price.

✗ **Marine Room Restaurant.** 2000 Spindrift Dr.; 619-459-7222 **$$$-$$$$**

The chef takes classic French and California cuisines to new heights of whimsy. Seafood is given a kick with surprising flavors (sambuca or candied endive, for instance). The Marine Room serves it all up with incredible ocean views.

LAGUNA BEACH *map page 271*

⊞ **Hotel Laguna.** 425 S. Coast Hwy.; 949-494-1151 **$$-$$$**
Old Laguna Beach at its best—and surprisingly comfortable lodging, considering this place dates back to the town's very beginnings.

⊞ **Inn at Laguna Beach.** 211 N. Coast Hwy.; 949-497-9722 **$$$-$$$$**
Above Main Beach and next to the Las Brisas restaurant; the very comfortable rooms have private balconies with ocean views.

✕⊞ **Surf and Sand Hotel.** 1555 S. Coast Hwy.; 949-497-4477 or 800-664-7873 **$$$$**
You can hear the ocean from every room. If you like the beach and have the cash, it's the only place to stay. The restaurant **Splashes** is very good, offering casual California/Mediterranean bistro fare. It's also well-named, as it's so close to the water the windows get splashed. Try to get a table at sunset.

✕ **Anastasia Cafe.** 470 Ocean Ave.; 949-497-8903 **$-$$**
A surprisingly inexpensive breakfast and lunch hangout for Laguna Beach's skinny fashion set. The food is scrumptious and beautifully presented; dishes range from simple muffins to poached eggs with basil, tomatoes, and thyme.

✕ **Five Feet.** 328 Glenneyre St.; 949-497-4955 **$$$**
Eclectic, Pacific Rim cuisine (with an accent on Chinese flavors) is served in large portions at this hip bistro. Admirers love the catfish.

✕ **Las Brisas.** 361 Cliff Dr.; 949-497-5434 **$$-$$$**
Overlooks Main Beach, surf, and ocean from south end of Heisler Park. Seafood with Mexican flair.

✕ **Wahoo's Fish Taco.** 1133 S. Coast Hwy.; 949-497-0033 **$**
Locally famous fish taco and other healthy Mexican dishes.

LARKSPUR *map page 65 (or 85)*

✕ **Left Bank.** 507 Magnolia Ave.; 415-927-3331 **$$**
At this pretty, upbeat eatery, chef Roland Passot serves French brasserie classics: steak and frites, steamed mussels, and roast chicken. Have brunch on the sunny patio.

LITTLE RIVER *map page 107*

✕⊞ **Heritage House.** 5200 N. CA 1; 707-937-5885 or 800-235-5885 **$$$-$$$$**
This classic coastal inn served smugglers of Chinese immigrants in the 19th century, when it was an isolated farmhouse, and rum runners during Prohibition.

There are 68 cottages, a lodge, and the old farmhouse, and it has a first-rate restaurant with an outstanding wine list—not bad for a little coastal hideaway. All room rates include breakfast and dinner.

✕▦ **Little River Inn.** 7751 CA 1; 707-937-5942 or 888-466-5683 **$$-$$$**
All of the 65 rooms have views of the ocean; some have fireplaces and Jacuzzis. The restaurant serves nicely prepared seasonal seafood dishes, meats, free-range chicken, and omelets in a beautiful garden setting. Oceanview bar. Special winter rates. There's an adjacent 9-hole golf course, plus championship tennis courts.

LOCKE
▦ **Al's Place Bar and Restaurant.** 13936 Main St.; 916-776-1800 **$$**
Known among locals as "Al the Wop's," this "Italian" restaurant is almost more of an institution than a restaurant. While it may be better appreciated for the quality of its cocktails than for its hearty meat-and-potatoes dishes, it's equally famed for steaks and for the peanut butter, jelly, and toasted bread on the table. (You spread the jelly on the steak.) Upscale motorcycle riders love this place.

LONG BEACH   *map page 271*
▦ **Queen Mary (Hotel).** 1126 Queens Hwy.; 562-435-3511 **$$$-$$$$**
The old *Queen* is getting a bit long in the tooth, but she still represents that once-in-a-lifetime opportunity: nowhere else in the world can you lodge on a classic ocean liner.

✕ **King's Fish House Pine Avenue.** 100 W. Broadway; 562-432-7463 **$$$**
The place in Long Beach for fresh fish, grilled or broiled, served with light but flavorful sauces.

MALIBU   *map page 271*
▦ **Malibu Beach Inn.** 22878 PCH; 310-456-6444 **$$$-$$$$**
On the beach, in a town that has virtually *no* hotel rooms of any kind, this place is a rare find—and can be hard to get into. Never mind the price; it's about the only way we peons can claim we spent a night in Malibu (unless you sleep in your car, as I did during my college days). Not to be confused with the **Malibu Inn** (22969 PCH), which is a surfer bar.

✕ **Beaurivage.** 26025 PCH (2 miles north of Malibu Canyon Rd.);
310-456-5733 **$$$-$$$$**
A Malibu institution. The kitchen turns out superb southern French cuisine in formal surroundings. A cliffside setting adds to its charms.

✕ **Neptune's Net.** 42505 PCH, 1 mile north of Leo Carrillo Beach; 310-457-3095 **$-$$**
Great lobster, french fries, and jumbo shrimp heaped onto paper plates are the order of the day at this low-key, friendly seafood joint.

✕ **Reel Inn.** 18661 PCH; 310-456-8221 **$$**
New England–style fishhouse with an array of seafood cooking. Order at the counter and wait for chowder, fish tacos, even Cajun-style blackened fish dishes, then dine at boardinghouse tables. There's a newer **Reel Inn** in Santa Monica at 1220 Third St. Promenade; 310-395-5538.

MANHATTAN BEACH *map page 271*

✕ **Cafe Pierre.** 317 Manhattan Beach Blvd.; 310-545-5252 **$$-$$$**
A very friendly cafe with good, simple, and elegantly prepared food. A wonderful bistro for the local beach crowd.

MARSHALL *map page 85*

✕ **Tony's Seafood Restaurant.** 18863 CA 1; 415-663-1107 **$$**
A great place for grilled oysters, with views of Tomales Bay from the deck.

MENDOCINO *map page 107 (also 141)*

✕▥ **MacCallum House.** 45020 Albion; 707-937-0289 **$$$**
The town's oldest B&B (built in 1882) offers rooms in a Victorian house and in garden cottages, with quilts and comfortable furnishings. You can also stay in the barn, with its stone fireplaces, or in the water tower suite, equipped with a Franklin stove. Under new ownership, with a new chef in the kitchen, the restaurant is better than ever. The **Gray Whale Bar & Cafe** offers lighter and less expensive fare in casual surroundings.

✕▥ **Mendocino Hotel & Restaurant.** 45080 Main St.; 707-937-0511 **$$-$$$**
An 1878 hotel, thoroughly updated with private baths in most rooms. In the bar you can sip drinks under the magnificent stained-glass dome or in front of the fireplace in a comfortable chair. California cuisine is served at all meals, dining in the plush **Garden Room** is a memorable experience, and the wine list may be one of the finest on the North Coast.

✕▥ **SeaRock Inn.** 11101 Lansing St.; 707-937-0926 or 800-906-0926; www.searock.com **$$$**
This family-run inn has comfortable cottages (with fireplaces, private baths, decks, and wireless Internet access) above a rocky beach at the north end of town. Breakfast

is sumptuous—best when enjoyed on the lawn, overlooking the headlands and ocean.

✕ **Mendocino Cafe.** 10451 Lansing St.; 707-937-2422 **$**
Reasonably priced fresh seafood, vegetarian dishes, and Asian and Mexican food.

MONTECITO *map page 223*

⊡ **Miramar Resort Hotel.** 1555 S. Jameson Ln.; 805-969-2203 **$$$$**
The only hotel in Montecito directly on the beach.

⊡ **Montecito Inn.** 1295 Coast Village Rd.; 805-969-7854 **$$$$**
An attractive if rather elaborate celebrity hangout established in 1928 by Charlie Chaplin and Fatty Arbuckle.

✕⊡ **Stonehouse.** At the San Ysidro Ranch, 900 San Ysidro Ln. (3 miles east of CA. 101); 800-368-6788, restaurant 805-969-4100; www.sanysidroranch.com **$$$$**, restaurant **$$$**
This old rancho and guest ranch in the Montecito foothills is now one of the West Coast's top luxury resorts. The comfortable creekside cabins have fireplaces and private terraces. In an old granite farmhouse, the rustic but intimate dining room turns out New American cuisine, sometimes with a Southern accent. Think dry-aged steak, perhaps served with an interesting horseradish sauce, and boldly prepared fresh fish.

MONTEREY *map page 177*

⊡ **Hotel Pacific.** 300 Pacific St.; 831-373-5700 or 800-554-5542 **$$**
A comfortable modern hotel designed to fit right in with Monterey's old adobes. Even though you're not right on the waterfront, you can hear the sea lions bark at night.

⊡ **Spindrift Inn.** 652 Cannery Row; 831-646-8900 or 800-641-1879 **$$$**
Right on Cannery Row and right on the water, where you can watch the sea otters float offshore from your window (if you get a room facing the water). The rooms are comfortable and elegantly appointed.

✕ **Cafe Fina.** 47 Fisherman's Wharf; 831-372-5200 **$$**
The Fisherman's Wharf restaurant most worth visiting. Good pasta and seafood.

✕ **Fresh Cream.** 99 Pacific St.; 831-375-9798 **$$$-$$$$**
This elegant room, up a spiral staircase, is the setting for French-California cuisine (lobster ravioli with two caviars, roast duck with black currant sauce). Fine view of the bay.

MORRO BAY *map page 223*

✕☷ **Inn at Morro Bay.** 60 State Park Rd.; 805-772-5651 **$$-$$$$**
This old inn has the kind of faded elegance that makes you feel cozy and at peace.
Sit by the fireplace in the lounge when it's cool, or on the deck in fair weather. Its
restaurant, Orchid (**$$$**), serves sophisticated preparations of local seafood, espe-
cially sea scallops and salmon, often in rich, creamy sauces, or in paella.

✕ **Dorn's Original Breakers Cafe.** 801 Market St.; 805-772-4415 **$$**
On the bluffs overlooking the Embarcadero and the harbor, this is a favorite hang-
out for Morro Bay old-timers.

✕ **Galley Restaurant.** 899 Embarcadero; 805-772-2806 **$$-$$$**
A very comfortable restaurant, right over the water, with beautifully prepared fresh
seafood and very friendly and accomplished service.

MOSS BEACH *map page 177*

✕ **Moss Beach Distillery Restaurant.** Beach Way & Ocean Blvd.(follow signs);
650-728-5595 **$$-$$$**
This place has been popular since Prohibition, when it was said to have served as a
speakeasy. A favorite Sunday brunch spot where patrons sit on low tables outside
on a deck above the beach. In chilly weather the waitstaff hands out blankets.

MOSS LANDING *map page 177*

✕ **Moss Landing Cafe.** 421 Moss Landing Rd.; 831-633-3355 **$**
An inexpensive, folksy place serving the area's trademark deep-fried artichokes, plus
crab cakes, squid and eggs, and other simple but tasty dishes.

MUIR BEACH *map page 85*

✕☷ **The Pelican Inn.** 10 Pacific Way (off Hwy 1, at entrance to Muir Beach);
415-383-6000 **$$$**
Cozy and comfortable in the way of a traditional inn, especially on stormy nights
when you can gather around the fireplace. Seven rooms on second floor, all with
private baths. Full English breakfast included.

NEWPORT BEACH *map page 271*

☷ **Newport Channel Inn.** 6030 W. PCH; 949-642-3030 **$**
Nothing posh, but clean, comfortable rooms in a motel on the off side of the
Coast Highway. Offers very reasonable rates, and staff who really know the area.

✕ **The Crab Cooker.** 2200 Newport Blvd.; 949-673-0100 **$$**
If John Wayne and Richard Nixon could wait in line, so can you. This down-to-

earth grilled and smoked fish place near the Newport Pier has been in business since 1951. Maybe it's the proximity of the fresh fish of the dory fleet, handled by a genius in the kitchen. The clam chowder is great.

OAKLAND *map page 65*
✕ **Oakland Grill.** 301 Franklin St. (Jack London Square); 510-835-1176 **$$**
A pleasant cafe whose large doors open onto Produce Row. A family spot.

OCEANSIDE *map page 323*
✕ **Beach Break Cafe.** 1902 S. Coast Hwy.; 760-439-6355 **$**
Diverse breakfast menu, or just go for bagels and croissants.

OLEMA *map page 85*
✕⊟ **Olema Inn & Restaurant.** 10,000 Sir Francis Drake Blvd.; 415-663-9559 **$$$**
This 1876 New England–style inn is comfortable and convenient to Point Reyes. The dining room serves great barbecued oysters. Cooking is straightforward (and good), plus there are a few California-style dishes thrown in, too.

PACIFIC GROVE *map page 177*
⊟ **Beachcomber Inn.** 1996 Sunset Dr.; 831-373-4769 or 800-634-4769 **$$**
Just up from the beach at Asilomar. Free bikes available for guest use. Fishwife Restaurant adjacent (see below), and within walking distance of the Links at Spanish Bay.
✕ **Fishwife Restaurant at Asilomar Beach.** 1996½ Sunset Dr.; 831-375-7107 **$-$$**
Across the street from the Asilomar conference center and a short walk from Asilomar Beach, this plain restaurant has some of the freshest and best prepared seafood on the Monterey Peninsula. The daily specials from the grill use only the freshest seasonal fish, like sand dabs; the seafood quesadilla is delectable.
✕ **Passionfish.** 481 Lighthouse Ave.; 831-655-3311 **$$$**
This casual seafood grill downtown is a fortuitous find. The seafood is fresh and prepared with just the right touch of seasonings; the wine list is well chosen (with low markups); the mood is relaxed; and the service is friendly and professional. No wonder the locals pack the place.

PESCADERO *map page 177*
⊟ **Costanoa Coastal Lodge & Camp.** 2001 Rossi Road at CA 1; 650-879-1100 *or* 800-738-7477; www.costanoa.com **$-$$** (Tents $60-95; cabin rooms $145; lodge rooms $175)

Rooms at this slightly odd but very upscale resort range from "basic" tents (on wooden platforms, with queen-sized beds and dual control electric blankets) to luxurious cabin and lodge rooms. Your "real" camping experience comes from hikes into the hills and redwood groves, or to windswept beaches. Afterwards, you can relax with a massage.

✗ **Duarte's Tavern.** 202 Stage Rd.; 650-879-0464 **$$**
Built in 1894 as a stagecoach stop, this old, comfortable building now serves as a tavern and restaurant regionally famous for its seafood dishes. Rock fish, sand dabs, and abalone (in season) are perfectly fresh and cooked just right. The fruit pies are made with fruit from the family garden.

PISMO BEACH *map page 223*

⛅ **Shelter Cove Lodge.** 2651 Price St.; 805-773-3511 **$$-$$$**
You can walk to the cove from this beachfront lodging. All rooms have ocean views.

✗⛅ **Shore Cliff Lodge and Restaurant.** 2555 Price St.; 805 773-4671 **$$-$$$**
This is a cliff-top place with astounding ocean views—99 rooms with outdoor pool and hot tub. Great food, presented in a light, California-continental style; there's a killer artichoke appetizer as well as perfectly fresh fish cooked to perfection. A great place for watching sunsets, and for observing the antics of shorebirds. The staff is friendly, relaxed and very professional. Sunday brunch is a local favorite.

✗ **Splash Cafe.** 197 Pomeroy; 805 773-4653; www.splashcafe.com **$**
A great place for watching the parade of visitors en route to the pier, while enjoying a bowl of clam chowder or fish 'n' chips.

POINT ARENA *map page 107*

⛅ **Coast Guard House Historic Inn.** 605 Arena Cove; 707-882-2442 **$$-$$$**
Bed-and-breakfast with ocean views, full breakfast, outdoor hot tub.

✗ **Arena Cove Bar & Grill.** 790 Arena Cove, at the foot of the pier; 707-882-2189 **$$**
Fresh fish, sautéed with garlic, done as fish 'n' chips, and blackened Cajun-style. Fishermen's hangout.

POINT REYES STATION *map page 85*

✗ **Station House Cafe.** 11180 CA 1; 415-663-1515 **$$**
Menu changes greatly but usually includes local seafood and locally raised organic beef and barbecued oysters. Shaded garden for summer dining.

✗ **Tomales Bay Foods.** 80 4th St.; 415-663-9335 **$$**
The best place to get chow for your picnic.

PRINCETON *map page 177*
X **Princeton Seafood Company.** 9 Jensen Pier, Pillar Pt. Harbor; 650-726-2722
$-$$
The fish is as fresh at this fishing-port restaurant as it was when the eatery started
out as a seafood market, some 20 years ago (it's still affiliated with the market).

REDONDO BEACH *map page 271*
X **Quality Seafood Inc.** 130 S. International Boardwalk; 310-374-2382 or
310-372-6408 **$$$**
A classic seafood market (selling live, fresh fish and shellfish) that's been around
since 1953. They'll broil or steam your selection for you. Outdoor seating. Beware
the gulls, pigeons, and sparrows. (Yes, sparrows.)

SAN CLEMENTE *map page 271*
▣ **Casa Tropicana Bed & Breakfast.** 610 Avenida Victoria; 949-492-1234 **$$$**
Champagne, Jacuzzi, and full breakfast.
X **Beach Garden Cafe.** 618½ Avenida Victoria; 949-498-8145 **$**
Soups, sandwiches, pizza, fish 'n' chips, omelets.
X **Fisherman's Restaurant & Bar.** 611 Avenida Victoria; 949-498-6390 **$$**
Perfectly fresh, beautifully prepared and presented seafood in a very friendly,
down-to-earth restaurant with great views. The bar across the pier is part of the
same establishment and even more friendly. The menu changes daily. Good selec-
tion of local microbrews. Don't be surprised to see pelicans sitting on the roof—
they know where the freshest fish is.

SAN DIEGO *map page 323*
▣ **Crystal Pier Motel.** 4500 Ocean Blvd., Mission Beach; 619-483-6983 **$$$**
The rooms of this elegantly refurbished waterfront motel are actually small cabins
jutting out over the beach on a private pier (but open to the public during daylight
hours). Needless to say, the views are splendid. An easy stroll (via the boardwalk) to
Pacific Beach's many attractions.
▣ **Pacific Terrace Inn.** 610 Diamond St., Pacific Beach; 619-581-3500 **$$$**
This lovely small hotel offers ocean views from the Pacific Beach cliffs.
X **Casa de Bandini.** Old Town San Diego State Historic Park, 754 Calhoun St.;
619-297-8211; www.bazaardelmundo.com/dining/bandini.html **$-$$**
The courtyard of this Old Town restaurant is a riot of colorful flowers and tiles; it's
a soothing place where sparrows splash and bathe in the courtyard fountain. The

food is Mexican, the service relaxed but professional. Highlights include the tostada de Bandini and the special Casa platter. Locals flock here for lunch.

✕ **Chez Loma Bistro.** 1132 Loma Ave., Coronado; 619-435-0661 **$$**
This tiny cafe housed in a Victorian has sophisticated service and wonderful French classics, such as roast duck and filet mignon with bleu cheese.

✕ **The Green Flash.** 701 Thomas Ave.; 619-270-7715 **$$**
The outdoor patio of this beachside restaurant is perfect for watching pelicans, for observing the characters walking, running, or skating by on the Pacific Beach boardwalk, and for waiting for a spectacular sunset that might display the famous green flash (a natural phenomenon) from which this very popular restaurant takes its name.

✕ **Hodad's.** 5010 Newport Ave., Ocean Beach; 619-224-4623 **$**
Utterly unpretentious place with the best hamburgers in town.

✕ **Laurel Restaurant & Bar.** 505 Laurel St.; 619-239-2222 **$$$**
While not exactly on the beach, the highly talked-about Laurel, located one block from Balboa Park, is worth a visit. The room exudes sophistication, but the friendly bartenders will put most anyone at ease. The impressive food—a combination of French, Mediterranean, and California cuisines—is never dull and always delicious.

✕ **Theo Bungalow.** 4996 W. Point Loma Blvd.; 619-224-2884 **$$**
Fancy French-inspired fare—savory roast duck with a black cherry or a green peppercorn sauce, seafood almandine, and desserts such as Grand Marnier soufflé—are served at this family-run longtime favorite. The bungalow itself is an architectural landmark of Ocean Beach. Excellent wine list—perhaps one of San Diego's best.

SAN FRANCISCO *map page 65 (or 36–37)*

▥ **Hotel Monaco.** 501 Geary St.; 415-292-0100 or 800-214-4220 **$$$$**
With its playful, technicolor style and chic vibe, the new hotspot in town attracts stylish out-of-towners; meanwhile, locals frequent the hyper art nouveau–style Grand Cafe restaurant and bar. Impressive sauna and gym.

▥ **Hotel Triton.** 342 Grant Ave.; 415-394-0500 or 800-433-6611 **$$$**
A comfortable hotel with quirky, almost surreal furnishings. Across the street from the Chinatown Gate and within walking distance of the Ferry Building and the Embarcadero.

▥ **Tuscan Inn Best Western.** 425 North Point; 415-561-1100 or 800-648-4626 **$$$**

Easy walking distance to Fisherman's Wharf and to the Red-and-White ferries (which serve Angel Island, Alcatraz, and Vallejo).

✕ **42 Degrees.** 235 16th St.; 415-777-5558 **$$$**
This China Basin restaurant feels industrial but cozy—concrete floors, yes, but giant, curvy banquettes, too. The menu draws from European cuisines at 42° latitude (Provençal, Southern Italian, et al.). You'll see hearty dishes like grilled salmon with white beans and chanterelles, roasted potatoes with aioli, and frisée with gorgonzola.

✕ **Farallon.** 450 Post St. (at Mason); 415-956-6969 **$$$-$$$$**
Pat Kuleto designed this aquatic wonderland of a restaurant inside an old mosaic-ceilinged swimming pool. He built another floor above the pool, then decorated every square inch of the place with oceanic-themed objects—sea urchin and jelly-fish lamps, a kelp lighting column, shell-like ceiling, octopus bar stools. The seafood-dominated menu can be just as spectacular. (Offerings include sea urchin shell filled with crab, truffled mashed potatoes, and orange salmon caviar.) Oysters, house-made caviars, and house-smoked fish are always available.

✕ **Greens.** Fort Mason, Building A; 415-771-6222 **$$-$$$**
Affiliated with the Green Gulch Zen Center, this converted warehouse right on the water is the city's most established vegetarian restaurant. (Vegans note: dairy and eggs are used liberally.) Have a brunch of asparagus omelet with roasted potatoes and enjoy the lovely room with its view, but be prepared to wait, as service can be slow. Prix fixe dinners on weekends.

✕ **John's Grill.** 63 Ellis St.; 415-986-0069 **$$**
This dark, wood-paneled dining room has been doing business since 1908. It has literary significance, because here Sam Spade ate a hurried meal of "chops, baked potato, and sliced tomato," before taking a cab to Burlingame in pursuit of the Maltese Falcon. The menu hasn't changed much since the days when Dashiell Hammett was still writing.

✕ **Tommy Toy's Haute Cuisine Chinoise.** 655 Montgomery St.; 415-397-4888 **$$$$**
This upmarket Chinese restaurant is famous for entrées like whole lobster with peppercorn sauce on angel-hair pasta. The elegantly presented food will cost you, but the gleaming surfaces and attentive service do exude luxury. You'll see lots of guests on cell phones here.

✕ **Zuni Cafe.** 1658 Market St. (at Rose); 415-552-2522 **$$-$$$**
Excellent service, moderate prices, terrific cocktails, and an informal yet tony atmosphere make this a favorite spot for San Franciscans. A copper bar runs along

one side of the front bar area toward the quieter dining room; two sides of the roughly triangular eatery are all window. The expertly prepared food is never precious: choose from an impressive list of oysters, then order Caesar salad or roast chicken with Tuscan bread salad.

SAN LUIS OBISPO *map page 223*

✗🛏 **Apple Farm Hotel.** 2015 Monterey St.; 805-543-4000 **$$$**
Built around an old millhouse and farm, this Victorian is furnished with antiques and fireplaces; there's also a swimming pool, Jacuzzi, and a pleasant, country-style restaurant specializing in grilled fish.

🛏 **Petit Soleil Bed & Breakfast.** 1473 Monterey St.; 805-549-0321 or 800-676-1588; www.petitsoleilslo.com **$$**
The former Adobe Motel on San Luis Obispo's main drag has been renovated with pleasant "Provençal" touches—bright flowers and colors—bringing a touch of Europe to San Luis Obispo. The breakfasts are big and very tasty.

✗🛏 **The Park Restaurant.** 1819 Osos St.; 805-545-0000 **$$$**
Chef Maegan Loring has made a regional reputation for herself for the way she prepares fresh local ingredients and matches them to local wines. The dining room is very comfortable; the service superb. The restaurant is near San Luis Obispo's old railroad depot.

SANTA BARBARA *map page 231*

🛏 **Santa Barbara Inn.** 901 E. Cabrillo Blvd.; 805-966-2285 **$$**
A recently renovated, comfortable motel across the street from East Beach.

✗ **Bay Cafe Seafood Restaurant & Fish Market.** 131 Anacapa St.; 805-963-2215 **$-$$**
Fresh fish at the market and in the restaurant. Fresh spiny lobster, live or cooked.

✗ **Brophy Brothers Restaurant & Clam Bar.** 119 Harbor Way; 805-966-4418 **$$-$$$**
According to locals, this small restaurant in the harbor serves the freshest and best-prepared fish in town.

✗ **El Paseo Mexican Restaurant.** 10 El Paseo; 805-962-6050 **$-$$**
A large, fun courtyard place in the heart of Santa Barbara with good food and great service.

✗ **La Super-Rica Taqueria.** 622 North Milpas St.; 805-963-4940 **$**
This rather plain eatery is the place the locals claim has the best standard (i.e. campesino or ranchero) Mexican food in California.

✕ **Wine Cask.** 813 Anacapa St.; 805-966-9463 **$$$**
Good food and good wine at the outer edge of El Paseo.

SANTA CRUZ *map page 177*

▦ **Chaminade at Santa Cruz.** 1 Chaminade Ln.; 831-475-5600 or 800-283-6569 **$$$**
A conference center and resort perched on a hill overlooking the harbor. The retreat also features hiking trails, tennis courts, and a pool, plus a completely outfitted fitness center.

✕ **Black's Beach Cafe.** 15th Ave. and E. Cliff Dr.; 831-475-2233 **$$**
Huge sandwiches and salads, plus more refined Pacific Rim dishes, served in an airy dining room near the beach. Ahi tuna might come with ginger and cilantro, a grilled chicken sandwich with plum sauce. Dinner weekdays; breakfast and dinner on weekends.

✕ **Oswald.** 1547 Pacific Ave.; 831-423-7427 **$$-$$$**
Probably Santa Cruz's most sophisticated eatery. A tiny spot serving French-inspired California cuisine. A recent menu included pork chops with roasted apples, and rack of lamb.

✕ **Stagnaro Brothers.** Municipal Wharf; 831-423-2180 **$$**
A restaurant with adjacent fish market. The fish at both is fresh, and the restaurant knows how to cook it.

SANTA MONICA *map page 271*

▦ **Shutters on the Beach.** 1 Pico Blvd.; 310-458-0030 or 800-223-6800 **$$$$**
The only hotel in L.A. that sits right on the sand, its three buildings are connected by trellises and awnings. Simple rooms, many with balconies. Expensive and chic, with a big Hollywood following.

✕ **Chinois on Main.** 2709 Main St. (bet. Ocean Park Blvd. and Rose Ave.); 310-392-9025 **$$$**
Wolfgang Puck's highest-rated restaurant is always packed with L.A.'s in-crowd. Try rare duck with plum sauce or a Shanghai lobster with ginger and curry.

✕ **The Galley.** 2442 Main St.; 310-452-1934 **$$-$$$**
Santa Monica's oldest restaurant has had its share of movie-star patrons, back in the days when the stars hung out at the Palisades instead of Malibu. Hard-drinking Errol Flynn and friends were regulars and put the place on the map. Today, the restaurant is mostly popular with businessmen who come to dine on the famous

steaks, lobster, and fresh fish. In keeping with its business image, The Galley bills itself as "cigar friendly."

✕ **Ocean Avenue Seafood.** 1401 Ocean Ave.; 310-394-5669 **$$$**
Stylish seaview dining at one of the best seafood restaurants in Los Angeles. There's a fine oyster bar here and a wonderful variety of desserts, including excellent banana pie.

SAUSALITO *map page 85 (or 65)*

⊞ **Inn above Tide.** 30 El Portal; 415-332-9535; www.innabovetide.com **$$$$**
This utterly—I'm tempted to say outrageously—luxurious inn is perched above the shore near the Sausalito plaza. The rooms are of course very comfortable, and the views are great. The sunrise over Angel Island can be spectacular. The staff is helpful and knowledgeable.

✕ **Angelino's Restaurant.** 621 Bridgeway; 415-331-5225; www. angelinorestaurant.com **$-$$**
Pasquale Ascona's unabashed southern Italian cooking has a very loyal local following. It's no wonder—the food's really delicious. This restaurant is also a great place for people-watching on Bridgeway, the town's main drag.

✕ **Sushi Ran.** 107 Caledonia St.; 415-332-3620 **$$$**
The best place for sushi in Sausalito. The restaurant has a hip feel too.

SEAL BEACH *map page 271*

⊞ **The Seal Beach Inn and Gardens.** 212 Fifth St.; 562-493-2416 or 800-443-3929 **$$$**
This restored 80-year-old inn has beautiful gardens, plus fine breakfasts and evening tea. One block from the beach.

✕ **Walt's Wharf.** 201 Main St.; 562-598-4433 **$$$**
Fresh seafood and good beer—just the right combination for après-beach—plus a great bar where the locals congregate over drinks and appetizers.

SHELTER COVE *map page 141*

⊞ **Shelter Cove Motor Inn.** 205 Wave St.; 707-986-7521 **$**
Basic motel lodging near the beach.

SOLANA BEACH *map page 323*

✕ **Fidel's.** 607 Valley Dr.; 619-755-5292 **$$**
Very popular, crowded cantina with some great, rather authentic Mexican fare.

STINSON BEACH   *map page 85*
✕ **Parkside Cafe.** 43 Arenal Ave. (off Calle del Mar, next to park parking lot); 415-868-1272 **$**
Omelets, blueberry pancakes, burgers, mussel linguini, seafood pizza, and more. The snack bar has a take-out counter serving burgers, fries, milkshakes. Breakfast, lunch daily; dinners Thursday through Monday.

SUNSET BEACH   *map page 271*
✕ **Harbor House Cafe.** 16341 PCH; 562-592-5404 **$**
The menu is heavy on burgers, omelets, and fried seafood, with variations. But it must work—the Harbor House has been around since 1939. Open 24 hours.

TIBURON   *map page 85 (or 65)*
✕ **Guaymas.** 5 Main St. (at ferry); 415-435-6300 **$$**
A terrific dockside location and an action-packed bar scene make this trendy regional Mexican restaurant a festive place to eat, if a tad pricey. The mesquite-grilled seafood and the tamales go well with the reliable margarita. The ferry to Tiburon lands here.

TIMBER COVE   *map page 107*
▣ **Timber Cove Inn.** 217 N. CA 1; 707-847-3231 or 800-987-8319 **$$$**
All 51 rooms have spas and wood-burning fireplaces.

TRINIDAD   *map page 141*
▣ **Bishop Pine Lodge.** 1481 Patrick's Point Dr.; 707-677-3314 **$**
Clean, relatively inexpensive motel on the road leading into town from the north.
✕ **Larrupin' Cafe.** 1658 Patrick's Point Rd.; 707-677-0230 **$$**
No credit cards. This place looks like a European country inn, though the fare is upscale American, with fresh seafood and barbecued pork ribs among the highlights.
✕ **Seascape Restaurant.** At the foot of the pier in the harbor; 707-677-3762 **$$**
A delightful place where local diners flock (and bring their visitors). Friendly, good service and fresh seafood prepared with flair have kept this dining room bustling for more than 35 years.

VENICE   *map page 271 (or 280)*
✕ **Chaya Venice.** 110 Navy St. (at Main St.); 310-396-1179 **$$$**
A typically upscale Venice crowd patronizes this trendy restaurant. Watch for

filmmakers and leading artists hovering around the sushi bar or making deals in one of the comfortable banquettes. Brunch here is an elegant affair.

✗ **Hal's Bar & Grill.** 1349 Abbot Kinney Blvd.; 310-396-3105 **$$$**
Venice's artsy crowd hangs out at this roomy, brick-walled bistro, home to the city's best Caesar salad and a number of fine grilled dishes.

VENTURA *map page 223*

✗🖬 **Pierpont Inn & Racquet Club.** 550 Sanjon Rd; 805-643-6144 or 800-285-4667; www.pierpontinn.com **$$-$$$**
This legendary inn (a historic landmark) has overlooked Pierpont Bay and the Ventura County coastline since 1908, and has been owned by the same family since 1928. The rooms have been remodeled; they're spacious and the grounds are secluded .

✗ **Jonathan's at Peirano's.** 204 East Main St.; 805-648-4853 **$$**
This pleasant cafe occupies the site of an old-time grocery store ("Peirano's") across the street from San Buenaventura Mission, next to a small plaza with tiled fountains and a short stretch of the padre's old irrigation canal (now clad in fancy Mexican tiles), the *zanja madre*.

INDEX

ACKNOWLEDGMENTS

■ FROM THE AUTHOR

A book is more than just the product of a single mind. I would, therefore, like to thank all of the many people who have made this book possible. Special thanks go to my editor, Diane Mehta, for guiding me through this update. Thanks also go to Paul Eisenberg, editorial director for Fodor's Compass American Guides. I would also like to thank Nyna Cox for her help with lodging and dining, and I must thank all those beach companions, surfers, beachcombers, fishermen, oyster farmers, sailors, innkeepers, winery owners, and restauranteurs who have given me information about the coast, providing me with a continuous, Kaleidoscopic vision. And I think fondly of the gulls and pelicans, murres and guillemots, sanderlings, snowy plovers, ravens and hawks who were my companions whenever I could not entice any humans to join me at the shore. Nor should I neglect to mention the sea otters, seals, seal lions, and whales who have entertained me with their antics.

This is also the place to mention those writers who helped me understand the coast and its history: Richard Henry Dana, Robert Louis Stevenson, Jack London, Gertrude Atherton, Robinson Jeffers, Henry Miller, John Steinbeck, and Dan Duane.

■ FROM THE PUBLISHER

Compass American Guides would like to thank the following individuals or institutions for the use of their illustrations or photographs. All photographs in this book are by Catherine Karnow unless noted below.

OVERVIEW
Page 14, Galen Rowell

LANDSCAPE & HISTORY
Page 17, Santa Barbara Mission Archive Library ▪ Page 19 (all), Galen Rowell ▪ Page 23, Bancroft Library, University of California at Berkeley ▪ Page 24–25, Library of Congress Geography and Map Division ▪ Page 26, Yale Collection of

Western Americana, Beinecke Rare Book and Manuscript Library ▪ Page 30, Moulin Archives/The Virtual Museum of the City of San Francisco

SAN FRANCISCO BAY
Page 46, San Francisco Maritime National Historic Park (photo by O.V. Lange) ▪ Page 56, Galen Rowell ▪ Page 68, Galen Rowell ▪ Page 73, Robert

Holmes/CalTour ▪ Page 76, John Hollingsworth/U.S. Fish & Wildlife Service ▪ Page 80, Corbis

MARIN COAST

Page 84, Galen Rowell ▪ Page 87, Galen Rowell ▪ Page 93, Galen Rowell ▪ Page 94, Galen Rowell ▪ Page 97, Galen Rowell ▪ Page 101 (all), Galen Rowell

SONOMA & MENDOCINO

Page 113, Galen Rowell ▪ Page 121, Galen Rowell ▪ Page 122, Galen Rowell ▪ Page 127, Galen Rowell ▪ Page 131, Peter E. Palmquist, Eureka ▪ Page 135, Galen Rowell

REDWOOD COAST

Page 142, Galen Rowell ▪ Page 146, Galen Rowell ▪ Page 147, Galen Rowell ▪ Page 152, Galen Rowell ▪ Page 154, Peter E. Palmquist, Eureka ▪ Pages 164–65, Galen Rowell ▪ Page 168, Galen Rowell ▪ Page 172, Special Collections Research Center, University of Chicago Library

GOLDEN GATE TO SAN SIMEON

Page 176, Galen Rowell ▪ Page 179, Galen Rowell ▪ Page 180, Galen Rowell ▪ Page 183, Galen Rowell ▪ Page 186, Harry Mayo ▪ Page 191, Galen Rowell ▪ Page 196, The Pat Hathaway Collection, Monterey ▪ Page 202, Seaver Center for Western History Research, Natural History Museum of Los Angeles County ▪ Page 203, Museo Naval, Madrid ▪ Page 204, Galen Rowell ▪ Page 213, Galen Rowell ▪ Page 214, Galen Rowell ▪ Page 218, Galen Rowell

CENTRAL COAST RIVIERA

Page 222, Galen Rowell ▪ Page 226, Yale Collection of Western Americana, Beinecke Rare Book and Manuscript Library ▪ Page 232, Galen Rowell ▪ Page 246, National Archives and Records Administration ▪ Page 247, Galen Rowell ▪ Page 249, Galen Rowell ▪ Page 252, Galen Rowell ▪ Page 260, Galen Rowell ▪ Page 263, Galen Rowell

L.A. METRO & ORANGE COUNTY

Page 275, Galen Rowell ▪ Page 281, Western History/Geneology Department, Denver Public Library ▪ Page 284, Chicago Historical Society ▪ Page 285, Galen Rowell ▪ Pages 288–89, Library of Congress, Prints and Photographs Division ▪ Page 294, Galen Rowell ▪ page 303 (bottom), Orange Public Library ▪ Page 308, USC Specialized Libraries and Archival Collections, University of Southern California ▪ Page 312, Galen Rowell ▪ Page 313, Galen Rowell ▪ Page 314, Galen Rowell

SAN DIEGO COAST

Page 331, Galen Rowell ▪ Page 334, Galen Rowell ▪ Page 338, Galen Rowell ▪ Page 340, Galen Rowell ▪ Page 346, Galen Rowell ▪ Page 349, Galen Rowell ▪ Page 350, Galen Rowell ▪ Page 355, USC Specialized Libraries and Archival Collections, University of Southern California ▪ Page 356, Galen Rowell

■ ABOUT THE AUTHOR

John Doerper has traveled the California Coast for almost 40 years, enjoying its beaches, inns, restaurants, and prime camping sites. He is the author of six books (and is working on a seventh) describing the pleasures of travel on the Pacific Coast, including several Wine Country titles for Compass American Guides. He has acted as editor and columnist for several publications, has published articles in *Travel & Leisure* and other national magazines, and was food-and-wine editor for *Pacific Northwest Magazine*. Mr. Doerper is the publisher of a gardening, nature, and travel Web site, *Notes from a Pacific Northwest Garden* (homepage.mac.com/jdoerper/).

■ ABOUT THE PHOTOGRAPHERS

Born and raised in Hong Kong, San Francisco–based photographer **Catherine Karnow** has covered Australian Aborigines; Bombay film stars; victims of Agent Orange in Vietnam; Russian "Old Believers" in Alaska; Greenwich, Connecticut, high society; and an Albanian farm family. In 1994 she was the only non-Vietnamese photojournalist to accompany General Giap on his historic first return to the forest encampment in the Northern Vietnam highlands from which he plotted the battle of Dien Bien Phu. Her work appears in *National Geographic, National Geographic Traveler, Smithsonian, French & German GEO,* and other international publications. She has also contributed to the *Day in the Life* photography series, including the books *Passage to Vietnam* and *Women in the Material World.*

The late **Galen Rowell** was one of the most prominent nature photographers in the United States. He was author and photographer of more than a dozen large-format books, including *Mountain Light: In Search of the Dynamic Landscape,* his valuable introduction to outdoor photography, and *Bay Area Wild.* A regular contributor to *National Geographic, Outdoor Photographer,* and *Life,* he was also a noted mountaineer, having climbed in Nepal, Tibet, Alaska, and Patagonia, as well as making more than 100 first ascents in California's High Sierra. Major exhibitions of his work have been held at galleries across the United States, including the Smithsonian Institution, in Washington, D.C., and San Francisco's California Academy of Sciences.